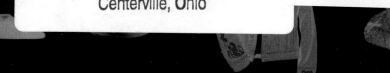
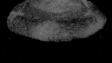

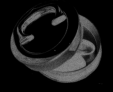

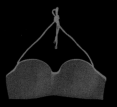

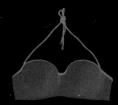

Claudia Piras & Bernhard Roetzel

LADIES

A Guide to Fashion and Style

Claudia Piras & Bernhard Roetzel

LADIES

A Guide to Fashion and Style

DUMONT monte

Original edition
© 2002 DuMont monte Verlag, Cologne

Text: Claudia Piras and Bernhard Roetzel
Translation and typesetting: Rosetta International, London
Design, layout, and typesetting: Malzkorn Kommunikation & Gestaltung, Cologne
Repro: PPP Pre Print Partner, Cologne
Printing and binding: Appl, Wemding

ISBN 3-8320-7067-2
Printed in Germany

Contents

The lady's style

A well-groomed appearance, well-made clothes, and good taste—these are some of the demanding requirements that women have had to meet since the beginning of the history of fashion. Added to this is the question of what the ideal image of a well-dressed woman should be, which is very different for every period. The list of what was "in" and "out" during the late Middle Ages is different from what it was during the rococo period and the belle époque, the years before World War I. In the 20th century the carousel of fashion began to move faster and faster. A lady in an outfit designed in 1905 would have been seen as a creature from outer space by the cheeky, bright young things of the wild 1920s. In the opulent, yuppie 1980s, no one would have believed that checked flared trousers and striped synthetic jumpers had been very fashionable just a few years earlier. In the 1990s, the business suit was taken back to the dressmaker to have the oversized *Dynasty* shoulder pads removed. Today everything that is "retro" is very interesting and our way of dressing includes "quotes" from other decades—but still we are finding it quite difficult to discover a particular fashion trend for the 21st century.

In order not to lose the thread completely when following the vicissitudes of the history of fashion, we have looked for actual style icons for each period. These fashion icons included ladies such as Madame de Récamier, Empress Sissi, Empress Eugénie, and the Duchess of Windsor, and what they wore was eagerly copied in high society. More recently the list of the "Top Ten" has included Jacqueline Kennedy, Audrey Hepburn, Grace Kelly, and Princess Diana. Thanks to the press, television, and the movies, their influence on the world of fashion was no longer limited to a limited select few but inspired thousands of other women throughout the world. Not surprisingly, the look of some of them now seems a little dated and it is doubtful whether items such as the little pillbox hat would still catch on today, but that is only because these ladies are no longer with us. Were Madame de Récamier and her fashionable sisters around in 2002, they would undoubtedly teach us a few things about fashion.

But what was really the secret of these "best dressed women"? What lay behind the particular charm of these ladies whose appearance still fascinates us today? Why is it that they have remained fashion icons, still admired by all today, in spite of the fact that today's designer fashion is completely different from that which existed in the past? The reason for this is they have set the right priorities. A distinctive style is not achieved by following the edicts of fashion and adapting our personality to the fashion of the season, but by allowing our personality to remain the guiding factor, regardless of what is shown on the cover of *Vogue* and *Harper's Bazaar*. Fashion is not a rigid requirement but a range of suggestions from which we can choose the ones that suit us best, that please us most, and that are the most fun. The more eccentric best-dressed women have clearly demonstrated how this game works: just think of Peggy Guggenheim, Marlene Dietrich, and Diana Vreeland. Another example was Coco Chanel, who was quite "revolutionary" in her way of dressing when she first became interested in fashion, so that she had to create the fashions that she wanted to wear herself.

But selecting something from contemporary fashion that will suit our own personality does not mean sitting in the front row at fashion shows twice a year. It is not always a matter of choosing among the latest trends in haute couture or ready-to-wear collections. A distinctive style means much more than merely checking the fashions of the present; it comes from a blending of three time zones, the present, the past and the future. The present contributes up-to-date elements without which a wardrobe would soon become dull and dated. The past plays a vital part in the classic wardrobe, full of those timeless "basics" that are always fashionable and form the foundation of a sound, tasteful wardrobe. The future provides the element of avant-garde that turns the lady into a trend-setter. A well-dressed woman will be guided by present-day fashion while respecting the past and looking at what the future has to offer. This will result in a style that combines personal taste with the developments of fashion. A woman in her mid-thirties does not need to deny that she has already seen more ups and downs of fashion than an eighteen-year-old. Those who have known the retro look in its original version will wear it differently from those who see it as new, exotic and fun.

The greatest style icons combined the present, the past and the future with an instinctive confidence. They are at the same time elegant and modern, conservative and avant-garde, reticent and daring. What kind of fashion developments we can expect in the next few years and decades is impossible to know. But what we can do now is to have a close look at the timeless "basics," those classics of the lady's style that will always remain fashionable and that are the most important and best-loved legacy of 20th century fashion. In this book we shall delve deeper into the historical study of costumes and undertake a voyage of discovery through the fascinating vicissitudes of the history of fashion. But above all we want you to enjoy fashion and all its accessories. Have fun!

Claudia Piras and Bernhard Roetzel
Cologne, May 2002

Classic, simple, timeless, elegant – there are many words to describe an elegant woman's style. But it is never exaggeratedly fashionable.

№ 1

Hair and skin

Ladylike from head to toe

Writing at the end of the 19th century and in the early years of the 20th, the American fashion journalist and cosmetic manufacturer Harriet Hubbard Ayer urged great caution in the use of artificial beauty products, because a woman who is visibly made-up is such a disgrace that further mention of the subject was out of the question. However, the flappers of the 1920s with their love of make-up clearly rejected Miss Harriet Hubbard Ayer's opinions, and if she had been able to see the colorful make-up applied by women in the 1970s she would have fainted from the shock. Nevertheless, even today an obviously "painted" face is still considered unacceptable in many situations. Especially for daytime activities and in business, the saying "less is more" remains appropriate so far as make-up is concerned.

Excessive interest in one's own image has always been considered vain, depraved, and a sign of a "loose" way of life. In addition to the use of make-up to improve one's looks, this also included any attempts made to retain a youthful appearance. But women were no more likely to give up on smooth, silky skin than cosmetic manufacturers were to abandon a healthy turnover. So, in order to avoid the accusation of vanity, the pioneers of the cosmetic industry decided to play the health card. They turned to test tubes and Bunsen burners, took a medical approach and declared that healthy skin depends on good skincare. After all, even the strict Harriet Hubbard Ayer was interested in selling her tubes and pots of beauty creams. Indeed, the medical approach proved to be a clever one. Today, many companies advertise and market their latest achievements with a scholarly attitude, and brands like Clinique or Prescriptives do carry a slight smell of laboratory and white coat.

A careful daily skincare routine involving several products is quite normal nowadays, and common even among the young. In 1962 Revlon launched its Eterna Series 27, specially developed for the woman over 35, which completely revolutionized the cosmetics market. This marked the beginning of increasingly aggressive marketing campaigns promoting youthfulness. Year after year, the cosmetic industry launches newer, better, more effective creams, capsules and ampoules to promote youthful skin. Extremely expensive substances such as liposomes, elastin and collagen promise to slow down the skin's aging process—in other words, people who look old have only themselves to blame.

Whether prompted by vanity, health concerns, the sheer enjoyment of colors and the pleasure of transforming one's appearance, or to prevent the formation of wrinkles, skincare and make-up products are now an integral part of the daily routine. The variety of products available on the market is impressive. But does the concept of a "lady's style" exist? No, there is no such thing as a lady's look. Usually, a woman knows her own mind as far as hair and skin are concerned. She also behaves in quite a special way. She usually prefers a discreet make-up that has been carefully applied. Her lipstick probably matches her nail polish (if she uses any), and this color usually goes well with the rest of her outfit. Her hair is well groomed and not excessively curly. If she wears open shoes in summer, her summery elegance will not be diminished by calluses on her feet. Her perfume will be noticeable upon getting close to her but not as soon as she enters the room.

In short: her cosmetics are chosen with great care and applied in appropriate amounts, tending toward the understated rather than being too flashy, too loud or too excessive. Does this sound boring and perfectionist? Not at all. People may joke about the idea of a "lady," but a lady always remains a lady, crumbling mascara no more affecting her mood than the few laugh lines she has acquired in the course of time.

Completely ladylike: the American country singer Shania Twain as the "face" of Revlon in 1999.

Forever young

From its earliest days, the high art of cosmetics has been divided into two categories: make-up and skincare. Make-up products help to improve and enhance the face's natural advantages, while protective, nourishing, and balancing creams, lotions, oils, and ointments aim to preserve these natural advantages for as long as possible.

Nivea advertisements always emphasized the all-purpose character of the cream. The product was very successful and quickly became a classic.

Indeed, Cleopatra was as famous for the daily baths in ass's milk that she took to keep her skin soft as for her striking eye make-up. Women in ancient Greece looked after their complexions by applying face masks made from breadcrumbs and milk, which they left on the face overnight. Each era in history has had its secret formulas that helped to slow down the damages of age and preserve a woman's delicate beauty. How easily this dream of eternal youth and beauty could be transformed into money was discovered at the end of the 19th century, when young cosmetic entrepreneurs began to sell tubes and pots of creams on a large scale.

One of the pioneers in the field was Harriet Hubbard Ayer who was born in Chicago in 1849. In 1886 she acquired the formula for a face cream during one of her trips to Paris. The advertising campaign organized by her husband claimed that this cream had already been used by Madame Récamier, a celebrated beauty of her time (1777–1849). In a very short time her "Récamier" cream had become a best-seller in America as well as elsewhere. Harriet Hubbard Ayer subsequently brought out many more miracle creams, among others the very popular anti-wrinkle cream "La Belle Cocotte."

The year 1911 saw another major milestone in the history of skincare. After years of research, three Germans, the entrepreneur Oskar Troplowitz, the chemist Isaac Lifschütz, and the dermatologist Paul Unna, finally discovered the active agent Eucerit. This is produced from lanolin (the fat from sheep wool). It is an emulsifier and can therefore be combined with water to make a smooth cream. It was now possible to produce for the first time a water-in-oil emulsion that remained stable instead of separating into water and oil after a while. This revolutionary discovery meant that it was possible to abandon the heavy creams made from animal and plant fats whose main disadvantage was that they quickly became rancid. Oskar Troplowitz owned the Beiersdorf company, which he had bought from its founder Carl Beiersdorf in 1890, and now he launched a new snow-white cream under the name of Nivea (from the Latin nix, nivis, meaning snow).

It was decided that the packaging should be in keeping with the image of the woman as seen at the time, namely fragile, delicate and soft. The box was yellow with elegant green art nouveau lettering and red decorative elements. Nivea acquired its well-known blue packaging with a white logo when it was re-launched with a new promotional campaign in 1924. The successful cream was soon followed by a sun oil and other beauty preparations, so that by the 1930s there was a complete range of Nivea beauty products. Nivea's advertising in Germany remained free of Nazi propaganda because of the influence of the economics graduate Elly Heuss-Knapp who worked as a copywriter for Nivea from 1934 onward. After the war, Elly Heuss-Knapp, a committed politician herself, became First Lady of the young Federal German Republic at the side of her husband President Theodor Heuss. Meanwhile, the cream in the blue box continued its triumphant progress throughout the world. Besides the classic Nivea cream, the composition of which has remained almost completely unchanged, there are now also several ranges of first-class cosmetics such as Nivea Visage and Nivea Beauté.

Whether they are products manufactured by exclusive cosmetic manufacturers or inexpensive own brands bought at the supermarket, skincare preparations can only enhance your skin if they are used regularly. The collection of beauty creams that is only there for decoration will not help on its own. Depending on the product it must be used morning or evening; in fact many can be used round the clock. But it is important to cleanse the skin thoroughly before any product is applied. Using old make-up and skincare products can lead to the formation of spots and skin irritation. In addition, the beneficial active ingredients will have little effect on an unprepared skin.

The characteristic blue background with white lettering was introduced in 1924. Apart from a few minor adjustments to satisfy contemporary taste, the design of the packaging of Nivea cream has hardly changed since then.

Beauty know-how

AHA
Alpha Hydroxy Acid, an acid that has a peeling effect on the skin

Allantonin
Found in wheat germ and used to soothe rough, cracked skin

Ceramide
Lipoids that hold the cells in the layer of the skin together, promoting moisture retention

Collagen
The connective tissue of the skin consists of 70% collagen; water-soluble collagen in cosmetics stimulates the formation of new collagen fibers

Elastin
Fundamental substance of the elastic connective tissue; applied externally, elastin promotes the formation of new elastin fibers that make the skin more elastic

Hyaluronic acids
Extremely hygroscopic (water-absorbent) acids with high moisture retentiveness; they keep the skin moist even in very dry conditions

Lipids
Fats and fat-like substances, used to counter wrinkles

Liposomes
These carry vitamins and other active agents deep into the skin

Panthenol
Vitamin B5, speeds up healing and has regenerative properties

Retinol
Vitamin A, stimulates the skin's self-protection and has regenerative properties

A smooth, unblemished complexion

A well cared-for, radiant complexion—since time immemorial this has been a symbol of perfect female beauty, but one that is never to be taken for granted. It is no wonder that women throughout the ages have always spent a lot of time, money and effort to achieve this image of perfect beauty. A closer look at the history of cosmetics is helpful in understanding this aspect of female beauty. During the baroque period in the 18th century, water was still suspected of spreading the plague and its use in daily personal hygiene was therefore taboo. Instead of water, people used plenty of powder and ointments that inevitably promoted the formation of pimples, pustules and blackheads. These were then concealed under a thick layer of make-up. The scars caused by smallpox, then a common disease, further damaged what was left of people's natural complexions. Although the situation had greatly improved by the beginning of the 20th century from a hygienic point of view, pale skin still represented high social rank, indicating abstention from all "unladylike" activities in the open air, such as work and sport. As a result, bleaching products containing arsenic and white Japanese rice powder were very popular. The use of make-up was thought unseemly and the purchase of such products was also quite risky since nobody knew exactly what they contained. There were many recipes that enabled women to prepare their own skin creams by mixing substances such as alcohol, mercury, glycerin or borax. But all these homemade products, as well as the bought ones, were difficult to apply, and when they dried on the skin they crumbled away at the slightest facial expression.

By the 1920s, improved powder and liquid foundations were eventually developed. By now make-up had become a generally accepted social custom and demand had increased as a result of the newly founded cosmetic empires such as those of Elizabeth Arden and Helena Rubinstein. Although pale skin was still considered chic, women were now developing interests in tennis, swimming and sunbathing, and the newly-developed Ambre Solaire soon became a bestseller. In 1935 Max Factor launched his revolutionary compact powder foundation, and this product was advertised by Hollywood movie star Lana Turner. The product was said to stay on for a long time and to conceal

In the 1970s, the natural, girlish type was the fashion: slightly waved hair, large eyes discreetly but effectively made-up, and full, glossy lips.

The typical make-up of the Roaring Twenties was applied much too heavily by today's standards and as a result was very dramatic. Black kohl was an absolute must-have at the time.

small skin defects while promising a "lovely new complexion." There were further advantages: the product saved time, and was also very easy to apply. From then on there was no excuse for appearing without make-up. Its use had developed from a tolerated female foible into a general obligation. Even during World War II and the post-war years, cosmetics remained available (although the quality was somewhat inferior) and women's magazines continued to advertise their use.

Because make-up had now become the norm, it was also subjected to changing fashion trends. In the 1950s, fairly heavy make-up, that would today be considered exaggerated, was fashionable. During the 1960s a pale complexion was often preferred while the growing tourism industry of the 1970s promoted a bronzed look again. Since the 1980s the trend in make-up has been toward a light, natural, transparent look. The new, modern, high-tech products of today care for dry, oily or combination skin, as well as incorporating an anti-aging formula, and may include sun-protection or have light-reflecting properties. The ideal of a perfect complexion is now more attainable than ever.

The demands made on modern cosmetics are constantly increasing. The Revlon Skinlights collection offers women professional products for use at home.

Rouge

Rouge or blush experienced the same difficulties in becoming socially acceptable as lipstick. Once the attribute of ladies of dubious virtue, it is today an indispensable item for everyone who wants to look fit, radiant and healthy at all times of the day and night. At the end of the 19th century, rouge was mainly used by men, especially aging dandies who used either theatrical make-up or a preparation of beet or strawberry juice. The first ready-made rouge preparations consisted of pressed color mixtures that were mixed with water or alcohol before being applied. Rouge only became part of women's make-up after World War I, when several cosmetic manufacturers launched make-up sets with blush, foundation and eye shadow. Now blush is available in all colors from pink to violet, from cherry red to brown, as a liquid product, a gel, a cream or a powder. Blush is perfect for shaping the face and solving the problem of a pale skin. Whether the cheek area should be more strongly emphasized or barely colored is now a question of current fashion and personal taste.

Lipstick (here Absolutely Fabulous Lipcream by Revlon) has a symbolic meaning. It represents femininity, beauty—and eroticism.

There are long-lasting liquid preparations as well as compact lipsticks to help produce an effect of dramatically red lips.

The color red

Diana Vreeland was the editor-in-chief of American *Vogue* in the 1960s and as a result she was the most influential fashion journalist in the world. She was an enthusiastic champion of the color red, which was present in every shade in her New York apartment and also in her eccentric make-up. She always wore bright red lipstick that contrasted strongly with her jet-black hair and pale complexion. Paloma Picasso also sported bright red lips and a black beauty spot on her left cheek, which became her trademark. It is no coincidence that her lipstick "Mon Rouge," launched in 1984, became one of the most successful products in her line of cosmetics.

In ancient Egypt women were already using red coloring to emphasize their lips, and in 16th-century France painted lips were a generally accepted phenomenon, even in convents and nunneries. There were various recipes for lip paint, many of them containing arsenic and therefore extremely hazardous to one's health. Others were made from animal blood and fat, thus jeopardizing a women's love life because they smelled unpleasant and rancid after a few hours. But the actual "birth" of lipstick in the modern sense of the word took place at the International Colonial Exhibition in Amsterdam in 1883. Paris-based perfumiers had succeeded in producing a comparatively durable, solid stick of color from beeswax, deer suet and castor oil, wrapped in silk paper and easy to carry about.

The celebrated actress Sarah Bernhardt, who had stirred audiences with her performance as the courtesan Marguerite Gauthier in *La Dame aux Camélias*, was among the first fans of this "lipstick" that she is said to have named "stylo d'amour" or "love pencil." But most respectable women of the late 19th century were at first rather reluctant to use it. It was only in the wild 1920s that red lips became an integral part of fashionable make-up and the bold gesture of applying lipstick in public was suddenly seen as an expression of a woman's emancipation.

This dramatic look with a heart-shaped mouth was inspired by the screen goddesses of

the time, a style that was then further promoted by the skillful beautician Max Factor. He started his career in St. Petersburg as a wigmaker to the tsar's family and later built up one of the largest cosmetic firms in America. As a make-up artist to the Hollywood stars, he created the screen face of many actresses including Gloria Swanson, Pola Negri, Greta Garbo, Carole Lombard and Marlene Dietrich. The theatrical lips he created were widely copied until after World War II.

Meanwhile, the cosmetic industry continued to develop better and less expensive lipsticks. In 1935, Germaine Monteil launched her celebrated "Chinese Red" and Elizabeth Arden created a set with different shades of red that was sold under the name of the "lipstick wardrobe." In the 1940s, Rita Hayworth advertised a Max Factor lipstick in an elegant gold case that apparently neither smeared nor dried the lips.

In the 1950s, eye make-up became more important, at the expense of the mouth. However, this did not mean that lipstick disappeared from the scene. On the contrary, a little powder and some discreet lipstick had by now become part of every woman's basic make-up. Women would never leave the house without make-up, and the

newly invented case with its twisting mechanism to expose the lipstick ensured that this practical beauty product could now be found in every handbag. The 1960s and 1970s continued the trend of heavily made-up eyes, while the disco era, with its fascination with everything glitzy, introduced the roll-on stick of lip gloss.

It was only in the ambivalent 1980s, which saw the invention of the straightforward business look with cool, discreet make-up as well as the admiration of the opulent elegance of the *Dallas* and *Dynasty* clans, that luscious red lips were allowed to make a comeback, at least in the evening.

The individualistic 1990s made it possible for every woman to decide for herself whether or not she wished to wear lipstick. Even so, it is a fact that 80% of women wear lipstick every day. But women are ever more demanding and today's products are required to meet increasingly high requirements: the color must last, the lipstick must be moisturizing, it must not "bleed," it must be hypoallergenic, and it has to include UV protection. In addition to these specific requirements, increasingly, women also want their lipstick to be free of petrochemicals, environmentally friendly as well as not tested on animals.

Brilliant red lips have been Paloma Picasso's trademark for decades. This photograph was taken in 1989, yet the look is timeless and classic.

1968 in Spain: Brigitte Bardot wearing the dark eye make-up typical of the 1960s during the shooting of the film *Shalako*.

Maria Callas's look was dominated by her dramatic eye make-up: thick eyebrows, eyelashes with heavy mascara, and strong eyeliner.

Eye make-up

The great era of eye make-up undoubtedly embraced the decades of the 1960s and 1970s with stars like Brigitte Bardot and Maria Callas who were famous for their use of eye make-up. Grooming tips at the time promoted the use of highlights, false eyelashes, mascara, and eyeliner, while eye shadow in the most strident colors was used in profusion right up to the eyebrows. It is true that eyes had always been made-up to a certain extent (the Roaring Twenties loved kohl), but the dominant feature of the face had always been the striking, dramatically painted lips. This now changed. The lips became paler (except in the case of Marilyn Monroe) and the eyes became the main, dominant feature of the face. Twiggy became the "Face of the Sixties" virtually overnight, particularly because of her large, made-up eyes.

The changing trend in make-up had already started in the years of European economic prosperity that began in the 1950s. Suddenly, companies were launching new eye make-up products almost every week: liquid and pencil eyeliner, powder and cream eye shadow, waterproof mascara, as well as a special remover to take eye make-up off again. There were also eyelash curlers that required some practice to use but were very effective, enabling everyone to have spectacularly curled lashes. Women who did not know how to combine these various new products could buy sets. Subtlety and understatement were not part of the vocabulary: combinations of lilac mascara, navy eyeliner and light blue eye shadow were the height of sophistication. These colors were also popular in the 1960s, but the areas where make-up was applied became larger and larger until the face looked painted rather than made-up. False eyelashes were obligatory. The continual development of innovative products ensured that women remained enthralled by these cheerful colors. Bold colors such as those in Mary Quant's collection caused a sensation. Bright metallic colors including gold, bronze and silver were also very popular, and they were subsequently also used by the disco generation, which added luminous eye shadow, glittery gels and white highlighter to emphasize the eye area. In order to help their customers find their way in this mass of colors, companies offered make-up suggestions for which at least five different eye make-up products were required. This was in addition to the various colors used for the face, lips, nails, and so on.

But how are these luscious colors produced? What substances are used to create the glorious ice blue or seductive fuchsia pink? Eyes have always been made-up, and in antiquity for instance, green eye-shadow was made from finely ground malachite. Even today, many preparations still contain substances of mineral origin. One of the main ingredients of eye shadow is talcum powder, which is a mixture of magnesium silicate and aluminum silicate. Seen through a microscope, the tiny particles that make up talcum powder look like small plates. This structure has three advantages. First, the small plates are so fine and transparent that they cannot be seen by the naked eye. Second, they lie flat on the skin without penetrating into the pores and blocking them. Third, the small plates glide easily on top of each other so that the eye shadow acquires a creamy texture and is easy to apply. The shimmering effect around the eyes is achieved by the addition of particles of mica (aluminum silicate), which is also made up of small plates; these break and reflect the light very effectively. Colored pigments are added, such as iron oxide and iron hydroxide (for red, yellow, blue, brown and orange), ultramarine (often synthetic) for blue, green, red and violet) or umber (kaolin, a clay substance with iron and manganese for brown shades).

Eyes are very sensitive and the conjunctiva often reacts to the slightest irritation by itching, burning, and reddening. This is why eye make-up products should be tested with great care. Many cosmetic manufacturers do this, but always check on the package that the product has been tested for allergies. There are ranges of eye make-up that are hypo-allergenic. If you wear contact lenses you should only wear mascara and eye-shadow that is declared to be "suitable for contact lens wearers." Otherwise you may damage your contact lenses as well as your eyes.

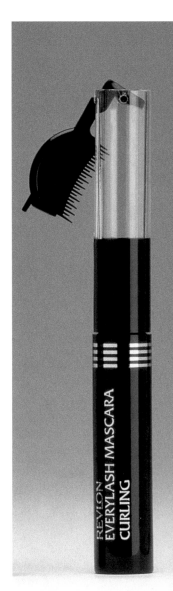

Mascara also adds volume and color to fine lashes. In order to ensure that the lashes do not stick together, manufacturers often include a little brush to separate the lashes.

Make-up artist Kevyn Aucoin checks and adjusts top model Linda Evangelista's make-up just before the beginning of a fashion show.

The art of make-up

The 1990s marked the end of uniform make-up, dictated by fashion. The look was no longer the most important aspect. What mattered now was the face with its individual features and the personality of the person. On the runways models were often seen apparently wearing very little make-up. In reality, they were wearing highly sophisticated make-up created by skilled make-up artists, in which the particular appeal lay in its obvious "natural" look.

This natural look was much favored by François Nars. The French-born make-up artist and adopted New Yorker is one of the most famous make-up artists of the present day, admired by designers such as Anna Sui, Karl Lagerfeld, and Dolce & Gabbana, as well as well-known photographers such as Herb Ritts and Irving Penn, and pop stars including Madonna. Nars's main aim is always to discover the various ways of bringing out the beauty of a face. Whether in natural, classic or extravagant manner, he does not believe in a standard look. The American make-up artist Bobbi Brown is also guided by the woman's individuality on which she then bases her make-up. "When a woman enters a room, it is her personality that should produce the effect and not her make-up," is one of the guiding principles of this former theatrical make-up artist. Bobbi Brown's make-up is very natural and often based on shades of brown that flatter the skin and do not look heavy.

In recent years make-up artists and the art they practice have acquired increasing recognition, as also has the interest in professional make-up methods and reliable products that are used to achieve a desired effect. Kevyn Aucoin, who is responsible for the Revlon face of Cindy Crawford, among others, reveals in his book everything there is to know about make-up, while the latest tricks for larger eyes or fuller lips are described in specialist magazines.

The trend toward the "Make-up of Make-up artists" was started by stylist Frank Toskan with his M.A.C. range, and François Nars, Shu Uemura, and Bobbi Brown have also launched their own ranges of cosmetics.

Tips and tricks

- Make-up should match the skin tone. Ask for a sample and try it on your face in daylight at home, not briefly in the store on the back of your hand.

- Do not apply foundation like cream, instead dab it on your face with your fingertips or pat it on with a sponge to achieve an even result.

- Pluck you eyebrows so as to achieve a natural look, but not too thin. An ice cube will reduce the pain as well as the swelling.

- Lashes will remain curled longer if the lash curlers are warmed up before use.

- In order to avoid the "spider legs" effect, separate the lashes immediately after applying your mascara, using a small eyelash brush or comb.

- Always match the blush with the foundation. Only use a cream blush on a liquid foundation, and powder blush on powder make-up. This will prevent blotches.

- Black kohl and dark eyeliner make the eyes look smaller. They should be used very sparsely.

- Red blush easily looks "painted on." Blush in shades of brown or pink looks more natural.

- Lips look fuller if you emphasize the pale outer contour of the lips with a lip liner and not the inner pink contour.

- Lip liner should match the natural color of the lips as well as the lipstick. Avoid very dark colors, otherwise the dark contour line will become obvious after the lipstick has begun to fade during the day.

- Dark red colors, chocolate browns and lilacs often look too hard and make the lips appear narrower.

- Rosewood, apricot or pale pink combined with lip gloss will make the lips look fuller.

- To ensure your lipstick stays on longer, apply some foundation to your lips, carefully line the lips, and apply the lipstick with a brush. Then blot your lips with a tissue before applying a second layer of lipstick.

The fragrance of a lady

Many famous women have adored it and many still do so. In the 1950s, Marilyn Monroe admitted publicly that at night she wore nothing but a few drops of it. Chanel No 5, in its classic square bottle, is still an incontestable legend in the world of perfumes, timeless and untouched by the vicissitudes of fashion, and the most successful fragrance of all time.

In 1920, Coco Chanel met the respected perfumer Ernest Beaux who used to work for Rallet in Grasse, the Mecca of French perfume in Provence. Beaux had just developed a new formula that, according to the story, he offered first to the famous perfume house of Coty. However, those in charge there soon lost interest when they discovered the price of the ingredients. Coco Chanel's reaction was quite different—sophisticated, expensive and exquisite, it was exactly what she was looking for. Beaux began working on the prototype perfume again. The ingredients were May rose, jasmine, ylang-ylang, neroli, civet, and musk, together with woody notes and vanilla. It was only when Beaux added aldehydes that the feminine, slightly synthetic character of Chanel No 5 began to take shape. Aldehydes are chemical compounds that in concentrated form smell like rancid butter but when appropriately diluted they exude a light, pleasant floral fragrance. In Beaux's composition, the presence of aldehydes added lightness and elegance to the otherwise rather heavy ingredients. Chanel No 5 was the first fragrance to contain aldehydes.

However, several developments had preceded the launch of Chanel's chemical perfume revolution on May 5, 1921, smoothing the way for the new perfume. Until 1889 perfumes were made from natural substances and produced using complicated methods that made them very expensive. However, since the middle of the 19th century, chemists had been analyzing natural fragrances and aromas in their laboratories in order to recreate them later. One of the first breakthroughs was the synthesis of vanilla in 1874, soon followed by the discovery of coumarin, the artificial green fernlike note. In 1904 the structure of musk was unraveled. The development of artificial aromatic essences not only made perfumes cheaper, but also paved the way for completely new compositions. Innovative perfumers such as Guerlain and Houbigant began to experiment with new chemical compositions. Jicky, launched by Guerlain in 1889, caused a stir in the world of fashion: in complete contrast to the usual floral fragrances customary at the time, the fragrance of Jicky was based on tonka beans, sandalwood and ferns, that is, coumarin. For the lily-of-the-valley scent in Quelques Fleurs (1912), Houbigant used a chemical compound for the first time, namely hydroxycitronellal, instead of the little flowers. Barely ten years later Coco Chanel celebrated her aldehyde success, and soon afterward this synthetic floral concept was copied by Lanvin with Arpège and by Worth with Je Reviens.

Modern perfume compositions may have up to 85% synthetic ingredients, a development that is observed with great skepticism by many perfumers. The old-established perfume houses swore that they would continue to use natural ingredients as the main components, as they had always done, and they believed that chemical compounds should not make up more than 15 to 20%. Guerlain firmly believed that only the quality determined the success of a fragrance and not the packaging or the clever marketing concept behind it. Perhaps Guerlain was not far off with this assessment, given that six of the most successful fragrances were created between 1861 and 1933 and they are still being produced. These include the famous Mitsouko, launched in 1919 and still sold in large quantities today.

The sumptuous Panthère by Cartier is a typical fragrance of the 1980s. The stopper of the glass bottle is embellished with the panther, a Cartier motif that dates back to the 1930s.

Cartier launched So Pretty on the market in 1995. It is a fine, feminine yet very modern fragrance.

Must de Cartier made its debut in the 1970s. Today its is one of the greatest fragrance classics of the house.

The favorite fragrances of the 20th century

1900–09
Fragrances that were based on one type of flower such as jasmine or violets were displaced by soft floral compositions: Rose Jacqueminot (Coty), L'Origan (Coty). Jicky (Guerlain), developed in 1889 and based on tonka beans, sandalwood, and fern, is still as popular as ever.

1910–19
The decade of Chypre fragrances: Coty created his legendary Chypre in 1917, followed by Guerlain's Mitsouko in 1919. Other scents were Quelques Fleurs (Houbigant) and the oriental Narcisse Noir (Caron).

1920–29
Aldehyde notes were considered modern: Chanel No 5 (Chanel), Arpège (Lanvin). Also Shalimar (Guerlain).

1930–39
Oriental fragrances dominated: Shocking (Schiaparelli). Also leathery fragrances such as Cuir de Russie (Chanel) and the floral-based Joy (Patou).

1940–49
Green fragrances such as Vent Vert (Balmain) and subtle Chypres such as Ma Griffe (Carven), Femme (Rochas), and Miss Dior (Dior), still very popular. Also Fracas (Piguet).

1950–59
In Europe Cabochard (Grès) became a bestseller, while in America the most popular fragrances were Youth Dew (Lauder) and Intimate (Revlon). Also Diorissimo (Dior) and L'Air du Temps (Nina Ricci).

1960–69
Floral fragrances such as Fidji (Laroche) and aldehyde-based scents such as Calèche (Hermès) and Madame Rochas (Rochas).

1970–79
All types are represented: Chanel No 19 (Chanel), Anaïs Anaïs (Cacharel), Chloé (Lagerfeld), Oscar (Oscar de la Renta), Nocturnes (Caron), First (Van Cleef & Arpels), Opium (St. Laurent), Rive Gauche (St. Laurent), Must (Cartier), Charlie (Revlon).

1980–89
Heavy floral and oriental fragrances such as Poison (Dior), Jil Sander No 4 (Sander), Loulou (Cacharel), Panthère (Cartier), Obsession (Calvin Klein), Samsara (Guerlain), Roma (Biagiotti), and Joop! (Joop). Also lighter floral scents White Linen (Lauder) or Calyx (Prescriptives), and some Chypre fragrances by designers including Armani, Paloma Picasso, Montana, and Fendi. Also: aromatherapy such as Eau Dynamisante (Clarins).

1990–99
The almost overpowering perfumes of the 1980s were followed by the return of softer fragrances and the launch of unisex ones such as CKone (Calvin Klein) and Paco (Paco Rabanne). Other favorites: Allure (Chanel), Cool Water Woman (Davidoff), Trésor (Lancôme), Obsession (Calvin Klein), Envy (Gucci), Casmir (Chopard), Rococo (Joop), Dolce Vita (Dior).

2000–
At the 2001 Fifi Awards, the Oscar of the perfume industry, the winners were as follows. In the Parfums Haute Couture category: 1. BLV (Bulgari), 2. Sensations (Jil Sander), 3. Intuition (Estée Lauder). In the Parfums Prêt-à-porter category: 1. Azurra (Azzaro), 2. Sui Dreams (Anna Sui), 3. Naomagic (Naomi Campbell). Shalimar launched by Guerlain in 1925 was declared the best classic perfume!

Fragrance families

Floral

The family of floral fragrances includes about half of all the perfumes available on the market. In addition, a distinction is made between fragrances based on a single type of flower (for instance, lily-of-the-valley in Diorissimo by Dior), and those based on several different kinds of flowers (for instance, Quelques Fleurs by Houbigant).

Floral-green

A mixture of floral notes and impressions reminiscent of green leaves, stems, and grass. Vent Vert (Balmain), Beautiful (Lauder).

Floral-fruity

Floral components with notes of pineapple, apricots, apples, raspberries, plums, or peaches. Byblos (Byblos), Eau de Givenchy (Givenchy).

Floral-fresh

The element of freshness is provided by bergamot or citrus components and the bright, floral notes by orange blossom, lily-of-the-valley, lavender or hyacinth. Moods Donna (Krizia), Valentino (Valentino), Romeo (Romeo Gigli).

Floral-flowery

This is the large group of the more or less pure floral fragrances whose main components are rose, jasmine, ylang-ylang, narcissus, tuberose, iris, and carnation. Eternity (Calvin Klein), K (Krizia), Lumière (Rochas).

Floral-aldehydic

In this group the floral components are complemented by synthetic aldehydes. Aldehydes have "fatty", "tallow-like" or "blown-out candle" smells. This may sound strange but aldehydes are used in many elegant, feminine fragrances—it all depends on the amount. Chanel No 5 (Chanel), Marbert Donna 2 (Marbert), Nonchalance (Mäurer + Wirtz), Scherrer 2 (Scherrer).

Floral-amber

These fragrances are also known as "floriental", the oriental touch being provided by the amber resin with its characteristic smoky, tar-like aroma. Loulou (Cacharel), Poison (Dior).

Oriental

These fragrances are dominated by the proverbial, seductive aromas, reminiscent of Arabia, namely exotic flowers, resins, spices, balms etc. They are mostly rather heavy.

Oriental-amber

This group combines components such as amber and vanilla with citrus, green notes or spicy aromas (artemisia, sage, rosemary, lavender). Must (Cartier), Roma (Biagiotti), Obsession (Calvin Klein), Magie Noire (Lancôme).

Oriental-spicy

Echoes of cinnamon, cloves, coriander and pepper combined with a touch of leather and resin. Cinnabar (Lauder), Coco (Chanel), KL (Lagerfeld), Opium (St. Laurent), Parfum Sacré (Caron).

Chypre

The mother of all chypre fragrances is Chypre by François Coty, which became the symbol of the generic family containing all those perfumes that are dominated by a fresh citrus note against a background of oak moss, labdanum and patchouli. Because it was originally associated with plants of the eastern Mediterranean, it was named "Chypre," the French name for Cyprus.

Chypre-fruity

A heavy, rich combination with pronounced fruity, often peachlike components. Y (St. Laurent), Azzaro (Azzaro), Femme (Rochas).

Chypre-floral-animal

Warm, rich fragrance with components of animal origin such as musk, civet, ambergris or castoreum. Jil Sander Woman Two (Sander), Mystère (Rochas), Ysatis (Givenchy).

Chypre-floral

In this group the dry, fresh chypre components become more pleasant and subdued with the addition of floral notes. Diva (Ungaro), Fendi (Fendi), Halston (Halston), Montana (Montana).

Chypre-fresh

This is chypre at its purest. 4711 Echt Kölnisch Wasser ("Real eau de Cologne") (Mülhens), Diorella (Dior), Ô (Lancôme).

Chypre-green

Tangy-fresh, dry interpretation of the chypre theme with spicy and coniferous components (pine and juniper). Armani (Armani), Alliage (Lauder).

The king of perfume

There is one thing that is needed above all to create a new perfume and that is the nose. The human olfactory organ is so important in the perfume industry that it almost symbolizes the perfumer himself; in France, the home of perfume par excellence, the person whose job it is to test fragrances by "smelling" is simply called "le nez" ("the nose"). Naturally, to become a "nose" you need some olfactory talent to begin with, but much more important is the sound training, which takes an average of five to six years. During this time the prospective perfumer (who today may also be female, since women have finally succeeded in penetrating this typically male domain) acquires his most valuable capital: the memory of fragrances. In fact, a perfume expert's sense of smell is not any better than other people's, but they are able to analyze their impressions of fragrance, identify them accurately, store them in their memory and retrieve them whenever necessary. While a layman can at best identify two dozen common fragrances, such as rose, vanilla and jasmine, the "nose" can accurately identify scents such as ylang-ylang, civet, neroli, cananga, or castoreum. With time, the "nose" is able to recognize about 2,000 smells, a skill that must be practiced every day in order to preserve the sensory skills. As well as acquiring knowledge of the sensory aspects of the business, the "nose" must also know the practical side. This includes having an accurate knowledge of natural and synthetic ingredients, that is, the raw materials of perfume, as well as the technical production requirements. Last but not least, some knowledge of the costs is required so that the product to be created later will sell for an affordable price.

When a designer or cosmetic firm commissions a new perfume, the lengthy development process starts for the perfumer, who must now create the desired scent. The final product will normally contain from 30 to 50 different scent components, although there are some perfumes that consist of several hundred components. First, a preliminary test formula is drawn up and mixed on a trial basis.

The perfumer also checks whether the fragrance remains stable or tends to smell completely different after a few hours. When a satisfactory formula has been found, it is then perfected further. Step by step, the importance of individual nuances is evaluated and the perfumer then decides on which version would be best. Perhaps a little more amber oil or perhaps a little less? Or possibly reduce the citrus aroma and increase the minty note? And so forth. When the perfumer has finally decided what the final fragrance will be, the formula must be adapted to the final product and medium. For instance, the product may be an eau de toilette in an atomizer, a bubble bath, a body lotion or something quite different, such as a scented candle for the home collection. When all further tests and experiments have proved successful, the final formula is given to the client company, which then takes care of the production and marketing of the new fragrance.

It is hard for non-professionals to describe such a sensory, intangible impression as a fragrance, but perfumers have created categories in which they can classify every single composition. These categories are based on three fundamental fragrance families, namely "floral," "oriental," and "chypre." Each of these families can be interpreted in several ways. For instance, a floral fragrance may have fruity or aldehyde-like characteristics, while an oriental scent is more dominated by amber and spices. These fragrances would be defined as "floral-fruity," "floral-aldehyde," and "oriental-amber" or "oriental-spicy."

Such nomenclature is not very interesting for customers. When buying perfume, women are entirely guided by their first impression. If it unconsciously reminds us of something pleasant, we shall like it immediately. If we do not, there is very little that even the best marketing can do about it.

The perfumer at the essential-oil factory of Haaman and Reimer in Holzminden, Germany. A perfumer has a highly trained nose for fragrance, typically being able to distinguish up to 2,000 nuances.

Scent and skincare with tradition

With Shalimar, launched in 1925, Guerlain created the first oriental fragrance and one of the most famous perfumes of the 1920s.

Perfumer Jean-Paul Guerlain, the great-grandson of the company's founder, has created many fragrances since 1959, some of which have become legendary.

Besides the famous haute couture and prêt-à-porter perfumes, there is a whole range of "independent" fragrances and skincare products. They do not bear the name of a famous fashion designer or perfumer but simply the name of their house. The house—like the formulas—is often a couple of centuries old. The popularity of these fragrant, well-established products is only enhanced by the reputation of these ancient houses. Many of their preparations are still produced by hand using natural products, following traditional methods, and they are also packaged by hand. Their customers include many stars and other famous people who appreciate the great care paid to the manufacture of these products and swear by their high quality.

The most ancient example is the Pharmacy of the Convent of Santa Maria Novella in Florence, the city that was already the perfume capital of Italy in the Renaissance. Since 1612 various essences, elixirs, ointments, creams, soaps and perfumes have been produced in these premises, which have been preserved in their original condition. Several of the preparations are still made according to the original recipes of the Dominican monks. In the 18th century, the monks' preparations began to be exported, acquiring a small but faithful following throughout the world. Any visitor to Florence should try the Convent's calming elixir or its pomegranate soap. Acqua di Parma also comes from Italy; this is a fragrance that has developed into a complete range that has been on the market since 1938. Audrey Hepburn and Ava Gardner were fans of this light fragrance that smells refreshingly of citrus, lavender and rose water, as Sharon Stone is today.

Guerlain is undoubtedly the symbol of perfume manufacturing in France. In 1828, Pierre-François-Pascal Guerlain opened his shop in Paris where he at first sold imported English fragrances. But soon he began manufacturing his own creams, soaps and ointments. In 1834, he launched the successful Crème Ambroisie, which is still in production. In 1842, he developed the first perfumes that immediately became favorites among Parisian high society, and he created the legendary Eau de Cologne Impériale for the Empress Eugénie in 1853. In the 1920s, the house of Guerlain dominated the world perfume market together with Coty and Houbigant. Responsible for countless classic fragrances, the company is still the most important representative of the art of perfume making in France.

The original Eau de Cologne comes from Germany and is called 4711 Echt Kölnisch Wasser. In 1792 Wilhelm Mülhens was given a parchment by the Carthusian monk Franz Carl Gereon Maria Farina as a wedding present. It contained the formula for an "aqua mirabilis," a miracle water. Mülhens immediately set about distilling this fragrant brew in his house, Glockengasse 4711 in Cologne, and sold it very successfully under the name of Kölnisch Wasser. The house number 4711 was registered as a trade name by Ferdinand Mülhens, the grandson of the founder, in order to distinguish it from the numerous copies that were available on the market. The precise composition has remained secret but citrus notes are clearly detectable, as are rosemary, neroli and lavender. This fresh-neutral, balanced composition made 4711 Echt Kölnisch Wasser the first unisex fragrance in the history of scent.

In 1760, James Henry Creed opened a tailor's shop in London. Shortly afterwards he started manufacturing perfumes that quickly became extremely popular at all the European courts. The Empress Eugénie, wife of Napoleon III, who loved perfumes, succeeded in persuading Creed to move to Paris in 1854. This ensured her daily supply of Jasmin Impératrice, a warm, powdery preparation based on jasmine, vanilla, sandalwood, and musk, which Creed had created for her. Queen Victoria preferred Indiana, while Empress Sissi of Austria loved the seductive vanilla fragrance of Vanisia. For the passengers of the Titanic Creed developed a special perfume, based on algae, seaweed and honeydew melon. Today, Olivier Creed is the sixth generation to run the family business. Creed still uses a remarkably high proportion of natural ingredients that are weighed, mixed, washed and filtered by hand.

As well as being Creed's birthplace, England is also the home of many other important perfumers and cosmetic manufacturers. These include the soap and perfume maker Bronnley, founded in 1883, whose motto is "Makers of the best soaps in the world," Penhaligon (1870), Floris (1730, now perfumers to Queen Elizabeth II), D. R. Harris (1790, also makers of the legendary revitalizing Pick Me Up elixir), and Yardley (1770, Old English Lavender), all making products much appreciated by those who love English preparations. The tradition of carefully produced cosmetics is being continued by young companies such as Lush. Lush produce soaps, lotions, creams and everything else that is needed for the daily care of body and soul. Its preparations, produced according to strict quality guidelines, are made predominantly by hand from carefully selected natural raw materials. "Bath Ballistics" bath cubes, the creamy "Massage bars," and new soaps with imaginative names such as "Banana Moon," "Pineapple Grunt," "Demon in the Dark," and "Ginger Man" have acquired a cult status in the bathroom.

The New World too has its traditional manufacturers, such as Kiehl's in New York, which is among the most famous. The company was founded in 1851 and it produces high-quality, handmade products that are sold in sober, plain packaging. With a reticence that is very unusual in America, Kiehl's does not advertise and it has only recently decided to have its own home page on the Web. But the quality of its shampoos, cleansers, creams, and lipsticks convinces its customers without the need for marketing. Winona Ryder and Sarah Jessica Parker are great enthusiasts of their beauty products, which are available from their always-crowded shop in Manhattan's East Village.

In 1914 Guerlain opened an elegant perfumery on the Champs-Élysées in Paris. But the firm's head office is in the Rue de la Paix.

Music for the nose: on this "fragrance organ" Jean-Paul Guerlain assembles the aromatic ingredients for his perfume creations.

A visit to Guerlain's store at 68, Champs-Élysées is an experience for its fragrances. The elegant, historic interior is also well worth seeing.

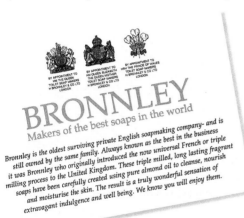

BRONNLEY
Makers of the best soaps in the world

Bronnley is the oldest surviving private English soapmaking company- and is still owned by the same family. Always known as the best in the business it was Bronnley who originally introduced the now universal French or triple milling process to the United Kingdom. These triple milled, long lasting fragrant soaps have been carefully created using pure almond oil to cleanse, nourish and moisturise the skin. The result is a truly wonderful sensation of extravagant indulgence and well being. We know you will enjoy them.

Many English women (and anglophiles as well) buy their beauty products at D. R. Harris & Co., a traditional store in London's St. James's Street.

From bobbed haircuts and blond bombshells to the natural look

Until the 1960s, the history of changing hairstyles could be summed up as a succession of different ways of systematically maltreating and forcing hair into the most unnatural shapes possible. Among the most popular instruments of torture were the curling instruments that were used for curly hairstyles or the famous "water waves" invented by the French hairdresser Marcel Grateau, which were burnt straight into the hair. No wonder the boudoirs of the Belle Époque always smelled slightly of singeing. If the hair survived this treatment, it was then colored with homemade dyes, while wigs, hairpieces, cushions and pads were used to achieve the voluminous pinned-up hairstyles.

The discovery of permanent waving by Karl Ludwig Nessler in 1906 did not improve the situation. Nessler soaked the hair in an alkaline solution, then wrapped strands of hair around metal rods that were heated with very hot tongs. The whole procedure lasted about six hours, burns and corrosion often being part of the process. Later the hot tongs were replaced by electric current so that the danger of burns was replaced by that of

electric shock. Gray hair has not always been feared; on the contrary, at the end of the 19th century women with prematurely gray hair were considered particularly attractive. Ladies who were not so fortunate as to have gone gray used hair powder to achieve this effect.

World War I and the 1920s with their love of everything modern put an end to the Pompadour hairstyle, and even women who had never cut their hair now made their way to the hairdresser to try the new hairstyle or bobbed haircut and show how fashionable they were. But by the 1930s women began to wear their hair long again, so curls and waves were back in fashion. In addition, platinum blonde, as sported by Jean Harlow, became the color of the decade. This necessitated the use of hydrogen peroxide to bleach the hair, which was quite damaging. The 1940s also favored mid-long to long hair as worn by Veronica Lake and Lauren Bacall. Fortunately, the "cold" permanent wave, in which the hair was no longer cooked, but merely warmed while a chemical treatment was applied to the hair then subsequently fixed, was developed in 1948. The 1950s were undoubtedly one of the toughest periods for hair. The reason was the invention of three new products. Hairspray developed from being a luxury product to a mass-produced item, the new Lockwell-Wickler system ensured the widespread use of the permanent wave, and hair dyes for home use flooded onto the market. Artificial, high teased hairstyles came into fashion, guaranteed to stay in place thanks to the new hairsprays.

However, there were also counter-movements that favored more natural looks. Audrey Hepburn launched the "ponytail" hairstyle whereby the hair was pulled tightly together at the back of the head, secured with a loop and allowed to hang loosely. This hairstyle was widely copied by a whole generation of jumper-wearing girls. Other women chose new types of short hairstyles that were cut with a cutthroat razor. The fact that hair could look good without hours of messing around, teasing and fixing with lacquer was proved in the 1960s by the leading hairdresser Vidal Sassoon with his revolutionary creations such as the Five-Point-Cut that only required an accurate cut. Such hairstyles no longer required lengthy sessions every morning but just a quick comb-through. The rediscovery of the natural look also led to a revival of long hair.

But how did the tired 1950s-look turn into the splendid healthy 1960s hairstyle? Naturally, this could not happen overnight. It needed time, care and a lot of patience—and the professional expertise of a hairdresser who would let hair grow instead of cutting it. The movement was led by long-hair guru George Michael, whose New York salon was a meeting place for movie and television stars. Hip-length and even knee-length hair were everyday occurrences there.

Since the free, relaxed hairstyles of the 1960s, people have been divided every season into those who favor elaborate hairstyles that require a lot of work and those who prefer simple chic with a few subtle highlights or lowlights. The elaborate, full hairstyles of Farah Fawcett-Majors were as representative of the 1970s as was the long, straight hippy hairstyle with a middle part worn by Ali MacGraw in *Love Story* during the same period. Well-defined "compulsory" hairstyles have not really existed since the 1960s, when most women started to wear their hair as they liked and as it suited them best.

More than washing,cutting and setting: top hairdressers and legendary salons

London society hairdresser Nicky Clarke gives his client a shaggy, layered haircut. His famous customer is radio presenter Emma B.

Hairdressers often have an almost magical sixth sense. They recognize and respect the complex personality of their clients, they guess their wishes before they have even expressed them, and they seem to know everything there is to know about women's hair. They conjure up hairstyles that make women look more attractive, more erotic, more authoritative, or more famous, as the case may be, but in any case a good hairdresser always makes a woman look better. Women who have discovered such a genius usually remain faithful to him for a very long time. If the client is well known, the hairdresser will also benefit from the publicity because, unlike the work of a couturier, his hair creations are inseparable from the wearer.

The 1950s produced a number of top hairdressers. Society ladies often wore their hair piled up high in elaborate hairstyles or with hairpieces skillfully incorporated into the hairstyle. In the evening, before going to bed, these magnificent hairdos had to be secured with bobby pins, clips and hairnets. Actually this did not help much because in the morning the hairdo was ruined and no one could straighten it, only the hairdresser who had created it. This led to a certain dependence on the hairdresser. Having a perfect hairstyle was society's acid test, so that women would patiently wait for hours for the privilege of having their hair done by the master. A top address of the 1950s was Alexandre de Paris, whose clients included elegant European high nobility and style icons such as the Duchess of Windsor.

The French capital was considered the Mecca of Haute Coiffure with artists such as Carita, Jacques Dessange and Jean-Louis David representing the highest art of hairdressing. In 1951 Rosy and Maria Carita opened their legendary salon in the Rue du Faubourg Saint-Honoré. The two sisters had the very innovative idea of offering their clients a complete beauty package: they would not only look after the hair but also after the whole body as well. Brigitte Bardot and Catherine Deneuve were among the first regular customers of this temple of beauty.

Today, the company (which now belongs to Shiseido) looks after the next generation of French film stars and it sells its products throughout the world. Jacques Dessange learned hairdressing in his father's barber's shop in Sologne. He subsequently moved to Paris where he worked for the great Louis Gervais among others. He soon developed the concept of natural, lively hairstyles, contrary to the still hairdo fashionable at the time. When he opened his first salon in the Avenue Franklin Roosevelt in 1956, he was already the favorite hairdresser of famous stars of the world of entertainment and cinema. The slogan of the now vast Jacques Dessange hairdressing empire is "I do not go to the hairdresser, I go to Dessange." Another hairdressing institution in Paris is Jean-Louis David, who also owns a network of franchised hairdressing salons and sells his own range of products. There are other chains such as Camille Albane (in the Dessange group) and Mod's Hair, which is particularly popular with younger women because of its trendy, perfect cuts without fuss.

Hairdressers in the English-speaking world were also and still are brilliant masters of the art of hairdressing. Vidal Sassoon began his hairdressing revolution in a small salon in London's Bond Street. In the 1960s he removed all the excess ballast from women's hairdos and went for a short, carefully cut look that emphasized the natural beauty of healthy hair—a completely new approach after the big, stiffly-lacquered hairdos of the 1950s.

The actress Nancy Kwan was one of the first to have a chin-length bobbed, layered haircut by the still unknown hairdresser, thus giving hair curlers and teasing a clear thumbs-down. Sassoon's hairdressing philosophy was based on the motto "wash and go," which did not need to be styled by a hairdresser. Sassoon clients could always be confident that their hair would still look fine on the following day. All it would need would be washing and combing. This new-found independence from hairdressers perfectly matched the new philosophy of the Swinging Sixties, represented by Mary Quant's miniskirts and Sassoon's Five-Point-Cut. Today Vidal Sassoon's hairdressing salons and hair products have become inseparable from hair care.

John Frieda also began his hairdressing career in London, having learned the trade in his father's hairdressing salon in the London suburbs. He became independent in the mid-1970s. The mention of John Frieda's salon soon became an insider tip and even the British royal family used his services. Lady Diana's layered haircut, as worn in the official engagement photograph, and later copied by thousands of women, is a John Frieda creation. John Frieda achieved cult status and opened six salons in Europe and the United States. He is also celebrated for his hair care products such as the "Thickening Lotion" for thin hair and the frizz-controlling lotion "Frizz-Ease" that works wonders.

Another figure in the British hairdresser's pantheon is Nicky Clarke, whose clients include royals, celebrities, and the glitterati. He has been entrusted with styling the fashion shows of Alexander McQueen, Calvin Klein, Jil Sander, and Givenchy. He also produces a range of successful hair care products with a turnover worth millions. Nicky Clarke is a modern top hairdresser in more than one sense—he is also the first hairdresser to have an entry in the English bible of VIPs, *Who's Who*.

In spite of all this, "star" hairdressers also have "normal" customers who know what they want. Indeed, today it is more often the woman who decides what her hairstyle should be, rather than the hairdresser.

In 1999 Vidal Sassoon was awarded a prize at London Fashion Week for his life's work. He firmly believes that a perfect cut is the basis of any hairstyle.

Classic hairstyles

1. In the 1950s **Jean Seberg** was known for her chic pixie look with very short blond hair. Before her, actresses like Audrey Hepburn and Leslie Caron had favored a similar style that they carried off with great confidence.

2. Long, straight hair was a popular hairstyle in the decade of the 1960s and early 1970s. Today this uncomplicated hairstyle without curls, which **Claudia Schiffer** has been wearing for years, still represents freedom and naturalness.

3. **Princess Caroline of Monaco** with her shoulder-length, slightly layered, dark hair. This is a typical hairstyle for the upper classes and prosperous high society. The cut expresses sophistication as well as simplicity and understatement.

4. **Jemima Khan**, English society lady and wife of the famous Pakistani cricketer and politician Imran Khan, wears her thick, lush, blond hair loose but always elegant and never bouffant.

5. The actress **Gwyneth Paltrow** likes to wear her straight, shoulder-length blond hair loose and unstructured. On special occasions, the hair can be pulled back into a simple, elegant bun or put up in an elegant chignon.

6. **Camilla Parker-Bowles** wears a practical layered haircut. Such a style is particularly popular with women who lead a busy outdoor life; they prefer an uncomplicated style that is easy to look after.

7. **Paloma Picasso** wears her thick, straight, jet-black hair—not layered—pulled away from her face. This classic, ladylike look is very popular in Mediterranean countries.

8. The not-too-short, layered, tousled look with blond streaks is a classic hairstyle of the 1990s. It was made famous by the American actress **Meg Ryan**. Today it represents the uncomplicated, sporty modern woman.

9. During her time as Prime Minister of Britain in the 1980s, the Iron Lady **Margaret Thatcher** had a typical "power" hairstyle. The rigid "hair helmet" symbolized power, importance, the ability to assert herself, and "no nonsense."

10. **Coco Chanel** was one of the first women in the 1920s to sport a fashionably short bobbed haircut. Later she adopted a slightly "wilder" version of this hairstyle that also became popular among older ladies.

The best time for a manicure is after showering or bathing because the nails and cuticles are then beautifully soft and clean. First carefully push back the cuticle using a rosewood stick but never cut it away because the soft transitional skin between the skin of the finger and the nail itself is necessary as a protective shield against dirt and bacteria. Then cut the nails with scissors and file to shape using a nail file, working from the outside to the inside to prevent the nails from splitting. Finish off with a buffing pad or polishing file to make them shiny. It is also very important to rub cream into your hands regularly, not forgetting the cuticles. Before polishing the nails they must be dry and free from cream. For a French manicure, first prime the white tips of the nails with a nail white pencil and paint the nails with colorless, beige or pale pink transparent nail polish. If painting the nails with a stronger color, first use an undercoat to prevent the nails from becoming discolored. Then apply a first coat of colored polish, starting with a wide brushstroke in the center of the nail and then further brushstrokes on the right and left of this central brushstroke. Do not apply the polish as far as the outer edge of the nail because this would make the nail look round and bulbous. To ensure a completely smooth surface, the first coat must be completely dry before the second coat is applied. A special protective coating will help the polish last longer.

Nails

Fingernails come in all shapes and sizes: filed short, or long and elegant, plain or polished, French-manicured and ladylike, or shocking red, with false nails for special occasions, or strengthened with long-lasting gel in a beauty salon, pierced with various items, adorned with transfers, and decorated with the wildest patterns. The range of products for nails is wider than ever. Very often the first experiments by little girls with colorful nail polish are their first initiation into the world of make-up and as exciting as using mommy's lipstick.

Neutral nail polish already existed at the turn of the century. Brighter colors only became fashionable in the 1920s when Hollywood stars began to paint their nails in the most strident colors. The disadvantage of nail polish at the time was that it did not stay on very long, so women wearing it had to sit around and keep their hands still to avoid damaging the polish. A few years later, manufacturers turned to the latest cellulose car paints, which enabled them to produce longer-lasting nail polish.

The first modern nail polish was developed in 1932. The brothers Charles and Joseph Revson turned to the chemist Charles Lachmann (hence the "L" in Revlon), and together they developed the first non-streaking, perfectly-covering nail polish, based on water-insoluble pigments. This use of pigments allowed the three men to develop a range of different colors. Revlon also created the trend of matching nail polish and lipstick colors. Revlon sets containing both products sold like hotcakes.

From then on women's enthusiasm for painted nails became unstoppable. Stars such as Marlene Dietrich launched the so-called "moon-manicure" fashion that left the half-moon (lunula) of the nail and often also the white tip of the nail unpainted, because it was thought that the nail might "suffocate" otherwise. It was only some years later when this fear was proven completely unfounded that nails were completely covered. Women with brittle nails that consequently never grew long could use artificial nails such as the

Any manicure starts with cleaning the nails. Dipping the fingers in a bowl of water softens the horny layer and makes it more supple. The cuticles are treated with a special cream.

American Nu Nails, launched in 1934. In the 1970s and 1980s women, especially in the United States, grew their nails extraordinarily long and decorated them with multicolored nail polish. This became possible with the development of various methods for lengthening nails such as the acrylic technique or modeling with light-hardening synthetic substances.

The new look with aggressively long nails even penetrated the world of sport. In athletics, the American sprinters Florence Griffith Joyner and Gail Devers impressed the spectators as well as their competitors with their threatening, brightly colored nails.

Whether long or short, polished or unpolished—nails will only look good if they are healthy and well-cut. This is achieved on the one hand by healthy, well-balanced diet and on the other by leaving your fingertips alone as much as possible. Are you one of those women who bites her nails, fiddles with them, or tears at the cuticle until there is visible damage to the nailbed? Then there is only one solution: you must stop this. At the beginning you might find that a coating of acrylic polish is helpful because it tastes of plastic which gives them a very unpleasant taste when you bite them. The cuticles can be treated with special creams and sticks, but the best remedy is undoubtedly the exertion of self-control. You will soon see the improvement and notice that your hands look much better than they did before.

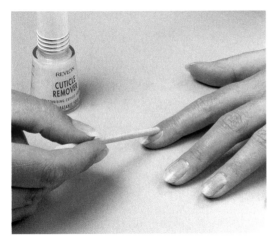

There are special preparations to ensure that the cuticles can be pushed back more easily. It is best to use a wooden stick.

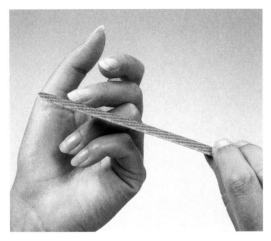

Shape the nail using a file. Always work from inwards from the outer edges to avoid them splintering.

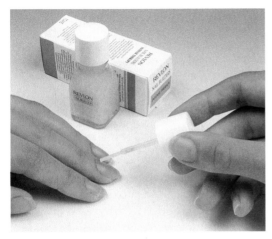

Protective, strengthening nail liquid should be applied under the polish. Nails treated like this may be left with the "natural" look.

A foundation of transparent under-polish will protect from discoloration. Then apply the first layer of colored nail polish evenly.

Often a second layer will be needed to achieve perfect covering and depth. Wait until the first layer is thoroughly dry before applying it!

Finally apply some hand cream, which will soften the skin and protect it from external aggression such as cold, hard water and so on.

Beautiful feet

Feet did not escape the nail polish euphoria of the 1930s. Since then toenails, painted red or other strong colors or perhaps more modestly in pale beige or shades of apricot, have become a colorful complement to painted fingernails, especially in summer. Painted toenails are even more attractive if the rest of the feet are well cared for. Horny calluses and thickened white hard skin on the heels look very unattractive. First soak the feet for ten minutes in a footbath, then remove the hardened skin with a pumice stone. Cut the nails straight across so that they do not become ingrown. Carefully push back the cuticle using a wooden stick and then rub special foot cream on the feet. If the hard skin is particularly difficult to remove, apply a thick layer of cream to the feet, put on cotton socks and leave the cream to take effect during the night. Paint toenails in the same way as the fingernails or leave unpolished.

№ 2

The lady's underwear closet

The most intimate of all garments

The fashion of undergarments has changed as dramatically in the last 100 years as has that of outer garments, the changing fashion of outer garments being accompanied by corresponding changes in the fashion of undergarments. In 1900 it took a long time for an elegant woman to get ready. A large part of the day was spent dressing, undressing and dressing again. This was not surprising since a lady would wear between four and seven pounds of undergarments: underpants, undershirt, various petticoats, corset, stockings and so on. In winter she would wear additional layers of woolly undergarments. A woman's bare ankle, meaning one not wrapped in several layers of clothing, would have been a scandal. Even boots were considered an undergarment that had to be concealed beneath voluminous, floor-length skirts. Going up or down stairs in the presence of a man bordered on exhibitionism.

Today people are no longer shocked by the latest trends on the runway, whether it be the lingerie look, the transparent look or, as it is most accurately described, the naked look. But away from the runway shows, our wardrobe has effectively become simpler and more natural: so uncomplicated, indeed, that the men and women of the German Allgemeine Verein für die Vereinfachung der Frauenkleidung ("General Society for the Simplification of Women's Clothing") would have rejoiced and approved. This practical association, founded in 1896, was set up to fight the spread of corset-mania represented by the old school, espousing the cause of "liberation from pressure and restriction of movement." Dress reform was a long, hard road whose first milestone was the "Artistic and reformed dress" movement. This played an important part in the history of costume but it was not influential on a wide scale.

Progress toward free and easy, informal dress was very slow. At the end of the 1940s Dior's New Look introduced the wasp-waist, which in turn led to the return of the waist-defining corset. Meanwhile however, women's obsession with dieting and being thin has become second nature to such a degree that it is no longer necessary to turn to monstrous, body-shaping garments. The perfect silhouette is achieved by shaping the body itself. Shaped with the aid of exercise and diet, the body will of course be clothed correspondingly in figure-enhancing underwear. Today underwear must be beautiful, sexy and, if the outer garments require it, body-hugging and invisible, as if no underwear was being worn. The American company Frederick's of Hollywood launched the first thong in 1981, thus reducing women's panties to the bare minimum. This type of panty has been extremely popular ever since it first appeared. Where in the past large areas of cotton and lace panties showed unattractively under the outer garments, now just a tiny piece of fabric is held in position by a narrow strip. What would the dressmakers of the Belle Époque have said?

The style of underwear that the modern woman prefers can only be discussed in a general manner. Indeed, this is a subject that belongs to the privacy of the bedroom, although all women will admit to loving beautiful lingerie. As early as the 1950s Sophia Loren complained that there was hardly any star whose underwear was unknown to the public, and Madonna has elevated sexy underwear to the status of an official stage outfit. Nevertheless, no one can tell what the Italian film star or the American pop icon may be wearing on an ordinary day with children or grandchildren, walking the dogs, meeting friends or checking their mail. That is only right because it is no one else's business.

However, without divulging the secrets of a woman's lingerie drawer to the public at large, most women will agree that good quality underwear is very important. As Christian Dior put it, "There is no fashion without a good foundation." Although women no longer wear corsets, beautiful lingerie contributes to the perfect outfit. Apart from the supporting, lifting, enlarging or correcting properties of many undergarments and the materials they are made of, lingerie is also fun—a completely private luxury that is indulged in for the wearer's own pleasure. It cannot be seen by others but it works wonders.

The waist-less, flowing fashion of the 1920s did not need the stiff girdles, bodices, and corsets of earlier years, but simply soft underclothes.

Shape! The changing fashion of body shapes

The soft and smooth "body" that emphasizes the figure has long been an indispensable part of a woman's underwear. Here is a model from Falke's current collection.

Although it is hard to believe after decades of fitness and figure-consciousness, there used to be a time when slender or skinny women were considered at best difficult and capricious, at worst spiteful and grumpy. In 1890 the ideal of beauty was plumpness, and looking more closely at the fashions of that time, the reason soon becomes obvious. A matronly silhouette with a prominent behind, large bosom and narrow waist was then considered the height of fashion. In order to achieve such an S-line, a tight corset was required, which would compress the body mercilessly into the desired shape. But this look could only work if there was enough to compress and lace up within the corset. Skinny women might show off their narrow waists, but in spite of added padding, they were unable to achieve the desired bulges and curves. There was only one solution: to put on weight.

The history of fashion is also the history of the changing shape of the female body. Which of the two determines the other? In the 1920s, women discovered sports and they became fitter and slimmer as a result. Was the fashion at the time specially geared to this new sporty type of woman—or did women diet and exercise more on the tennis court in order to be able to wear these new, fashionable clothes? The avant-garde fashion designer Elsa Schiaparelli held the view that one should never adapt the garment to the body but that one should form the body into the right shape for the garment. Whether or not she was right, there are women at every period who are fortunate enough to have the right body shape for the fashion of the time, all the others depended on boring diets or on undergarments that help them to achieve the desired shape. In the 1920s, an androgynous figure was very fashionable. This meant that women had to be tall, slim and very bony, and breast-binders were an indispensable undergarment for those with a larger bosom who still wanted to achieve the desired flat-chested boyish silhouette.

In the 1930s and 1940s, fashion began to promote the feminine figure again. This trend culminated in Christian Dior's New Look of the late 1940s and 1950s, for which women needed a narrow waist and rounded hips. Yet again many women required the help of a figure-molding corset to wear this fashion style. But although women loved this glamorous new style after the restrictions of World War II, most of them were reluctant to squeeze into uncomfortable undergarments such as corsets. This new, voluptuous fashion could also be worn in a casual way, as was demonstrated by Brigitte Bardot and Anita Ekberg.

The 1960s drew a temporary line under bosoms, stomachs and bottoms. Tall, skinny models like Twiggy made it clear to all women that the youthful-naive fashion of that period looked best on childlike bodies, which led a whole generation of girls starving themselves to self-destruction to achieve this ideal. Those who were not so young refused to follow this Twiggy style, but they caught up in the 1970s. By that time women had realized that excessive dieting could lead to serious health problems, but no one wanted to give up on the slim-line fashion. This resulted in the opening of countless dance and aerobic studios across the Western world, and the making of fitness videos by famous personalities such as Jane Fonda, to help those striving towards a slim figure. "Fitness for all" was the motto of the time, supported by various diet and health programs.

This attitude has now become such integral part of life that most women feel guilty if they do not exercise regularly and eat healthily. This health-conscious attitude was briefly interrupted by the heroin chic of emaciated, hollow-cheeked models with straggly hair and sunken eyes who made their appearance on the runway during the late 1990s. But even this kind of look was not entirely new, since at the beginning of the 20th century there was a short period during which women would stay awake all night, drinking large amounts of coffee without eating anything in order to look pale and worn out the following morning. Even in the 21st century there appears to be no end in view to the fashion for slim models. The most popular ones are very slim without any subcutaneous fat but at the same time having large breasts. This is not always possible without plastic surgery.

Round hips, narrow waist and a generous bosom: Jane Russell and Marilyn Monroe in *Gentlemen Prefer Blondes* (1953). This type of hourglass figure was fashionable in the 1950s.

During the 1920s the androgynous figure was favored. The bosom was flattened by wearing breast bandages.

Almost back to the style of the 1920s: the super-slim model Twiggy in the early 1970s during a photo shoot in London.

Corset glossary

Corset
Mostly strapless, tied either at the front or the back, and strongly stiffened, it molds the waist and stomach. It is either made to measure or adjusted in a specialist shop.

Corsage
The corsage may sometimes be reinforced, but not invariably. It is strapless and can reach down as far as the hips.

Corselet
The corselet is an all-in-one figure-molding garment for the bosom, waist, stomach and hips. Unlike the corset, it is made mostly from an elastic material. It has shoulder straps and suspenders and is always bought ready-made.

Teddy
All-in-one sleeveless undergarment that combines a camisole-like top and panties and often fastens at the crotch. May be loose, or figure-hugging when made from elastic material. Loose teddies are sometimes called camisoles.

Leotard
Originally worn by ballet dancers when training, this is a garment similar to the body, a tight-fitting combination consisting of short leggings and a top that often has sleeves. Many leotards are worn with a skirt or trousers so that only the top is visible.

Bodice
Light, barely reinforced top, often made from elastic material. Sometimes also used as a synonym for a full corselet. In national costumes the bodice is worn as an outer garment.

Bustier
Close-fitting, bodice-like garment, made from tricot or stretch fabric. When strapless and cut straight, it is known as a "tube top" or bandeau.

Girdle
Very tight-fitting undergarment that extends from the waist down to the hips, usually made from elastic material. With or without garters.

Guêpière or Merry widow
Bodice girdle, launched by Marcel Rochas in 1946 to achieve a narrow or wasp waist, curving over the hips. Worn with Dior's New Look clothes.

How the corset has survived

Some see the corset as a unpleasant relic of body oppression while others love it because of its erotic implications. Since the early 1990s when Madonna appeared on stage dressed in an exclusive corset designed by Gaultier, no one is any longer indifferent to the garment.

Fastened as tight as possible, the corset has, since antiquity, met the demands of fashion to achieve the ideal of beauty of each period. This means that sometimes it was the décolletage that had to be emphasized, and in other periods it was the waist that was constrained. Sometimes the garment with its whalebone, leather, wood or metal stiffeners went from the armpit to the thigh, while at other times only the waist was emphasized. In the 19th century, the corset even became the symbol of morality. Respectable women were not allowed to avoid wearing a corset, and it was unthinkable to go out socially without being tightly squeezed into one. Meanwhile, even men began to wear tight bodices and many children were forced to wear them too because people believed that this encouraged a straight back. It is true that there were some enlightened minds who warned about the dangers to health of wearing a corset: constant breathing difficulties, fainting, constriction of the inner organs and so on. Nonetheless, the excessively rigid reign of the corset lasted well into the early 20th century.

Then the reform movement pleaded for more health awareness, the suffragettes campaigned for involvement and participation, and World War I inevitably brought about more independence for women, since people who were asked to work in the fields or look after the wounded in military hospitals could hardly do so wearing corsets. So gradually new kinds of undergarments were developed that supported the body and made women look slimmer without constricting the body so drastically. In 1920 corsets made in a new type of jersey fabric were launched. The growing interest in sporting activities and the development and

The corset is always said to have died but it is often rediscovered as an object of passion. This corsage by the Munich-based designer Stephanie Rapp is an example of a modern reinterpretation of the theme as an elegant fashion garment.

patenting of ever more elastic synthetic fibers led an increasing number of women to wear comfortable bodices rather than stiff, constricting corsets. Unfortunately, in the early 1950s the corset made a brief and ultimately unsuccessful comeback as a result of the fashion for narrow waists.

The social, fashion and textile revolution of the 1960s finally threw out corsets, corselets and those monstrous rubbery bodices. But it was not quite forever, because in the 1980s and 1990s corsets and bustiers began to make their appearance on the runway. Admittedly, in this period corsets came in more presentable forms, turning the former undergarment into an elegant, erotic outer garment. They had indeed never disappeared from the repertoire of lingerie manufacturers.

Not entirely socially acceptable—Madonna's stage outfits (seen here in Gothenburg in 1990) were a little too risqué and extreme for everyday wear. But there is no doubt that they were sexy.

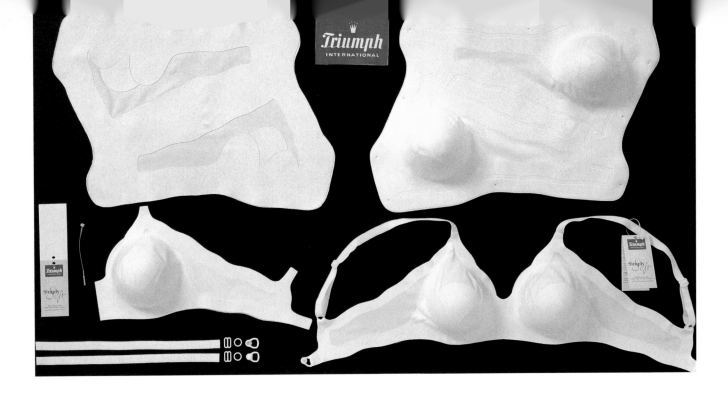

From bodice to Wonderbra

Modern textile technology enables the cups to be made without any annoying seams. The parts are then sewn together and fitted with straps and fasteners.

When in the early 1970s a new generation of feminists began to change the image of women in society as well as women's own perception of themselves, women also began to question the kind of clothes they wore. The garment that became the symbol of anti-feminism was the restricting bra, and the general call to women was "burn your bras." Admittedly, the rejection of the bra was not as spectacular as that of the corset a few decades earlier, but underwear manufacturers had to react in some way to the new trend. The only kind of bras that they could persuade emancipated young women to wear were sporty, plain garments without lace, made from soft material, without padding, non-wired, and without cups. Thus they were hardly detectable when worn. In fact Rudi Gernreich, the American designer and inventor of the "topless" fashion, had already paved the way for the new trend a few years earlier with his ultra-light, almost transparent No-Bra Bra.

The present-day bra is a development of the late 19th and early 20th century bodice, although it is impossible to pinpoint the actual inventor. As early as 1891, a patent had been registered by the Bohemian industrialist Hugo Schindler for a "bust-holder." This was followed in 1899 by the "woman's bodice as a bust-holder" invented by Christine Hardt of Dresden, and in 1904 a Swabian corset manufacturer also invented a "bust-holder." In 1905 Sigmund Lindauer from Cannstadt created a new type of bra that he patented seven years later under the name "Hautana bust-holder." Other sources state that the American Mary Phelps Jacob, who later called herself the Caresse Crosby, was the original inventor of the bra. In 1914 she used two handkerchiefs and a strip of fabric to produce the first fully un-reinforced, featherlight bra. The Kestos by Rosalind Klein was based on a very similar principle. The then manager of the Kestos company sewed together two triangular-shaped pieces of fabric that overlapped a little in the middle. She attached strips of cotton jersey to the top and side corners that were crossed at the back and fastened to the "cups" with buttons. From then on underwear manufacturers developed the most varied models. In the 1940s, a woman's underwear consisted of the combination of bra, panty-girdle and garter belt to hold up the stockings (pantyhose did not yet exist).

What a lady wears "underneath" is a matter of taste. But underwear should always be beautiful, like this elegant set by Palmers.

The alternative design to the simple sports look pays more attention to the decorative aspect. This set by Palmers is almost too elegant to be hidden under a shirt and sweater.

Fashion trends also affected the shape of the bust. In America in the 1950s, very uplifted, pointed "rocket breasts" were the fashion. This was achieved by wearing rigid, reinforced bras. Women's fashion during the 1950s was dominated by the admiration for large breasts. Curvaceous movie stars such as Jane Russell, Elizabeth Taylor, Marilyn Monroe, and Jayne Mansfield contributed to emphasizing the wonderful effects of the bra on the big screen. Then the androgynous 1960 promoted flat chests, putting a sudden end to the era of the opulent chest.

It was only at the end of the 1980s and the early 1990s that breasts and low necklines were discovered again. Suddenly there was a demand for supporting bras that appeared to enlarge the breasts. The American underwear manufacturer Frederick's of Hollywood launched a series of push-up bras that strongly emphasized the roundness of the breasts and came with additional padded fillings for insertion in pockets in the cups if necessary. In 1990 Gossard launched the Ultrabra and in 1992 British *Vogue* named the Wonderbra by Playtex as the accessory of the season. But women who did not want the Wonderbra look were also catered for. Many companies included sports underwear in their ranges, thus taking advantage of the fitness craze of the 1980s. Women who did not care for the "bosomy" look of the Wonderbra wore a comfortable Calvin Klein or Fila bra.

"Unmentionables"

Bloomers, drawers, culottes, boxer shorts, pantaloons, slips, thongs, panties, passion killers—the names and shapes of female briefs or panties are legion, although they are a relatively recent addition to the family of undergarments because these "unmentionables" only made their appearance in the 19th century. At first these "drawers" were long and baggy because they were supposed to conceal the woman's legs, which in 1805 were still an extremely private part of the body. Later they became less baggy and also shorter, ending at the knee. In 1914 some slightly more modern "drawers" were launched, which were cut in one piece with the rest of the garment and secured with elastic at the waist. They were known as panties. During the 1930s, 1940s, and 1950s, almost all women wore a tight panty-girdle made from elasticized fabric that provided firm control for the stomach, bottom and top of the thighs. Naturally, such underwear was completely unsuited to the mini-skirt fashion of the 1960s. This led to the creation of the short, leg-less panty. Since the lingerie boom of the 1980s, panties and thongs have come in all sorts of shapes and sizes, and every woman has her favorite type. One of the most important aspects is that they should fit well and be comfortable. Panties that are too tight are very uncomfortable. Moreover, they should not be visible under tight clothes. A "visible panty-line," as Woody Allen called it, completely spoils any elegant outfit.

Fabric ABC

Acetate
Synthetic, cellulose-based fiber with a silky appearance.

Acrylic
See Polyacrylic.

Calais
Very delicate, soft, woven lace from France.

Cotton
Fibers from the seed capsules of the cotton plant. One of the most popular natural fibers used in the manufacturing of underwear, it may be used on its own or in combination with other fibers.

Cupro
Cellulose-based fiber, similar to viscose but softer.

Dorlastan
Trade-name for elasthan produced by Bayer.

Double-rib
Classic knitwear used for underwear. Two plain (knit) and two purl stitches are visible at the same time.

Elasthan
Abbreviation for "elastic polyurethane", a synthetic elastic fabric that when combined with other fibers produces an elastic fabric that holds its shape. Elasthan fibers can be processed "naked" or "encased."

Fine rib
Plain stitches are visible on both sides. Only when the fabric is stretched is it possible to distinguish the plain (knit) and purl stitches. Very stretchy, soft fabric.

Georgette
Extremely delicate, transparent fabric made from crêpe yarn.

Interlock
Like fine rib, this knitwear fabric only shows plain stitches on both sides. However, Interlock is produced on other machines.

Jersey
General term designating stretchy, comfortable knitwear of various kinds.

Linen
Natural fiber made from flax. Cool, smooth fabric that creases a lot.

Lycra
Brand name for a Nylon material combined with elasthan produced by DuPont.

Lyocell
Pleasant to wear, easy-care cellulose-based fiber.

Mercerized
As a result of being treated with a special alkaline solution, the fabric becomes shinier and smoother, more resistant and easier to dye.

Meryl
Brand name for microfiber by Nylstar. An extremely soft, comfortable, permeable, crease-resistant material.

Microfiber
Extremely fine synthetic fiber, usually polyamide. Extremely comfortable and very permeable.

Modal
Cellulose fiber, very soft and fluffy although very hard-wearing.

Natural fiber
Natural fiber of plant or animal origin, for instance cotton, linen, silk or wool.

Nylon
Brand name for polyamide fibers produced by DuPont.

Perlon
Another brand name for polyamide fibers.

Polyacryl
Synthetic fiber with soft, woolly appearance that does not felt, does not shrink and is easy to care for.

Polyamide
Non-tear, abrasion-resistant synthetic fiber that keeps its shape and is very easy to dye.

Polyester
Easy-care, hard-wearing, crease-resistant synthetic fiber that keeps its shape very well.

Satin
General term for sateen fabrics with a shiny surface. Can be made from different materials, for instance silk satin, cotton satin.

Silk
Natural fiber made from the cocoon of the silk worm. There is a distinction between wild silk and silk produced by the specially bred silkworm moth. Very fine textile raw material with a characteristic sheen, light, soft, and cool in summer, and warm in winter.

Singed
Small projecting fibers are singed off to produce a particularly smooth surface.

Tactel
Brand name for polyamide-based fibers produced by DuPont. The outer surface is shiny while the inner surface feels pleasantly soft on the skin.

Viscose
Fiber based on cellulose. Soft, smooth fabric, pleasant on the skin with a silky sheen.

Wool
Natural fiber of animal original. It can come from sheep, rabbits (angora), goats (mohair, cashmere) and certain types of camels (alpaca).

Fabrics

Whether it is a sports bra, a figure-controlling "teddy" or an elegant lacy camisole, underwear should always be comfortable. The comfortable, well-fitting underwear of today was still a long way away in the late 19th and early 20th century when women wore unwieldy, voluminous underwear, secured with ribbons and made predominantly from coarse woolly fabrics. Soft fabrics such as crêpe de Chine, muslin or silk were reserved for the super-rich. In winter, women had to endure scratchy "drawers" made from a mohair and wool fabric. It was in the 1920s that the first cellulose-based fabric was developed. This artificial silk fabric contributed to the democratization of underwear because now even less well-off women could afford beautiful underwear. However, World War II put an end to this luxury. During the war, underwear was made from ordinary plain jersey fabrics, parachute silk or even knitted from wool remnants.

After the war, synthetic materials were introduced from America into Europe. This completely revolutionized the underwear industry. In 1938 the American company DuPont had developed polyamide, which it marketed under the trade-name Nylon. Perlon was invented about the same time in Germany. Meanwhile, new manufacturing processes had been developed to produce these and other synthetic fibers in quantity.

So it was that the 1950s and 1960s experienced a real boom in man-made fabrics. Nylon stockings and tights came to symbolize modern living. Also popular with young women was Lycra, another revolutionary fabric developed by DuPont, a highly elasticized, very light material that also provided gentle control. It was only in the 1980s that cotton made a comeback, resulting from the growing awareness of the need to protect the environment. However, because women did not want to lose the advantages offered by synthetic fibers, underwear was now produced in mixed fibers. In fact, today underwear would be unthinkable without a certain percentage of polyester, elasthan and polyamide. This is not to say that cotton and silk have completely disappeared from the market but their share has greatly diminished.

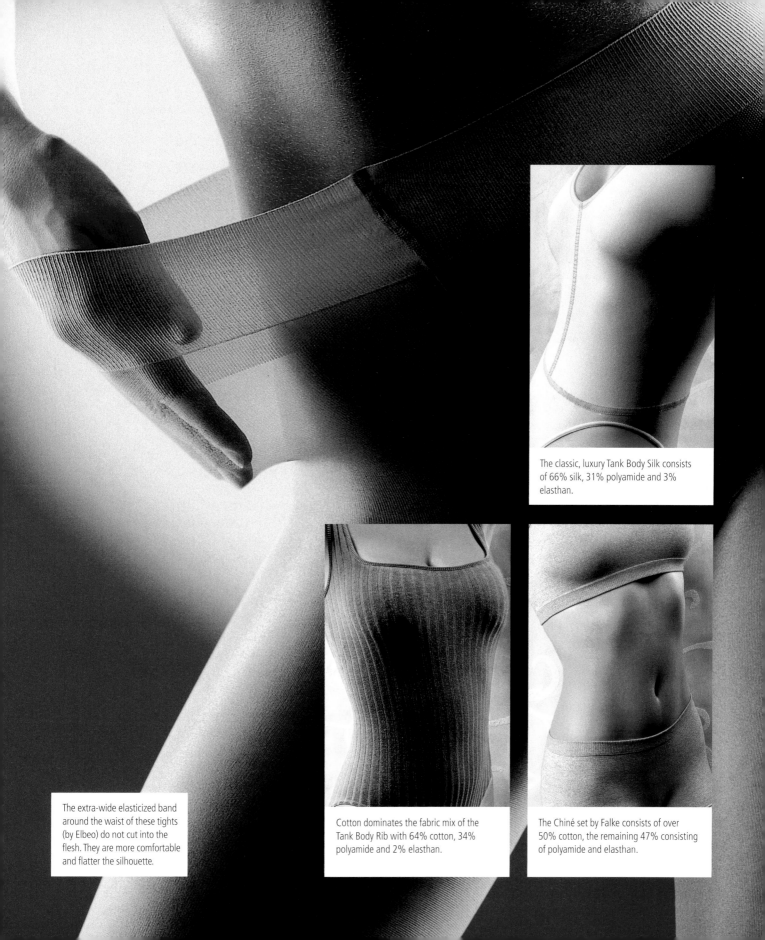

The classic, luxury Tank Body Silk consists of 66% silk, 31% polyamide and 3% elasthan.

The extra-wide elasticized band around the waist of these tights (by Elbeo) do not cut into the flesh. They are more comfortable and flatter the silhouette.

Cotton dominates the fabric mix of the Tank Body Rib with 64% cotton, 34% polyamide and 2% elasthan.

The Chiné set by Falke consists of over 50% cotton, the remaining 47% consisting of polyamide and elasthan.

Classic lingerie for every taste

La Perla

Founded in 1954 by the Italian designer Ada Masotti, La Perla had its international breakthrough in the 1980s with the extremely successful Malizia collection. Today it is a synonym for luxury lingerie made from the best materials. The La Perla group is now also famous for its exclusive beachwear, outer clothing, perfumes and so on.

Victoria's Secret

Victoria's Secret, which was founded in the U.S. at the beginning of the 1970s, is a real woman's enterprise because over 80% of the managerial staff are female. The underwear ranges from traditional to highly erotic lingerie and is available by direct mail and through the Internet all over the world. One of the company's most popular garments is the Miracle Bra, which ensures a wonderful low neckline.

Triumph

The underwear company Triumph was founded in 1886 by Gottfried and Michael Braun in Heubach in Württemberg, Germany. It soon became a market leader in Europe. It produces several classics including the comfortable, hard-wearing Sloggi range made from a cotton and Lycra mixture as well as the BeeDees range.

Left page:
Top left: plain, black set by Palmers with transparent straps.

Top right:
A white set consisting of tanga and bra, like this one by Triumph, has a clean, sporty, and discreet effect.

Bottom left:
Elegant and seductive, black lace has always been a favorite for underwear.

Bottom right:
Romantic white lace looks best against a tanned skin.

Damart

Damart supplies warm undergarments for those who feel the cold in winter. A special feature of Damart underwear, which is produced in France and England, is its particular elegance. In the early days of the company the Despature brothers discovered an insulating fiber called chlorofiber, which is now marketed under the brand name Thermolactyl. They combined this with natural fibers to produce thermal underwear.

Chantal Thomass

At first, the French designer Chantal Thomass only created her fashionable, very feminine underwear as a sideline, but it became so successful that in 1975 she launched her independent lingerie collections. As before they were a "must" for women who love expensive, luxury fabrics. Catherine Deneuve is one of her clients.

Rigby & Peller

As befits a traditional English House, Rigby & Peller has a department for made-to-measure lingerie catering for the rich and famous, as well as their off-the-peg clothes. Founded in 1939, Rigby & Peller was awarded a Royal Warrant by Queen Elizabeth II in 1956 as suppliers to the royal court.

Gossard

Originally an American company, Gossard made its bold move to London in the 1920s and subsequently became known for its successful collections of elegant, understated underwear. It has produced classics such as the Ultrabra and in the 1970s it created the highly transparent Glossie collection.

Berlei

Berlei was founded in Sydney in Australia in 1917. Originally a corset factory, the company opened its first successful branch in London where it specialized in elaborate, sophisticated bras and girdles. Today Berlei is famous for its excellent sportswear such as the classic Shock-Absorber bra.

Sidelights on the history of stockings

A woman with bare legs? Such a sight has only been imaginable in the last few years and even now not on all occasions or in all countries. In the United States for instance, stockings or pantyhose are worn at work even on the hottest days. It just would not be the "done" thing to go to work without pantyhose. This is easier to appreciate when it is remembered that all banks and offices in America have air-conditioning all year round, which makes these premises rather cool. In Europe, both in the colder North and in the warm South, the situation is more relaxed. Bare legs are quite acceptable in many places, especially if they are flawless and slender, smooth and not hairy, perhaps slightly tanned under a skirt that is not too short. But in these countries too, it is best to wear stockings or pantyhose for an important business appointment or a formal meeting.

Stockings have undergone various changes in their development toward becoming a fashion item. At first they were purely practical, to protect the legs from undergrowth and insect bites. They later developed into the silky epitome of seduction or the blue stockings of emancipation. At the beginning of the 20th century, brightly decorated, embroidered, and patterned stockings were the fashion, but World War I put a sudden end to this decorative approach. From then on all wool and cotton stockings were in dark colors. Once again it was the Roaring Twenties that brought new life into the market, including the legs, because the stocking industry had invented a revolutionary new fiber, artificial silk. In addition, underwear designers had discovered the garter belt, which prevented stockings from sliding down. Indeed the unwieldy corset that had previously been used to hold up stockings was extremely unpopular in the era of the tango. Admittedly the early artificial silk or rayon stockings did not compete very successfully with the genuine silk originals because they were very shiny, and the coarse seam at the back revealed that they were not quite the real thing. Nevertheless, the invention of artificial silk also made possible the democratization of stockings because in the following decades existing materials were improved and new materials such as nylon and Perlon were discovered. This meant that it became possible to produce increasingly better and less expensive stockings, thus making them affordable to an ever large number of women.

But women had first to survive World War II. Elegant stockings were as rare as they would have been useless for most women. Instead, thick, knitted stockings that protected the wearer from the cold were now preferred by nearly all women. After the war, the much sought-after nylon stockings became available and in many parts of Europe could only be bought on the black market. Those who did not have the means to barter or were not on good terms with the American forces were forced to resort to special leg "make-up," using an eyebrow pencil to draw the seam at the back. Beauty salons specializing in "leg make-up" opened everywhere. Women would visit them every morning before going to work to have "stockings" painted on.

In the 1950s, manufacturers launched the first seamless stockings, which however were received with less enthusiasm than had been expected. The seam was considered not only erotic but also an advantage for those with slightly shorter or thicker legs. So why get rid of it? But the days of the stockings were numbered in any case. Barely ten years later the introduction of transparent pantyhose was greeted with great enthusiasm by all women because it was ideal for wearing with mini-skirts. It would have been unthinkable for garters or garter belts to show under mini-skirts, and only pantyhose guaranteed the perfect sixties look. So stockings lost their status and were relegated to the back of drawers.

It was only in the 1980s when beautiful lingerie was all the rage that women discovered the pleasure of luxury stockings again. Besides the traditional models that were held in place with a garter belt, there were now also Stay-Ups (in fact an invention of the 1950s) whose top edge was lined with strip of elastic or silicone that enabled them to stay up without a garter belt. Since then women have had the choice: practical or feminine stockings, in a discreet beige or exciting black, with or without seam, plain or patterned.

After World War II, nylon stockings were an extremely rare and very expensive luxury commodity. Those who had none would have the characteristic stocking seam drawn on their legs.

Advertising played an important part in introducing the new stockings to women. The lady on this 1960s poster wears an elegant cocktail dress, matching gloves, and stockings by Falke.

Advertisements by Palmers for the "stylish heel" launched in 1954. Ladies' stockings were still relatively expensive in the 1950s.

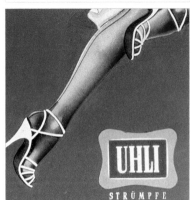

Uhlmann advertised their Uhli-stockings not only on posters but also in commercials in movie theaters, for instance with the title "My best friend."

At first quite unusual, seamless stockings only appeared in the mid-1950s. In 1961 Palmers advertised them as the "most beautiful in the world."

Denier and decitex

Denier and decitex are units of measurement that define the strength of the yarn or, in other words, its fineness. The fineness is determined by the ratio of the weight of a particular length of yarn. Denier indicates how many grams 9,000 meters (about 10,000 feet) of a yarn weigh. Decitex converts this somewhat esoteric unit of measurement into a decimal figure, which indicates the number of grams weight per 10,000 meters.

For instance, take a yarn of 10 denier. The weight of 9,000 meters is 10 grams, indicating that it is a fairly fine material. Expressed in the decitex system, 10,000 meters of this yarn would weigh 11.1 grams, so it is an 11.1 decitex yarn.

The production of fine synthetic yarns has made enormous progress in the last few decades. At the beginning of the 1960s, 60-denier yarn was a recent achievement and ten years later 20-denier yarn was launched. By 1992 Wolford had developed a 9-denier yarn in collaboration with DuPont. Only a year later Wolford launched 7 and 5 denier pantyhose and stockings.

Finest stockings from Austria

Legs on the move: the feet stretch, they are put on the ground and raised again, the knees bend, the muscles work. How is it possible to dress this complicated human running gear without restricting it? And how can anyone be certain that the effect is elegant? These were the questions that the early stocking manufacturers began to ask themselves. At the very beginning stockings were made from woven fabrics that were then sewn together. But this solution was rather unsatisfactory because the fabric hardly stretched, resulting in unsightly folds at the right angle between the shin and the foot. The use of knitted materials produced better results. The first stockings were knitted by hand using two needles and later sewn together with a seam. In 1589 the Reverend William Lee invented the knitting machine for stockings where all the stitches of one row were produced simultaneously, which meant that it was

much quicker than hand-knitters. In 1767 Samuel Wise developed the circular knitting machine, which made it possible to produce seamless stockings for the first time. Previously this had only been possible by hand-knitting using 5 needles.

It is true that seamless stockings only became widespread in the 19th century, although the mechanization for the production of stockings had been in full swing throughout Europe for a long time already. Naturally, contemporary stocking factories have little in common with the early industrial mills: they are much more like a high-tech company. So it is with Wolford, which is one of the largest manufacturers in the field. It was founded by the industrialist Reinhold Wolff and the retail trade entrepreneur Walter Palmers. Registered as a tradename in 1950, Wolford specialized mainly in the production of stockings. This was at the time of the

Perlon revolution. In 1954 the young company launched the first seamless Perlons and thus acquired their reputation for being the pioneers in the manufacturing of ladies' stockings. The seamless stockings were followed by countless other innovations such as the beltless stockings with adjustable garter (1968), the first hipster tights that could therefore be worn with low-waist trousers and short-cropped tops (the "Hipsters" of 1970), the first runproof tights ("Luxor", 1975), and the first support tights that looked fashionable and attractive rather than medical and inelegant ("Miss Wolford", 1977). Wolford had already expanded its range of ladies' knitwear in the 1970s and 1980s, when it also included aerobic outfits. In the 1990s, the company launched the famous seamless "bodies" and completely seamless tights that caused a sensation when they appeared. Wolford has also been at home on the runway for quite a while; it has made exclusive developments and collaborations with Lanvin, Chanel, Claude Montana, Chloé, Jean-Paul Gaultier, Chantal Thomass, Thierry Mugler, La Perla, Kenzo, Sonya Rykiel, Helmut Lang and many other major names. In 1998, another world premiere took place in Tokyo, the launch of "Starcknaked", a multi-wear garment designed by Philippe Starck that consisted of a seamless, knitted tube over 8 ft (2.5 m) long with integrated tights. There were nine different ways of wearing it and it weighed only 7 ounces (200 grams).

Wolford's innovative spirit is reflected not only in its fashionable designs but also in its constant search for new yarns. In this context, it has developed a close relationship with DuPont, the leading American fiber specialist, as well as with European suppliers. Helanca, Cantrece, Banlon, Skinlon and Synergie are are but a few of the significant milestones in the development of the yarns used by the company. In 1992, the legendary "Le 9" was launched. The lightest pantyhose in the world, weighing only just over 1/2 an ounce (16 grams). This time, too, the yarn, an ultra-fine bicomponent fiber, was developed by DuPont. Even finer yarns were developed for "Aura" and "Fatal." All these high-tech fibers were knitted on ever-improved machines according the company's high standards.

However, even the most sophisticated machines cannot replace humans in every field, which explains why about 400 seamstresses are employed at the Bregenz production plant. Some 16 different stages are necessary to make a single pantyhose, 25 to make a "body" and up to 45 to make a "swimbody." The process always starts with the choice of yarn. Then every single spool is carefully tested by highly skilled experts before it is allowed into the knitting department. Each knitting machine takes between four and fifteen minutes to knit a single pair of pantyhose—the finer the knit the longer it takes. The item now goes to the sewing department where the feet parts are closed with very fine stitches (so that the seam does not press on the foot), the leg parts are assembled, and the diamond-shaped gusset is sewn in. The tights are then dyed and treated with special plasticizers. The final stage is the molding department where they are given their final shape. There are constant meticulous controls between the various stages. It is only after the pantyhose has passed all 18 quality tests that it is packed and sent out to be sold all over the world. It is quite an expensive process but one that pays off because the high-quality products from Wolford have long ago achieved a cult status in the world of fashion.

High-tech is just as important as experience and craftsmanship in the production of fine stockings and tights.

The dye works building at Wolford's headquarters in Bregenz has a magnificent glass facade nearly 700 feet long. The innovative architecture succeeds in merging the inside and outside world together.

Nightgown versus pajamas

However nice it is to snuggle in "his" pajama top, elegant ladies' pajamas such as this model by shirt manufacturer Emanuel Berg are something special.

It is not known for certain when in the history of costume people started to make clothes especially for sleeping at night. But it seems likely that the nightshirt or nightgown made its first appearance in Renaissance Italy. Until then, it had been customary to sleep naked or at best in a day-shirt. Very soon the rather plain, knee-length unisex garment developed into a ladies' and men's version. The ladies' version became increasingly elegant, better cut and lavishly decorated until at the beginning of the 20th century it appeared to be suited for everything except sleeping in comfortably. Luxury models decorated with lace, flounces, ruches, frills and elaborate embroidery became semiofficial garments, worn at home for greeting close female friends and family. Beautiful, feminine nightwear was considered very important. No woman at that time would have dreamed of wearing trousers and a matching short top, buttoned at the front, to sleep in.

Ladies' pajamas made their first appearance in the 1920s. Avant-garde fashion had already thrown away many of the rules of dressing, so the triumph of pajamas, still a male preserve, was almost inevitable. The resistance of traditionalists was more a formality than a serious protest. While men's pajamas were made from rather stiff cotton, the new ladies' pajamas were made from comfortable silk and synthetic fabrics. Pastel colors, decorative lace, imaginative details and a soft, flowing cut all helped to turn the simple pajamas into a luxurious outfit for the bedroom.

From then on pajamas became an indispensable part of a woman's wardrobe and ranged from very feminine to classically sober. In 1960 the designer Irene Galitzine caused a sensation with her palazzo-pajamas at the Florence Fashion Fair that took place in the Pitti Palace. The wide-cut trousers and loose tunic-type top had become socially acceptable—at least as casual leisure wear.

But not all women were willing to give up their nightgowns, which also developed to reflect contemporary fashion. Thus the question "dress or suit" became a fashion statement. The "Baby Doll" style made its appearance in the late 1950s and early 1960s when pajama parties were all the rage, and the garment was extremely popular with the young. This mini-combination consisted of a top that reached below the bottom with puff sleeves and a gathered, ruche neck, worn over short harem pants. Later the top acquired spaghetti straps. In 1956 the actress Carroll Baker became famous for wearing such an outfit in Elia Kazan's controversial movie *Baby Doll*.

Women who did not like such frivolities found an alternative model on the big screen in the person of Audrey Hepburn in *Roman Holiday* (1953), who showed how irresistible a woman could look in a man's pajamas, in this case ones belonging to Gregory Peck. Even today, "his" roomy pajamas, comfortable and maybe even still smelling of his after-shave, are still much appreciated by a woman in love.

This lady is still living in the sheltered world of a princess, and so far there are no man's pajamas in sight: Audrey Hepburn wearing a girlish nightdress in the movie *Roman Holiday* (1953).

Clothes for private moments

Many centuries ago the clothes worn at home and those worn on grand social occasions were completely different garments. Getting ready for a grand occasion, such as appearing at court or attending official events, demanded that the woman wear a very special gown, enhanced by precious jewelry. These preparations took a very long time. A lady was then expected to spend hours in this heavy, uncomfortable gown with corsets, bustles and crinolines without displaying any sign of tiredness, let alone fainting. When not absolutely required, all this finery remained in the wardrobe and the woman wore instead a private or semi-private garment. These clothes much more accurately reflected the fashion of the time than the traditional court dress dictated by strict protocol.

Even at the beginning of the 20th century there was still a very clear division between private and official dress. Admittedly, it was no longer a question of wearing the correct dress to appear at court, but social life and even the simple activities of daily life were regulated by a set of rules whose transgression was synonymous with social suicide. No wonder that home was considered a haven of freedom from a fashion point of view. Garments were designed for both men and women that could be worn at home and were very comfortable. It is true that today we would consider the magnificent tea-time dresses, negligees or house dresses, which often required bulky underwear and a corset, as more akin to formal ball gowns. But in the past they were considered very casual and would never be worn except in the company of family and close friends, and certainly never outside the house.

Even in the Roaring Twenties, a well-dressed woman would still have many items of clothing in her wardrobe that were reserved for her private mornings and afternoons at home. For instance, the negligee was a kind of elegant dressing-gown that was worn over a matching nightgown or a simple shirt with straps. The dressing-gown or "peignoir" was originally worn to protect the woman's precious clothes from powder while getting ready, and it subsequently developed into a soft, fine cape. The dressing-gown was made of a light or thicker fabric depending on the season and it was so elegant that it could even be worn to receive guests. The expensive combination of silk pajamas with a matching coat was so comfortable that women often did not feel like getting dressed "properly." Women who loved books were able to indulge their passion for reading in bed, wrapped in comfortable, soft bed jackets or capes.

In the 1950s, all these items of clothing were increasingly classed under the all-embracing concept of a dressing-gown or bathrobe, and the elegant, fashionable clothes worn to entertain at home lost their role in women's wardrobes. This was partly caused by the fact that fewer women spent entire mornings or long afternoons in their boudoirs.

Nowadays women no longer have time for such a life of leisure. Schedules are full of appointments and meetings, and women are generally busy from morning till evening with business or private activities. However, in spite of having very little time for private moments at home because of the hectic way of life, the idea of the "boudoir" clothes of the past has not been entirely given up. They are no longer specially designed for the purpose but are comfortable leisure garments selected from the varied collections of sportswear.

Admittedly few women openly confess to preferring baggy old jeans and a loose sweatshirt that may have been a fashion statement over twenty years ago, or old leggings (which naturally no woman officially admits to owning), or some similar comfortable garment. Nevertheless, most ladies have their very personal favorite items for those private moments that they do not share with the public. And if by any chance she has to open the door to an unexpected visitor she can always throw on an outrageously expensive but irresistibly stylish Hermès dressing-gown.

In the 1930s, clothes were always matched to the occasion. At home they would be sporty and practical yet correct, while for going out they would be chic and elegant.

Warm, soft, comfortable, and perfect for an evening at home. Worn with a sweater, Falke's stylish version of leggings are perfect for feeling comfortably relaxed.

№ 3

Classic day clothes
and the business look

Outfits for an active day

The 1920s were known as the "Roaring Twenties" but the period described by this phrase actually lasted only a few years, from the middle of the decade until the beginning of the great depression of 1929. Nonetheless, these years saw a complete revolution in ladies' fashion, leading to a new approach to the concept of fashion that is still valid today at the start of the 21st century. During the Roaring Twenties, magazines, novels, and movies celebrated the "new woman." The description of this "ideal woman" would have been accurate when seen on the television of yesteryear, and it still is today on the Internet, because the attributes used to describe her remain unchanged. The "new woman" of the 1920s was independent, unattached, working, open to the world, sporty, confident, prepared to experiment, and emancipated. She enjoyed going out in her free time (without a male escort) or taking short trips (in her own car). The modern lady was always on the move and never had enough time. A wristwatch was an indispensable accessory and the concept of stress was invented then, coming to be seen as an attribute of women who were sought after, chic and successful. All aspects of a woman's life had changed from one generation to the other, and this naturally resulted in a change of dress habits.

Because of the dramatic loss of life in World War I, there were many young women living alone in the large cities who had to survive on their own. For the first time there was a specifically female labor market: every day new businesses were started up and these urgently needed secretaries and bookkeepers. Even government and industry began to employ women. Admittedly the salaries were low and management positions were almost inaccessible, but the traditional gender roles had gone for the time being. A man was no longer the automatic breadwinner who made a career for himself outside the house, and a woman no longer necessarily stayed at home to look after the family. Women now had their own position in the world of work and women from every level of society worked in shops, offices, and factories, because with postwar inflation even better-off families could no longer afford to rely entirely on a male breadwinner to support them.

Naturally fashion had to react to these completely new circumstances. Suddenly there was a demand for clothes that not only looked good but were suitable for work. The concept of business clothes was born. In addition, other clothes were needed on the weekend for leisure activities and sports, clothes that today would be described as sportswear or casual wear. In the evening, office workers filled bars, hotel lounges, dance halls, and variety shows. They therefore needed fashionable, seductive clothes that made the women wearing them feel like vamps but were still comfortable enough for dancing the night away.

There was nothing new in the fact that women wanted to be elegant on social occasions and especially in the evening, but chic, elegant business outfits and day clothes were a new concept. There was no better source of inspiration for these new kinds of clothes than men's outdoor wear. Hard-wearing but attractive tweeds proved themselves to be very reliable fabrics, knitwear was ideal for sports because it moved with the body, and the sober, plain, straight cut of men's suits partly inspired by uniforms were adapted to women's clothes. The simple shirtwaist dress, pantsuits and suits of the 1920s show how the new elements were adapted and integrated. This "clean-cut" look was ideally suited to the new working woman and this is still the case. As today, there was an overlap between business wear and sportswear. For instance, in the 1920s the popular sweater with the indispensable calf-length pleated skirt was the height of fashion, and it was also a popular outfit for the office. Today such an outfit would be considered slightly too casual in some work places.

When women started going out to work in the 1920s, the question was how to dress suitably for a job in an office.

Mini-Minor, mini-skirt and mini-bag—in the real world elegant women do not go to the office like this. Falke's posters were probably designed by men.

Elements of everyday wear

Defining a classic, elegant outfit for private or business purposes is not an easy task today, because the strict rules that used to dictate when what should be worn where hardly exist anymore. Ultimately, what a woman wears to walk around town on a free afternoon is entirely up to her, while there are many places of work where women are allowed to create their own personal business look. In Paris you will see French women in Chanel suits with Kelly bags rushing along the Rue Saint-Honoré to do their shopping. They do not consider their outfit unusually elegant but rather as a normal, functional, everyday way of dressing, a fact that is reflected in the rather worn look of the bag, the slightly frayed seam of the skirt or the tiny coffee stain on the jacket. In London on the other hand, you will see owners of advertising agencies who come to the office in sneakers, black pants and tight little sweaters. This is in spite of the fact that England used to be a stronghold of well-established dress conventions.

In recent years, rules are becoming increasingly liberal, to the point of almost disappearing, not only in Great Britain, but all over the world. This has created endless new possibilities, and a large number of new styles and trends have been developed for wearing during the day. But this has also led to some uncertainty, especially in the case of important occasions, as to which outfit would be most appropriate to the situation. We are constantly worrying whether we are "underdressed" or "overdressed" and often it is best to rely on our own feelings.

Even the many examples provided by the world of fashion are of little help in this respect. For daytime, fashion designer Alberta Ferretti favors romantic dresses with shoulder straps worn with comfortable cardigans in black, dark-blue or burgundy, while designer Paloma Picasso prefers straight gray flannel pants combined with a light-colored shirt or some other simple top, preferably by Hermès. American ladies

often combine understated, off-the-rack chinos with equally understated tailored shirts by Charvet. A politician such as Hillary Clinton is hardly ever seen in anything but a pantsuit, suit or sober shift dress with matching coat.

Although all these dress concepts appear very different at first sight, they do have a few points in common. Good daywear and business outfits should be as classic and as plain as possible. Jewelry or accessories may be used to add a decorative touch. These outfits are usually in plain, neutral colors, mostly suited for all seasons, unaffected by fashion trends, while the various garments can be combined with each other. These clothes are made from first-quality fabrics, and the tailoring and fit is absolutely perfect.

This sounds like a rather costly approach to dressing, but it need not be particularly expensive. By investing in a few absolutely classic, timeless basic elements such as a couple of well-cut shirts and a formal dress, you will have built the foundation of a wardrobe that can be varied and pepped up with some cheaper, fashionable items. A dark-colored, top-of-the-range, off-the-rack or tailor-made suit that fits like a glove always consists of two parts that can be worn separately with other items, thus creating a different outfit every time. Although it is not old-fashioned, it is unfashionable in a positive sense so it will last for years without ever appearing dated.

Looked at in this light, buying classic, first-quality clothes will save you time and money, because you will not need to constantly buy new clothes from the latest season's collections. This is an aspect that is much appreciated by everyone, by both the prosperous and the less well-off. Everyone dislikes paying vast sums for a trendy little item that will look dated after a few months; a timeless classic is a much better investment. It is vital, however, that one's weight remains constant so that the garments which will last for years will also fit all this time.

Far left, top:
Shoes and accessories are what decides whether this dress can be worn for leisure purposes or at the office.

Far left, bottom:
There are many variations on the suit. Here is an interpretation designed for summer.

Top left:
Whether at the office, strolling through the city or sitting in a bar, the classic trouser suit is ideal for any situation.

Bottom left:
A separate jacket can be combined with a skirt or trousers, depending on the occasion and your taste.

The dress

Whether made of a romantic Laura Ashley-style floral print or as a sober straight-cut variation, a dress is, as it has always been, one of the most elegant, feminine outfits for a lady. This is in spite of the fact that combinations of a skirt and top or pants and a top tend to predominate the modern woman's wardrobe.

Dress-type garments are as old as mankind itself and the history of costume includes a large number of interpretations of this garment, ranging from the simple shirt-like garment worn by the Babylonians to the tunic worn in ancient Rome, and on to the medieval coat made from a coarse woolly fabric. Until the 14th century the dress or tunic was a neutral garment that was worn by both men and women. It was only some time later that women's clothes began to differ from those worn by men. Both the fabric and the cut of dresses changed considerable and frequently throughout history. Depending on the fashion current at the time, it was either tight or loose, and it either emphasized the shape of the body or concealed it. Sometimes it would enhance certain parts of the body by means of stomach, hip, shoulder or posterior padding; it might have a low-cut, revealing neckline or a demure high neck, embellished with decorative elements such as ruches, frills, lace, embroidery and edging. Special occasions required special dresses, thus leading to the development of sumptuous evening dresses, bridal gowns, ball gowns, practical travel dresses, light summer dresses, indoor dresses, and ordinary everyday dresses that could be worn on the various occasions. One feature of the dress remained virtually unchanged until the early 20th century—it was always long. The development of the dress as we know it today started in the 19th century with the so-called artist's dresses and reform dresses. These were to take the place of dresses with artificial silhouettes created by wearing tight corsets, favoring a natural line instead. However, at the time these loose garments did not appeal to many women and therefore they did not spread. Nevertheless, these garments were a source of inspiration to the new haute couture because in 1905-1906 fashion designers such as Poiret, Erté and Fortuny launched their new creations, simple dresses that could be worn without a corset. Five years later Paul Poiret invented the hobble skirt, a very tight ankle-length skirt that forced women to walk with a mincing gait. Although it was not particularly popular, it was an important milestone in the history of costume. For the first time, the hem of the skirt was raised from full-length to ankle-length, a fashion sensation as well as a moral one. This paved the way for the revolutionary fashion of the Roaring Twenties, when a series of popular classics that are still popular today became socially acceptable. These included the comfortable shirtdresses and jersey dresses, the straight-cut flapper dresses, the simple button-through and pinafore dress (the first female work uniform, which was even worn in shops and offices), and last but not least, the little black dress, the first knee-length dress for festive occasions.

The shape of these dresses changed constantly throughout the following decades. Sometimes they were longer and then they became shorter again; sometimes the skirt was full and widely flared, sometimes it was tight and emphasized the hips; sometimes full sleeves were all the rage and at other times straps were considered the height of fashion. Then in the 1960s the image of the dress changed much more drastically with the invention of the miniskirt.

The simpler the cut, the more important the details. This sophisticated low-cut back shows a lot of skin but still looks very "dressy."

There is one name that incorporates the quintessential English style: Laura Ashley. Her clothes evoke images of garden parties and picnics in the country.

The various types of dress

Dress and jacket combination

The dress and jacket combination is one of the most elegant variations on the dress, and it is one that can also be worn on formal daytime occasions. The ensemble usually consists of a simply cut dress and matching jacket made from the same material or from some other perfectly coordinating fabric. It was particularly fashionable in the 1930s and the 1950s, and it is still seen today as a timeless outfit. Such a dress and jacket combination is too formal for everyday business wear but it is still very popular in traditional circles or for official events.

The shift dress

The shift dress is a straight dress that fits closely at the waist and hips, often sleeveless and with a low neckline. It made its first appearance on the fashion scene in 1918, and in the 1920s it was often worn as an evening dress. In the 1990s Princess Diana revived the shift dress, which was now worn as a day dress. A well-cut shift dress can be endlessly varied with different accessories and jackets and it also looks very good on festive occasions.

Slip dress

The slip dress is usually knee-length, loose-cut, and held up by narrow straps. It has a flared cut or low-set skirt or flounce. Because of its lightness, it is mainly worn as a summer dress. The original slip dress was the "Charleston" dress, which could be seen everywhere in dance halls between 1925 and 1927. The simplicity of the cut contrasted with the lavish decoration that included braiding, fringes, embroidery, beads, and sequins.

Shirtdress

The shirtdress is a combination of a man's shirt-like top (turn-down collar, with visible or concealed rows of buttons and sleeves with cuffs), joined onto a straight or flared skirt. Until the 1960s, this dress was a comfortable everyday outfit that was extremely popular with all women. The first shirtdresses, made from soft, flowing fabrics such as jersey and cotton knitwear, were designed by Coco Chanel in 1916.

Laura Ashley dress

The typical Laura Ashley dress is calf-length with ruches and other romantic decorative elements, and it is usually made from printed cotton fabrics with a floral pattern. It is a delightful old-fashioned dress that has been popular since the 1960s with young women who have a yearning for the countryside. In the early 1970s the popularity of this "traditional" dress was so great that the crowded Laura Ashley shop in London's Fulham Road was selling about 4,000 dresses a week.

Coat dress

This practical garment between a coat and a dress was first seen in the 1940s. It usually has long sleeves, a collar with lapels, applied pockets and, like a coat, it is fastened at the front by a row of buttons. The fabric is warm enough to give protection from the cold but light enough so that in winter a real coat can still be worn on top. Often the waist is emphasized by a belt. Current coat dresses usually reflect the shape and details of the coat fashion of today.

Lena Strothmann (left), responsible for the ladies dressmaking department at the Gütersloh couturier Kleegräfe & Strothmann, discusses a design with workshop manageress Angelika Ulbrich.

Modern tailoring differs from earlier dressmaking only in that it uses contemporary fabrics and accessories, such as buttons, zippers, and so on. The tools are the same.

Style to measure

Everyone will have experienced this: the sleeves are too long, the legs are too short, the waist is too high or too low, the jacket is perfect but the skirt is too tight, the coat is long enough but two people could almost fit in it. These are the traditional problems that women have with off-the-rack clothes. Unfortunately we have become accustomed to the bad fit of many ready-made clothes and ascribe it to our own physical shortcomings rather than to the clothes themselves. A further problem is that the sizes indicated on the label are only approximate, being calculated on a statistical average. The "standard" woman has a height of such-and-such and weighs so much. But that is the "standard" woman—the real one is not so well served with standard off-the-rack clothes.

Factory-produced clothes have been in existence since the late 19th and early 20th century but the phenomenon only became widespread after World War II. Before that many women went to a dressmaker or tailor who would make their clothes to measure. The person was first measured

and the garment made to the individual's measurements. As a result, the clothes fitted perfectly, unless there had been significant changes in a person's weight in the meantime.

Now the widespread custom of made-to-measure clothes has gone out of fashion. Some say that this is the result of the high prices asked by tailors—an argument that can only be partly true in view of the cost of designer off-the-rack clothes that are often equally expensive. Others say that it is because tailor-made clothes would look unfashionable after one season and are therefore not worth the expense. This is not a very valid argument either, because a classic off-the-rack Armani pantsuit is not bought to wear for just a few months and then put aside.

The main difficulty in going to a dressmaker lies more in the possible misunderstandings between the dressmaker and the client. Both will have their own ideas and it is absolutely vital that they should exchange views and come to an agreement at the outset. The dressmaker must take the wishes of her client seriously. For instance, if the dressmaker

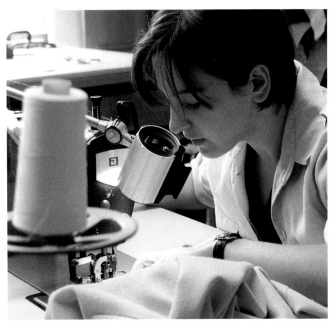

The dressmakers at Kleegräfe & Strothmann make clothes that fit perfectly, of course, but they also make sure that clients end up with a unique garment in which they feel comfortable, one that reflects and underlines their personality.

It is not difficult to persuade potential clients of the advantages of made-to-measure clothes. It is much harder, however, to find a skilled workforce for their workshop.

thinks that puff sleeves, box shoulders or a very low neckline down to the belly-button are a bad idea, she must say so immediately rather than change the details on the quiet, which would undoubtedly lead to disappointment all around. By the same token, the client must be able to describe exactly what she wants. It can be very helpful if she can show the dressmaker a photograph of a similar outfit. Similarly, if a new jacket will be worn with an existing skirt, she should wear the skirt when she visits the dressmaker or at least bring it with her. The same applies to accessories such as shoes, purses or scarves that will later be worn with this skirt.

When the client feels she can trust her dressmaker and there is a good communication between them, made-to-measure clothes are always a success because they fit perfectly and meet all the requirements and wishes of the wearer. In addition, because they have been hand-finished they will last longer than off-the-rack clothes. Obviously, this way of acquiring clothes is more time-consuming than buying them in a store because sev-

eral visits to the dressmaker will be needed and it may take several weeks—sometimes even months if the dressmaker has a lot of work—to produce the finished garment. This lengthy process must be taken into account if the garment is to be worn on a special occasion, since it means going to the dressmaker well in advance so that the garment can be finished in time. In fact, a garment for a special occasion is not the best introduction to the world of made-to-measure clothes. The task of a dressmaker is to produce a first-quality garment that fits and gives pleasure to its owner because it makes her look good. It would therefore be a pity not to enjoy this pleasure as often as possible, if not every day. Women who have no use for a smart suit should not bother to ask the dressmaker to make them one, but should rather opt for a casual piece that can be used as an everyday garment, such as an elegant blouse or well-fitting pants. There is no point in letting "good clothes" waste in a wardrobe, and in any case, made-to-measure clothes are too expensive for that.

The dressmaker's workshop: stylish made-to-measure clothes

Made-to-measure clothes take time to make and as a result demand a completely different approach to buying habits. Instead of spending an afternoon shopping in town or at the mall at the beginning of the season, several visits to the dressmaker's will be necessary. These visits should of course start several weeks or even months before it is cold enough to wear the new winter coat or warm enough to wear the new summer dress. The first visit will be spent discussing the item of

The choice of fabric is another very important point that should be discussed at the first meeting. Many dressmakers have a few fabrics in stock but naturally not a full selection since this would require a large storeroom for which few dressmakers can spare the space or the money. If the client does not find any fabric to her taste, the dressmaker will buy it, or the client may go and buy the fabric herself, having ascertained how much is needed. But it is the dressmaker who will look after the other necessary materials such as padding, interfacing, yarn, and zippers.

As soon as the fabric has been purchased, the first "version" of the garment can be made. First the pattern is cut out. To do this the dressmaker draws all the separate parts that make up the garment on special pattern paper. If the garment is not too exotic and the client has a more or less normal figure, the dressmaker can simply alter a standard pattern. The pattern is then transferred onto the fabric, which is then cut out according to the pattern. The dress, jacket or pants can now be assembled, ready for the first fitting. How far the garment is advanced at this stage will depend on whether the dressmaker has worked several times with the client before or if it

Here a seamstress in the workshop of the Munich-based haute couture house Max Dietl is sewing pearls onto a made-to-measure evening gown.

clothing. The client must explain as clearly as possible what she wants and the dressmaker may draw a few sketches to make sure that they both understand what is required. If the client has been going to the same dressmaker for a while, it will only be necessary for the latter to ask if her measurements have changed, but a new client will be carefully measured and the measurements noted down.

is the first time, and whether the garment is straightforward or complicated. So at the first fitting the client may try on an almost finished garment or just a roughly basted together garment without interfacing, pockets and fastenings. The dressmaker makes the necessary corrections with pins and asks the client for her first impression. This is the moment of truth. If there is anything you do not like you must say so now! It will be too late if you do not. At this point changes can still be made easily but it will be much more difficult at the next fitting. This second fitting is the time to discuss details such as the buttons, possible decorative elements, and also the length of the garment.

The semi-finished garment then goes back to the workshop. If the fitting was fairly successful the corrections will be within reasonable limits, but if the garment did not fit at all it may be necessary to take it completely apart, alter the pattern and re-assemble the garment piece by piece. It is also at this second stage that the final finishing of the garment takes place, including the hemming, sewing on of buttons and trimmings, and sewing in the lining. The pockets that were only marked on the garment are now cut open and the pocket pouches attached. The reason for delaying the cutting open of the pockets until this stage is that the height of the waist can be adjusted after the first fitting without affecting the pocket positions.

If the client is an old customer the finished garment may now be sent to her, but new customers will be asked to attend a last fitting so that the dressmaker can check that all the alterations have been carried out successfully and that everyone is satisfied with the result. If there are still a few small problems, the garment is sent back to the workshop with the alterations indicated with pins. But usually the proud owner will be able to take her new garment home. Unlike clothes purchased from large stores and boutiques, it is always possible to go back to the dressmaker after months or even years if the hem has become unraveled, the zipper is stuck, or the garment needs some repair or alteration. In addition, your dressmaker will often know a good place where tears and burn holes can be invisibly mended, and she will probably also be able to recommend a reliable dry cleaner. Most women will derive such pleasure from their made-to-measure garment that they will soon go back to "their" dressmaker to order the next item of clothing.

In the 18th century, all clothes were made by hand by dressmakers. Those who could not afford made-to-measure clothes wore old cast-offs.

A little about fabrics

Fabric forms the basis of any garment, and the manufacturing of fabric is one of the oldest achievements of mankind. It is a very complex process, consisting of two different stages or techniques: spinning to make the yarn, without which there can be no fabric, and weaving. Already in the 7th century B.C. the inhabitants of Mesopotamia wore clothes made from magnificent woolen fabrics, while Egypt was famous for its linen and China was producing silk by the 3rd century B.C.

Over the centuries spinning and weaving techniques were constantly improved, as were dyeing processes. Thus every period in history developed its own textile innovations that were then enthusiastically adopted by the court, the aristocracy, and the more prosperous middle classes. Admittedly, expensive fabrics such as velvet and brocade were reserved for special occasions, as were delicate fabrics such as muslin, tulle, and chiffon that would not have been suitable for everyday clothes. Ordinary clothes were usually made from wool, cotton or linen fabrics.

In the 20th century, clothes were made from a wide range of fabrics and weaves. The first cellulose-based artificial fiber had been developed in 1890, while after World War II, numerous chemical fibers were created from coal, tar, natural gas, and oil. There were also countless mixed fabrics that combined natural fibers such as wool with silk, or cotton with linen, and also natural fibers with synthetic fibers.

However, elegant daywear would usually be made from natural fibers or combined with just a very small proportion of synthetic fiber. This is particularly true in the world of business where most working clothes are made from light to medium weight woolen fabrics, fine cashmere, delicate silk, and cool linen.

Raw materials for precious fabrics

Wool

The manufacturing of all wool fabric starts with sheep-shearing. Sheep are shorn once or twice a year when around ten or twelve pounds of wool or fleece are removed and then used to make warm woolen garments of every kind. The best fleece is produced by the merino sheep, a breed originally native to Spain which then spread to the rest of Europe, to Britain, and ultimately to Australia, which is now the largest producer of wool. Even when very fine, woolen fabrics are quite hard-wearing and relatively crease-resistant. They have temperature-balancing properties, which is why they are also used for summer clothes. The terms "virgin wool" and "pure new wool" guarantee that the wool was shorn from live sheep and then made into fabric. Wool that is not so designated may be made from production remnants and recycled garments.

Cashmere

Cashmere pantsuits, suits and coats are among the finest garments anyone can buy. They are made from the soft under-fur of the cashmere goat, which is not shorn like sheep but carefully combed. The yield is extremely small—a billy-goat yields six or seven ounces while a nanny-goat produces a mere four ounces of usable raw material. The highest quality cashmere comes from Central Mongolia. Cashmere fabrics have an unmistakable sheen, feeling wonderfully soft while being as hard-wearing and pleasant to wear as fine wool fabrics.

Mohair

The angora goat takes its name from the Turkish town of Ankara in whose surroundings these goats used to graze as far back as the 12th century. The fine, long silky hair is rarely used on its own but usually in combination with pure new wool to produce a much sought-after mixed fabric that is very light, crease-resistant and wonderfully pleasant to wear. The presence of mohair gives the fabric an attractive sheen.

Angora

Very confusingly, angora does not come from the angora goat but from a completely different animal, the angora rabbit. The very fine, light hair of this rabbit is mostly used in combination with pure new wool. In spite of its lightness, fabric containing angora is usually very warm and pleasant to wear because it has insulating properties.

Silk

Silk is produced from the cocoon fibers of the silk worm, a type of moth native to Asia. After removing the larva's cocoon, the silk is dissolved in water and the fibers are then put together and spun. This precious fabric is used on its own or in combination with other materials. Silk is cool in summer and warm in winter and relatively prone to creasing.

Vicuña

Even better than cashmere is vicuña. This comes from llamas, or to be precise from Lama vicugna, the smallest species of llama, native to the Andes. Until the 1950s these animals were still being killed for their fine hair but then strict hunting laws were passed that forbade the hunting of these animals to ensure the survival of the species. These protective measures led to a decrease in the amount of vicuña fibers available on the market, which in turn led to a steep increase in the price. Today vicuña is collected by gathering individual hairs shed naturally by the animals from the ground and bushes. Consequently a vicuña coat is one of the most luxurious and most expensive garments anyone could wear.

Alpaca

Abb. 265. Alpaka.

The alpaca is a South American llama, Lama pacos. The fine, soft, shiny hairs can be used on their own or with pure new wool and other fibers. Fabrics containing alpaca are very pleasant to wear and crease-resistant. Besides the alpaca the guanaco, another animal related to the camel, also produces hair that is much sought after.

Linen

Linen is a fabric of vegetable origin, made from the bast fibers of the flax plant that are spun into yarn. Pure linen fabrics are wonderfully cool in hot weather but they have the disadvantage that they crease very easily. Those who do not like the creased look should not wear pure linen, choosing mixed linen fabrics instead to achieve the appearance without the creasing.

Cotton

Cotton is made from the seed heads of the cotton plant. In the past this much sought-after raw material was gathered by hand, the seed heads were dried, and the fine fibers pulled off from the kernel. Cotton fabrics were therefore rather expensive. Today, the separation of the fibers from the kernel is carried out by machines, but very high quality cotton such as Maco Egyptian or Sea Island cotton are still luxury fabrics. Cotton has become one of the most important fabrics used in everyday and business wear. It is available in a wide variety of yarns, types of fabric, and mixtures, on its own or used in combination with other natural or artificial fibers. Cotton can be very warm or quite cool, depending on the finish of the fabric. Its only disadvantage is that it creases easily.

Variety of fabrics

Exquisite cashmere, elegant herringbone, fine-quality worsted, formal pinstripes, cool wool mixtures—the choice of fabrics and patterns in ladies' fashion seems to be endless. But this diversity is simply the result of constant variations on a few basic characteristics. The weaving process itself provides only a small number of significantly different ways of making fabric, because fundamentally it always consists of the regular interlacing of lengthwise warp threads and crosswise weft (or woof) threads. But the possible variations on these types are almost infinite.

The weaving process determines the structure and appearance of the fabric. There are three types of basic weaves: calico or plain weave, twill weave, and satin weave. The simplest and most important type of weaving is plain weave. Here the weft threads run alternately over and under the warp threads, and in the next row the same process is repeated but running over and under the warp threads. Calico or plain weave (called taffeta weave in the case of silk and cotton weave in the case of cotton) has smooth, similar surfaces on both sides. In twill weaves the weft thread goes under one warp thread and then over the next three. Then after each weft thread, the raised warp is displaced to the right by one thread so that a clear diagonal structure is created. Serge and herringbone fabrics have a twill weave.

The third type of weave is satin weave. In this type of weave only every fifth warp thread is raised by a weft thread. This means that from row to row the weave moves three threads to the right. Because there are never two weaving points next to each other with this type of weave, there is a smooth surface without structure on which the light breaks uniformly. Shiny satin is a typical example of satin weave. As mentioned above, these three types of weaves can not only be varied endlessly but several types of weaves can be combined and alternated in the same length of fabric, thus creating the most varied woven-in patterns.

The selection of a weave is one thing while the choice of yarn is another. A plain weave fabric can be made from all kinds of materials, such as wool, linen, silk, cashmere, chemical fibers, or a mixture of yarns and fibers. In addition, there are smooth and slightly "hairy" yarns. Smooth yarns or so-called worsted yarns consist of very fine, long fibers and they produce equally smooth, fine fabrics. The "hairy" or "carded" yarns consist of short to medium-length fibers. Because these fibers cannot be twisted entirely parallel and smooth, there are always a few fibers that stick out, which produce that hairy effect. The comfortable, woolly tweed is a typical example of fabric made from carded yarn.

The beauty of this plain cut pants suit by Belvest lies in the fabric—the material need not always be pinstripes.

Classic fabrics and patterns

Atlas
Shiny fabric made from silk, wool, cotton, or a mixture of materials using satin (atlas) weave.

Bouclé
Fabric with a knobbly, frizzy surface made with bouclé yarn. Suitable for dresses, coats and sports outfits.

Bourette silk
Also known as floss silk, this fabric is made from waste silk fibers.

Canvas
Hard-wearing cotton fabric, similar to sailcloth, used for jeans and sports shoes.

Carded yarn
Coarse fabric with a soft, woolly feel, made from short-fiber carded yarn.

Chalk stripe
Variation on the pinstripe pattern but with broader stripes.

Chenille
Term used both for the fabric and yarn. Chenille yarns are yarns with dense tufts of fibers that project at right angles along the thread.

Cheviot
Refers both to the Scottish breed of sheep and the wool produced by them, which is a heavy worsted yarn used to produce fabrics in twill weave.

Cord
Generic term used to designate fabrics with more or less pronounced ribbing in the direction of the warp.

Corduroy
Cotton pile fabric with lengthways ribs, used for dressed, blouses and coats.

Crepe
Fabric with crinkled surface made from twisted or crepe yarn, either in ordinary weave or special crepe weave.

Double-face
Fabric with two different sides. One side shows the positive pattern, the other the negative one. Can be worn with either side showing.

Flannel
Warm, soft fabric made from wool, cotton, chemical fibers or mixed fibers with a nap on one or both sides.

Fustian
Coarse twill fabric of cotton and wool with a nap on the reverse side, similar to flannel.

Gabardine
Thick, hard-wearing twill fabric, made from wool or cotton, used for suits and light coats, as well as raincoats and trench coats.

Georgette
Light, granular crêpe fabric in plain weave, suitable for dresses and blouses.

Glen check
Refers both to the special woven design and the fabrics with a characteristic pattern of ground check and overcheck, made in worsted fabrics for suits.

Herringbone
Herringbone patterns occur in twill weave. They are frequently associated with coarse tweeds but this pattern also looks very good in worsted fabrics.

Houndstooth check
Two-colored check pattern in which the checks are linked to each other by their jagged corners. Also known as dog's tooth check.

Jersey
Jersey is machine-knitted on special machines, not woven conventionally with a warp and weft on a loom.

Pinstripe
Fabric with very fine stripes, a classic cloth for business suits.

Pepita
Check design with checks linked together by two diagonally opposite jagged corners.

Ribs
Generic term used to designate fabrics with lengthways and diagonal ribbing, created by the weave but also by a strongly differentiated weft and warp.

Satin
Fabric in satin weave with very shiny surface, made from silk, wool, cotton or mixed fibers.

Saxony
Soft, warm woolen fabric in twill weave with warp of worsted yarn and weft of carded yarn.

Serge
Twill weave fabric used for suits and pantsuits.

Taffeta
Silk or artificial silk fabric in plain weave, used for dresses, blouses and linings.

Tweed
Traditional carded yarn fabric whose pattern is created by the weave or by the use of mottled yarns. Harris tweed and Donegal tweed are among the best known.

Twill
Twill-woven fabric made from wool, silk or cotton.

Worsted fabric
Generic term used to designate fabrics made with smooth, long-fibred yarn, known as worsted yarn. This type of fabric is used for elegant, formal pants, jackets, dresses and suits.

Pepita: black-and-white pattern, for any occasion.

Dog's tooth check: ideal for sports jackets.

Chalk stripes: less severe with its slightly blurred pattern.

Pin stripes: the timeless classic for business outfits.

Glen check: all-purpose fabric for all kinds of garments.

From the sheep to the wardrobe: how woolen cloth is created

A fine woolen fabric is very popular and an ideal fabric for classic, elegant clothes. It is pleasant to wear, warm in winter, cool in summer, generally crease-resistant, hard-wearing and considerably less expensive than the luxury cashmere. We are all so used to having woolen garments in our wardrobe that we are hardly aware of the enormous logistical, technical and creative expenditure that is required to produce just a yard of this fabric.

The long production process starts with the shorn wool of the sheep, the fleece. The fleece is separated and sorted according to which part of the animal it comes from, the trunk, neck, belly or rear. Often the wool is washed at this point. After sorting, the various parts of the fleece and different qualities are sold at large auctions.

Before the weaving process can begin, the loose fibers and hairs are spun into long, uniform threads and yarns. First, the various parts of the fleece are fed into the willower or teaser that separates it into small tufts or flocks. These flocks are then thoroughly washed in a kind of enormous washing machine. The wool is now clean but it still clings together in tufts. In order to disentangle them and arrange the individual fibers parallel to each other, they are conveyed through pipelines into a carding machine. This consists of several powerful rotating rollers positioned opposite each other, each fitted with millions of very fine wire needles. Called scrapers, these catch the clusters of fibers and pull them carefully apart while at the same time getting rid of any remaining dirt. The resulting veil-like gauze is then gathered into ribbons. If worsted yarn is to be spun, the wool fibers of this gauze ribbon are stretched even further, made parallel, carded or combed, and drawn out or slubbed. The refined gauze ribbon is known as woolen slubbing. The coarser, woolly carded yarns that are used to make fabrics such as tweed are not combed or slubbed. In this case the gauze is merely put through the carding machine, separated into strips and reeled up to form the preyarn. But let us now return to slubbing.

Balls of woolen slubbing weighing up to 800 pounds are delivered to the spinning mill. At this stage the wool is either left in its natural color or dyed, depending on its later use. The process of dyeing can take place at various stages in the processing of the wool. The fibers may be dyed at the flock stage, that is, immediately after the fleece has been separated into flocks and washed. Alternatively, dyeing can be carried out when the wool has been slubbed or the yarn already spun. Fabrics of lesser quality are often dyed once they have been woven, after they have come off the loom. On arrival at the spinning mill the woolen slubbing is gathered together in spinning batches. A single spinning batch may contain over a dozen woolen slubbings, because the color of a yarn is the result of a measured and therefore always repeatable combination of woolen slubbings of various colors. A dark blue yarn, for instance, will contain several shades of blue but also gray, brown, red, and green. A colored yarn that is made up of several colors usually gives the fabric a refined, complex shading, which makes it look much more special and interesting than a fabric dyed all in a single color.

After mixing, the slubbings are further stretched until they form a thin pre-yarn. This pre-yarn then goes to the spinning machine where the actual spinning starts. During the spinning process the fibers of the pre-yarn are twisted together under tension by a rotating spindle. The result is a high quality yarn of the required length. After spinning, the yarn may be twined or twisted further. In the case of simple twining, two threads are twisted together but more can be twined if desired. Depending on the number of threads, the twined yarn is called three-ply, four-ply, and so on. Because each of the threads twined together has a separate tension, the twine is treated with steam in order to smooth it. At this point the finished yarn is wound on large spools that then go to the weaving mill.

Above left:
To the side of the large loom is the small test loom used for trying out new fabrics and patterns under production conditions.

Above:
The fabric increases in length with every weft thread that is shot through the warp threads that are stretched lengthwise.

Fabric today is produced on ultra-modern, highly automated looms, but the skills of the weaver still play a major part. Only an experienced craftsman can adjust the machine correctly, check that the weaving process is progressing as it should, and intervene immediately if necessary. First the warp threads are arranged on the loom. In the weaving process, a proportion of these lengthwise threads is raised in a particular pattern so that the shuttle with the weft, the crosswise thread, can be "pushed" through. To produce a simple fabric in plain weave, every other thread (the first, third, fifth, seventh etc.) of the first row is raised, while the second, fourth, sixth, eighth etc., remain down. The weft is then threaded through and pushed against the part already woven. Then, for the next row, the loom lifts the alternate threads (second, fourth, sixth, eighth etc.) while the first, third, fifth, seventh, etc., remain down. Then the weft is moved across again and the whole process is repeated for the next row. This creates a continuous fabric.

In the same way that several colors were used to dye the yarn, the fabric is made up of threads of different colors. Even a plain colored fabric such as dark blue is not made up entirely of dark blue weft and warp threads. It is the combination of different colors that is responsible for the fact that an apparently plain colored fabric suddenly acquires a reddish, greenish or violet sheen in different light situations—an interesting effect that is lacking in fabrics dyed in a single color. Sometimes different yarns are combined: for instance, the warp thread that will form a pinstripe may be a silk yarn while the other warp threads and the weft is made up of woolen yarn.

When the finished fabric is removed from the loom it still has little in common with a soft, high-quality cloth. The fabric is hard and creased, and there are likely to be small weaving defects. So the cloth then goes to the quality control department where numerous patient seamstresses carefully check every inch of the fabric for minute defects such as small knots

and tears in the yarn. They repair these defects using tiny little needles, specially designed for the purpose. Once all the defects have been successfully repaired, the fabric goes to a finishing company, where it will be further refined and finished.

On this site, the fabric is washed in a giant drum with soap and water. This procedure ensures that all the dirt particles unavoidably picked up by the fabric during the spinning, weaving and repairing processes are removed; it also softens the fabric. The degree of suppleness or softness is specified by the client, interpreted by the weaving mill. Because suppleness is a relative concept it comes down to the feeling and experience of the person in charge. The desired effect is achieved by determining the length of the washing process. In most cases this assessment can only be made by a human and not by a computer. These highly skilled experts are indispensable for the weaving mills—an incorrect judgment will result in the fabric being ruined. The right "inspiration" at the right time will turn an average

quality fabric into an absolute first-quality cloth. After washing, the fabric is put in spin driers to remove most of the water. It is then carefully dried by being guided through a kind of rotary ironing machine consisting of heated cylinders, a process that also stretches the fabric. Then any protruding fiber ends are singed off. Next the pile fibers are cut to equal length by the cloth shearing process. This is carried out by rotating spiral cylindrical knives that work like a cylindrical lawn-mower. Any sheen that may have been created during the drying process is removed by an operation called decatising. Between each stage the fabric is treated with steam, stretched and pressed. If required, the fabric may be coated with a particular finish to make it water-resistant or flame-retardant, for instance.

Finally, the fabric is sent back to the weaving mill, and then on to manufacturers or directly to dressmakers, taking some time for this fabric to find its way into your wardrobe, for first it must be made into a garment.

Above left:
After the fabric has been washed and dried, it is moistened again with hot steam, then slowly and carefully stretched over hot rollers.

Top right:
The fabric is now placed between cardboard and pressed overnight under heat. The gives the fabric a very special sheen that cannot be achieved by any other method.

Buttons

Buttons are as old as the history of fashion. These small practical accessories were invented somewhere in central Asia from where they traveled to ancient Greece and Byzantium. In Central Europe large clasps, brooches, ribbons, and hooks and eyes were used instead. But in the 13th century when the crusaders brought the button back from the East, it immediately became widely popular. Anyone who could afford it would wear lavishly decorated buttons made from precious materials. As a result this simple everyday object had become a status symbol. In the 16th century, buttons were even used as a means of payment, and by the beginning of the 17th century there were decorative buttons embellished with miniature paintings or adorned with miniature clocks or precious stones.

Buttons can be made of almost any material. The earliest buttons were made of wood or bone, but later they were also made of ivory, coconut, mussel shells, horn, tortoiseshell, ivory nut, and metals such as iron, aluminum, and brass. China and enamel have also been used and in the 19th century buttons were also made of polished glass and glass backed with a mirror coating. Sometimes buttons are covered in leather or fabric matching the garment, or made from cord and braid as decorative trimming (the double silk knots worn today by men and women as a fashionable substitute for cuff links are very reminiscent of these cord buttons). The great spread of artificial fibers in the 20th century has also led to a staggering range of colorful, new plastic buttons that can be used to produce very interesting effects. Unfortunately, this also means that traditional materials have been replaced by inexpensive substitutes. This is a great pity because cheap buttons on a suit made of fine wool or expensive cashmere will spoil the whole outfit. For instance, a beautiful cotton or silk shirt should have mother-of-pearl buttons, not plastic ones. Buttons play an important part in an outfit, adding a particular character—and fortunately they are easy to replace. When a dress, jacket or suit does not feel quite right or no longer pleases you, try replacing the buttons with a set of beautiful new ones.

The traditional materials used to make buttons that are becoming increasingly rare are ivory nut, mother-of-pearl and horn. The ivory nut, also known as the tagua nut, is the seed of the ivory palm. Originally native to Peru and Colombia, the ivory palm also grows in many tropical countries. Its fruit contains from 80 to 120 seeds ranging from chestnut to hen's

egg size. On the outside they look like wrinkly potatoes in color and structure but inside they are ecru-colored. Because of their hardness, ivory nuts must be worked on a lathe and they can only be cut after soaking in water for a long time. Mother-of-pearl is obtained from the shells of various kinds of mollusks. The most valuable buttons are the larger ones, because they require thicker, and therefore more expensive shells. Smaller and medium quality buttons are made from thinner shells or leftover fragments. Horn buttons are usually made from cattle or buffalo horn. These buttons have a beautiful dark brown to black color and a fine yet strong structure. The best buttons are made from the solid tips of the horns but the sides can also be used. Lower quality horns and left-over pieces are soaked, heated and then pressed into plates from which buttons are punched out.

What makes good buttons expensive is not just the rare and expensive raw material but also the skilled manual work and craftsmanship involved. The skills required are an eye for measurements, sensitivity, and experience—all skills that cannot be provided by a machine. Consequently, because of the craftsmanship involved in the manufacturing of ivory nut, mother-of-pearl or horn buttons, the process takes much longer than the fully automated production of good imitations made from synthetic materials.

As an example, a horn button may go through up to ten stages before it finally ends up in a store or in the workshops of top clothing manufacturers and dressmakers. First the raw material must be carefully selected so that the finished buttons match together—horn is never dyed or stained. Then the blank button is cut, sawn or punched out. These button blanks are laid on a light table where they are sorted again according to color and shading. Next the back and then the front are cut to shape. The most important operation is

still to come: making the holes. Every hole in each button is made separately and by hand, two or four holes being drilled in each button depending on the model. Finally the buttons are placed in a polishing drum where they are whirled together for many hours with an abrasive material consisting of a mixture of small wood chips and cubes of wax. All in all, a lot of work is involved in making such a small object, but it is fully justified because style is all in the details.

The suppliers of these high-quality buttons that enhance the style of the garment are vanishing fast. Many have had to give up because of the overwhelming competition from plastic buttons. One of the last representatives of its kind is the German button factory Carl Schneider & Söhne in Augsburg. This traditional button factory dates back to 1894. Naturally, production methods have changed since then, and indeed some of the processes are still highly guarded secrets, but the raw materials are still the same. These luxury buttons produced by the Augsburg button factory are not only highly regarded in all tailor's workshop around Flensburg and Munich but they are also very sought after by international fashion labels and designers.

What are ready-to-wear clothes?

The 19th century was a period of great economic and social upheaval. Industrialization completely changed the old production methods, increasingly more efficient machines were invented, and factories were set up everywhere. Industrialization also played a major part in the world of fashion, paving the way for the ready-to-wear clothes industry. However, before dressmakers' workshops could be replaced by factories with efficient industrial machines, a few prerequisites had to be met.

First of all, fabric was needed in large quantities to ensure that the investment in factories was worthwhile. This meant there had to be enough spinning and weaving capacity to guarantee a sufficient supply of fabric. In addition, a system of sizing had to be established to ensure that the clothes fitted the potential customers. In this connection, a fashion for loose, flowing clothes was helpful because a bad fit would not be so obvious. Last but not least, an effective work system and a large number of workers were required to cut and sew these garments. In order to ensure a high output, the system had to operate rapidly and smoothly.

The problem of fabric supply had already been solved in the 19th century because the industrial revolution had resulted in the invention and development of elaborate, very fast spinning machines and weaving looms. Manufacturers based their sizing system on the standard uniform sizes of the period and the fashion of simple shirtdresses worn in about 1800 was not too demanding so far as the fit was concerned. However, there was still the question of how to organize the work and make it as efficient as possible.

There was a breakthrough in 1850 with Isaac Singer's improved sewing machine, which because of the great demand was mass-produced in the spirit of the time. Another great help was the development of the paper pattern in 1863. This could be bought in any size thus making cutting much easier. In about 1880, division of labor was introduced into Britain. This meant that a single seamstress was no longer responsible for an entire garment but only for a particular stage of the process, for instance, sewing in the sleeves or the lining or making the buttonholes. Admittedly, this was quite a tedious business for the seamstresses, but routine helped to speed up the work. Until about 1900 most of the stages were carried out by outworkers. Then electric sewing machines were developed, as a result of which factories set up electrified work positions on their own premises. Nevertheless, a few companies preserved the system of outworkers while others combined both systems. After World War II the ready-to-wear industry had become firmly established everywhere. Women's, men's and children's clothes were now mostly bought off-the-rack, thus leading to the inescapable decline of the tailor's trade as a private occupation.

Left and right pages:
The fashion house Peek and Cloppenburg, founded in 1901, first started its ladies' and girls' section in 1936. These advertisements dating from that time illustrate the rather sporty outfits they produced.

Today there are ready-to-wear clothes of various qualities and prices, ranging from the reasonably priced ranges marketed by the large clothing chains to the luxury prêt-à-porter collections, produced under license for a particular designer or haute couture house. A variation on the off-the-rack concept are the so-called made-to-measure clothes. In this case, the dressmaker does not make up her own pattern but uses a standard pattern that is altered to suit the wishes and measurements of the client. Well-tailored made-to-measure can be a very sensible compromise between traditional custom dressmaking and off-the-rack.

It is worth looking for a good manufacturer of ready-to-wear clothes, including those companies that originally specialized in men's clothes but now also include women's clothes in their collections. Traditionally, men's ready-made clothes are better made than women's, generally using fabrics of higher quality. A company that has always specialized in men's clothes is therefore more likely to apply the same high standards of quality to their women's clothes.

Luxury Italian clothing manufacturers, such as Belvest for instance, are known for their well-made garments. This company, based in the Veneto region, offers a fashionable interpretation of classic, elegant suits, jackets, and pantsuits. Since its foundation in the 1960s very little has changed in the company's expensive production methods, which in a positive sense are reminiscent of the very early days of industrial clothing manufacture. Both men's and women's clothes are sewn by hand by highly skilled dressmakers. There are overstitched lapels and hand-finished buttonholes while the fabrics come from the best weaving mills in England and Italy. The buttons are made not of plastic but of horn, mother-of-pearl, and other natural materials.

Unfortunately, such high standards are becoming increasingly rare today in women's clothes. This is why it is so important that these high standards are still being preserved by some manufacturers.

The suit

Today the classic suit is seen as a the symbol of an elegant woman, more serious, more elegant, more ladylike, and in particular more feminine than the pantsuit. Indeed, a jacket and skirt, combined with a beautiful shirt is the favorite outfit of most women for daywear, whether for business or private purposes. It is extremely versatile as well as practical. You can wear a suit to see your bank manager, to get married, to go to a birthday party, or simply to go shopping. In addition to creating the perfect image, suits are easy to wear and accessorize: a matching top, a suitable pair of shoes and a handbag will create a stylish, businesslike effect. For convenience the ensemble rivals the ease that men have in putting on their business suit in the morning.

The suit has always been recognized as a simple, uncomplicated but elegant way of dressing for everyday purposes. In order to emphasize this concept of soberness and simplicity, the cut of the jacket is often based on that worn by men. The first suits—admittedly with long skirts—date from the second half of the 19th century. This was the time of the first women's emancipation movements, women were beginning to play an increasingly active part in society, and many practiced sports. The jacket style was the perfect top, and so-called travel suits had men's style jackets with wide lapels, sturdy seams and large buttons. By about 1913 there were also suit jackets tailored like tail coats that were fastened with a large button at the waist.

Because these "masculine" suits proved so good for daywear, ladies began to go to gentlemen's tailors to have their suits made to measure. These timeless "tailored" suits that were outside fashion were always very well made and they lasted forever. In addition, women also benefited from the excellent fabrics used to make men's suits. Marlene Dietrich had her suits and tail coats made by Vienna's famous tailor Knize, who also made her husband's suits. In the 1940s, Lady Edwina Mountbatten had her entire military wardrobe—which she needed as a regimental commanding officer—made in Savile Row, the Mecca of English tailoring.

Lady Edwina Mountbatten in the famous uniform suit she wore in the 1940s. Fashion legend has it that it was made in London's Savile Row.

The ladies' suit actually has a sports background and it can therefore also be made from woolly, country-style fabrics.

A well-cut, classic suit will remain chic and wearable for many years. This is why it is worth investing in good fabric and first-class tailoring.

Belvest has created a suit that strictly speaking is not one, because on close inspection it becomes apparent that the jacket and skirt are not made of the same fabric.

Chanel

Coco Chanel's contribution to what is defined today as the classic ladies' style cannot be rated too highly, given her strong, long-lasting influence on the image of the modern woman and on women's fashion in general. Coco Chanel (her real name was Gabrielle Chanel) was born on August 19, 1883, in Saumur on the river Loire. Shortly after the turn of the century, this young girl from a family of modest circumstances began her career as a sales assistant in a shop selling household linen and baby clothes. Soon she found financially powerful patrons who also opened the doors of society to her. In 1909, with the help of her friend Arthur Capel, she opened her own milliner's shop in Paris. The venture was so successful that only a year later she moved to Rue Cambon no. 21. From 1913 onward she also began to make outer garments as well as hats. Fashion houses opened in Deauville and Biarritz, the popular resorts that were haunts of the smart set. In 1919 Coco Chanel decided to concentrate exclusively on haute couture and opened a boutique at no. 31. These premises, just a few yards from the discreet back entrance of the Ritz Hotel, have housed the Chanel headquarters ever since.

The fashion guidelines that Chanel learned in her youth were those of the Belle Époque with bustles, flounces, crinolines, ruches, corsets, and gigantic hats that forced women to sit still for purely practical reasons; consequently they were hardly suitable for helping them overcome the passivity that had been forced upon them over the centuries. The clothes that the newly-fledged designer now proposed to women were quite different. Her clothes were intended to serve women and not the other way around. At that time it was a revolutionary concept to put women's personal needs, their enjoyment of an active life, and their independence

Coco Chanel herself always wore the style of clothes she recommended to her clients. Her favorite outfits were soft jersey suits with which she wore costume jewelry.

at the forefront of fashion considerations. Henceforth, fashion was also judged from the point of view of usefulness and wearability. Admittedly, Chanel had not freed women from the corset—this was achieved by the fashion designer Paul Poiret. But the perfect fit, the simplicity, the outstanding finish and the soft, smooth material promoted much greater ease of movement, reliability, and comfort for whatever women wanted to do in these clothes.

Chanel reduced clothes to their essence—today she would be called a purist—and Jean Cocteau, one of Chanel's numerous intellectual and artist friends, fittingly described her designs as a "revolt against frippery." Her collections included simple pullovers, plain pleated skirts, straight cut shirt-waist dresses, and sporty suits made from jersey or tweed that were extraordinarily sober for the time and yet radiated irresistible charm. Although Chanel was much influenced by men's fashion, she also designed very elegant, lavish evening dresses. She made costume jewelry socially acceptable, often combining it with real precious jewels. Indeed Chanel, who always insisted on being addressed as "Mademoiselle" right up to her death in 1971, was rarely seen without her sumptuous pearl necklaces. Meanwhile Chanel is still one of the most famous luxury designer labels, not least because of Karl Lagerfeld's wonderful designs contributed since 1983. The couture creations by the founder of the house were costly, and even today Chanel is still at the expensive end of the scale. Nevertheless, the style created by Chanel contributed to moving the idea of ladies' fashion out of its elitist ivory tower back to real life. The far-sighted fashion designer created a simple line that suited almost all women. She used simple fabrics such as tweed, cotton jersey, knitwear, and artificial silk. All the garments could be combined with each other. The look was completed by reasonably priced costume jewelry. Accessories such as silk flowers were not sewn on but used as brooches so that they could be worn with other outfits.

Chanel was not only interested in doing away with frippery, she also wanted to create a timeless wardrobe that would last not only through the next season and the one after, but for many years because of the simple functionality of the clothes. This claim is still valid for all Chanel's clothes today, because, as in the past, a classic Chanel piece is still an investment. Whether a suit, a pair of shoes, a handbag or a small accessory, everything is always perfect, and experience suggests that they will remain in the Top Ten of everyone's wardrobe for a very long time.

Coco Chanel remained faithful to the fashion concepts she had created for the whole of her life, thus demonstrating most impressively that style and elegance were not a question of age.

Skirts

A skirt is actually a simple, rather unremarkable item of clothing. It consists of a small amount of fabric sewn together, drawn in at the waist, of varying length, easy to make, not requiring serious dressmaking skills. Yet skirts have always reflected the latest trends in women's fashion.

In the 20th century, with its fast changing trends, skirts have experienced a dramatic development. From 1820 or 1830 onward it began to be worn as an independent garment, not joined to a top to make a dress, and it was usually worn with a blouse and jacket, fitted at the waist. But it was only in 1880 when suits became more important that skirts really began to hold their own as a separate garment. In about 1900, straighter skirts became fashionable, and the sumptuous petticoats that had provided volume became redundant. In 1910, Paul Poiret launched his "hobble" skirt, which was so tight at the bottom that women had to walk with tiny, mincing steps. In order to ensure that women did not take too large a step and tear the skirt as a result, special "shackles" were used to lock the calves together.

However, this fashion did not please everyone and many women preferred the more comfortable trendsetting designs of Coco Chanel and Jeanne Lanvin. After World War I, hems, originally ankle-length, gradually climbed higher and higher until they finally reached the knee in the 1920s. Straight cut and pleated skirts remained the dominant shapes until the end of the 1940s. The economic upturn of the 1950s was reflected in new fashion trends, such as a narrow waist with very full, calf-length skirts that required vast amounts of fabric. But the straight skirt remained fashionable, especially now that the seam at the back of the skirt was no longer sewn all the way down to the hem but left open to a certain height, the so-called "Dior-slit." Not only were the skirts more comfortable to wear as a result, but they were also considered quite erotic.

The Swinging Sixties were entirely dominated by the miniskirt, launched by Mary Quant in 1965. The calf-length skirts or midis that appeared at the beginning of the 1970s received a very luke-warm welcome, as did ankle-length maxiskirts, because women still preferred their miniskirts. Even in the 1980s skirts played an important part in business suits, usually knee-length and very tight, although mostly combined with broad-shouldered jackets.

The decade of the 1990s was dominated by the concept of individuality, so there is no longer such a thing as the "right" length for a skirt. This is much better for many women since they can choose the length that suits them best. Women with beautiful legs will undoubtedly look great in a miniskirt but others will do better with skirts that are knee-length or just above the knee. It is important that the length of the skirt should suit the overall proportions of the figure and be in harmony with the length of the other garments in the outfit.

A straight skirt just below the knee look very good with high boots. This model by Belvest is teamed with a sleeveless pullover that further emphasizes the slim silhouette.

It need not always be a mini-skirt—calf-length skirts that show hardly any leg can be sexy when they are tight-fitting on the hips. (Model: Trastornados)

Maxi or mini? Since the 1990s skirt lengths have been peacefully co-existing. Women now wear what they like best, or what suits them.

The leather skirt has made a vigorous comeback in the 21st century after having fallen out of grace in the 1970s and early 1980s. This stylish example is by the German house of Etienne Aigner.

Today pants are seen as an acceptable alternative to the skirt and they are considered just as correct and suitable in almost any situation. Women who prefer not to show too much leg need not do so.

Pants

Turn-ups are particularly suitable for straight-cut pants in sports style. The legs are cut slightly shorter in this model, so that flat shoes can also be worn with them.

Pants for women? Although today we take pants completely for granted, this option is relatively recent. Pants made their first appearance in the world of women's fashion as sportswear because full skirts were extremely impractical in activities such as cycling and horseback riding, and were even dangerous. This fact soon became obvious to clothing designers, and culottes or divided skirts were consequently sold at first on the basis of their safety aspect; indeed in England such a riding costume was known as a "safety-habit."

Between 1911 and 1914 designers experimented repeatedly with the concept of pants for women. Parisian haute couture houses such as Drecoll and Paquin designed ankle-length divided skirts or culottes. Paul Poiret, who in 1910 had been responsible for the rather unsuccessful "hobble" skirt that forced women to mince rather than walk, later launched the pantsuit, and even overalls. It is true that these designs were extremely functional and comfortable but they still felt like tentative suggestions or proposals—pants were the power symbol of men.

It is therefore little wonder that the emancipated "garçonnes" or tomboys of the 1920s caused such a stir wherever they appeared in pants. Even in the 1930s only a living legend such as Marlene Dietrich could sport an androgynous look with impunity. Marlene Dietrich looked stunning in her wide-legged, front-pleated, cuffed pants that were clearly inspired by classic men's pants. But it would be some time before such pants became socially acceptable as day dress for all women. At first pants remained strictly restricted to sport, beach, and home activities.

That ladies' pants could also exist in professional and official circles became clear during World War II, when many women were obliged to wear pants as part of their uniform. But the war had barely ended when pants were returned to the closet and at best would only be taken out again for leisure activities. It would never have occurred to the few professional women of the 1950s to go to the office wearing pants. As business wear, pants only began to appear in the mid-1960s, and even then rather tentatively. They were tolerated because the alternative would have been miniskirts, and superiors saw pants as the lesser of two evils.

Even today pants are still not always welcome in certain more conservative circles, and if pants are to be worn, they should be pleated-front pants and not too tight, or as part of a pantsuit. In those professional circles where attitudes are more relaxed, almost every type of pants can be worn, even those normally worn in leisure time or at home, with the possible exception of Bermuda shorts or jeans. Ultimately, what is acceptable and what is unacceptable depends on the company and the company's dress code.

Left:
Like the hems of skirts, pants lengths vary according to the changing fashion. But straight-cut pants that are not too short will always look elegant with high heels.

Shirts and blouses

Shirts or blouses by Emanuel Berg do not need additional accessories because of the interesting, unusual cut, fabric and details.

Fine silk blouses and slim-fit, straight shirts made from the finest cotton are indispensable items in the classic, elegant wardrobe as well as the fashionably sporty one. Whether plain, striped, polka-dotted or checked, whether lavish or sober, whether fastened with buttons or merely slipped on, these light tops always add a touch of class to the outfit. They are also wonderfully versatile because they can be worn on their own or under a blazer, pullover or cardigan.

The blouse made its first appearance in 1820 when skirts and separate tops began to be worn as well as dresses. The earliest designs were fitted and worn on top of a corset. But by 1880 blouses had already become what they still are today: they became the standard top worn with the suits that have always been the favorite outfit of active businesswomen. Until the 1920s women's blouses were significantly different from men's shirts, because they were still lavishly decorated and very feminine with ruches, pleats, and wide sleeves. It was only after World War I that women's blouses became more like men's shirts, adopting pointed Peter Pan collars, cuffs, applied breast pockets, and button facings. Today the term blouse refers mainly to more feminine versions of the shirt made of fine silk.

It is important to have a small but carefully chosen selection of shirts and blouses in your wardrobe because they are the foundation of business and daywear. They can be worn in a variety of combinations with suits, skirts, pants, and jackets. The selection should also include a least one white shirt or blouse as well as a black and a light blue one. Apart from these basic colors, the colors of the others will depend on what colors you usually wear. Those who prefer wearing earthy, autumn colors such as brown, red, green, orange, and yellow will need shirts and blouses in different colors from those who usually wear black, white or red. The simpler a top is as far as color and cut are concerned, the more versatile it will be. Even the most nondescript shirt or blouse that looks uninteresting in the shop will often prove extremely versatile and ideal for combining with a wide range of outfits.

Shirts and blouses are everyday clothes and should be treated as such. If they are worn directly against the skin or close to the body, they should be washed every time they have been worn. This is also true for fine silk shirts, which unfortunately have to spend a large part of their existence at the dry cleaners. Cotton shirts, on the other hand, can be washed and ironed at home and have a lifespan of several years—if they are good quality. Good quality shirts may shrink a little at first but after the third wash this should stop. The fabric should be easy to iron and become smooth after ironing. The better the shirt, the finer and stronger the seams will be. Mother-of-pearl buttons look better than plastic ones. Many women favor chic sports shirts with button-down collars, preferably by Polo Ralph Lauren. Others prefer more classic shirts such as those found in London's Jermyn Street or made by the celebrated Paris shirtmaker Charvet.

Many companies that originally specialized in men's shirts now also make beautiful ladies' versions, which are extremely well-made. Those who prefer can also have them made to measure. If it is a first order, a fitting will be absolutely necessary.

The white shirt

The white shirt is a classic of a particular kind. As indispensable as the black turtleneck sweater and the dark blue blazer, the white shirt is extremely versatile and can be worn on all kinds of occasions. It is like a white sheet of paper on which you can write your own personal fashion statement. The conservative elegant lady will probably go for the calf-length Black Watch tartan skirt, while the younger woman will probably prefer a Burberry miniskirt or jeans, but in both cases the white shirt will be the perfect accompaniment to create a chic, sophisticated look. Unlike many other items, the white shirt need not be a designer item and it does not matter what the label on the collar says. It does not matter whether it is an expensive shirt made by a luxury shirtmaker, a trendy designer version or a no-name product from a department store—a white shirt is a white shirt. The only feature they have in common is the color; the rest varies depending on the style. It may have button cuffs or French cuffs, a standing collar, tie collar or a collar like a man's shirt. It may have fancy ruches, fabric-covered buttons or a smooth front, and it may be made from silk or cotton. Whichever kind of shirt you choose, a white shirt will always add a touch of freshness and sophistication. In the past, fine white clothing was always a prerogative of the upper classes, completely unsuited to any type of work. This is maybe why white shirts still have a certain aristocratic charm. Today everyone has a washing machine, so that what was once the preserve of the idle rich is now the perfect accompaniment for business suits and perfect for wearing to the office. But it is not restricted to that! Combined with a knee-length skirt, pumps and a Hermès scarf you can achieve a casual chic look, and when worn with jeans or khaki pants, loafers and a sweater around the shoulders, the white shirt will get a sporty touch.

A classic shirt in a white fabric is an indispensable basic in any woman's wardrobe. Important: a flattering collar.

Finest Swiss cotton:
from the design to fine fabric

The fabric designer is responsible for the pattern or design that is then executed by the weaver. The finisher is responsible for the feel of the fabric. This last stage is critical and in spite high technology it still depends on the sense of touch: does the fabric feel good to the touch?

What else is there besides cotton?

Linen

Ranging from near-transparent to really heavy, there is a kind of linen to suit every occasion. Thin linen is really cool in summer. But be warned—linen shirts crease extremely easily.

Silk

For many the height of luxury! Good silk shirts look very much like extremely fine cotton.

Wool

This might be expected to be scratchy, but good quality wool is as soft as silk. A woolly shirt is very warm and ideal for the country. It is therefore a popular fabric for sports shirts.

Wool and cotton

Widely used for traditional winter shirts and very popular with a check pattern giving an English country-style look. Anyone allergic to wool should not wear this mixture because of the itching it may cause.

The little Swiss town of Appenzell is famous for its delicious cheese and for Alpenbitter, the herbal liqueur that is a perfect digestif after a fondue. Both are excellent reasons to go to this picturesque town, but most of the designers of the major international fashion labels and shirt manufacturers have a different reason for their visit. They are interested in the finest Swiss cotton produced by the very select weaving mill Alumo, which is one of the finest cottons in the world. The reputation of this isolated little town is not surprising since Switzerland has been famous since the 19th century for its fine batiste, voiles and poplins. In the Alumo design studios we will find out how the fabrics are produced.

The world of fashion lives and works according to its own unusual schedule. Collections are presented and sold in fairs and showrooms one whole year before they appear in stores. This is why designers have to start working on their creations in plenty of time, and why they travel twice a year to Paris for the Première Vision Fair, the most important fabric fair in the world. Weaving mills from all over the world gather here to present new trends and fashions in the world of fabrics, and designers draw inspiration from it for their new creations. Although the fair attracts all the major companies in the field of weaving, many fashion houses prefer a more individual service. Instead of going to Paris to see what everyone else can see as well, they commission the weaving mills to design fabrics especially for them. Such a service is provided by Raphael Sommer, the designer of Alumo Textil AG.

A fashion designer will not necessarily come to Appenzell with a specific design in mind, for instance a lime-green gingham design in Oxford fabric or a black-green-violet striped full-twill poplin. Most visitors are fairly vague about what they want, bringing with them more or less usable pattern designs, sketches, and clippings from magazines. Raphael Sommer is happy with this because his creativity does not need much prompting. If necessary he can always translate the client's vague descriptions into usable drawings from which the client then chooses, usually finding something to their satisfaction. Although Raphael Sommer enjoys this freedom, he also likes working with people who know precisely what they want, presenting him with accurate, detailed drawings of what they have in mind. The more the client knows about fabric, the more the expert will be stimulated.

How Raphael Sommer sets to work when creating a new design depends on the type of fabric. Raw or natural-colored fabrics are usually woven from light-colored yarns and then lightly dyed or bleached, but strongly colored fabrics are woven with colored yarns so that there is no need for subsequent dyeing. Sometimes both methods are used at the same time, with dyed and un-dyed yarns being woven together, then dyed or bleached later. Natural-colored fabrics are first test-dyed to determine the right shade, while colored fabric designs are assembled on a computer screen using different colored yarns, then printed out and finally test-woven. The first method is a procedure that requires great technical and chemical skill as well as an aesthetic sense that demands much experience and an instinctive feeling for colors and shades. Designing a colored pattern also requires creativity and artistic drive, but a thorough knowledge of the various weaving techniques is also essential, because otherwise the physical translation of the printed design onto the loom would be impossible. Raphael Sommer has a perfect command of all weaving techniques and knows exactly what is feasible on a loom and what is not. Sommer's clients benefit greatly from his expertise and he is responsible for many of the fabric designs used by the great international fashion houses.

Finest Swiss cotton refers to very high quality cotton, available in a wide range of colors, patterns and weaves.

Cotton classics

Batiste

Light, plain weave fabric made from very fine, high-quality yarn. The most popular fabric for shirts.

Cotton flannel

Soft, fluffy fabric in plain weave or twill, ideal for sports shirts, comfortable leisure shirts, and warm nightdresses.

Cotton twill

Thick fabric for sports shirts, for instance shirts with button-down collars, with the typical diagonal weave of a twill fabric. A twill shirt looks very good with canvas pants.

Cotton poplin

Plain fabric weave with considerably more warp threads than weft threads which, depending on the yarn used is called single-twill, half-twill or full-twill poplin. The traditional fabric for business shirts.

End-on-end

A type of fabric woven with two warp threads of different colors in order to achieve a characteristic multi-color effect (also called fil-à-fil).

Oxford

Soft, slightly grainy fabric woven with warp and weft yarns of different colors. The multi-colored shimmering effect of Oxford fabric is ideal for the traditional shirts with button-down collars.

Voile

Gossamer-thin, gauze-like and transparent, one of the finest fabrics for shirts and blouses. In spite of its fineness, good quality voile is quite hard-wearing and hardly creases.

The perfect combinations

Tops are the most important items in your everyday wardrobe. Let us assume that you have only two "bottoms" in your wardrobe, straight-cut pants in dark blue or charcoal gray and a classic straight cut knee-length skirt, also in a muted color. Boring? Not in the least, because with your various tops worn in different ways, you can create different "looks" by constantly varying the combinations of "top' and "bottom."

The most festive and formal option is a white shirt or blouse with stand-up collar or tie-collar in a beautiful, soft material such as satin silk. With a dark blue blazer or matching suit jacket you will be prepared for any official function. Somewhat less formal is a white cotton shirt with fabric-covered buttons, cut like a man's shirt with a turndown collar. If this is too plain it can be worn with a silk scarf to add a touch of color. Sometimes pure white looks too glaring or dazzling. A more subtle but equally effective look can be achieved with shades like cream, champagne, pale beige or ecru. If you combine white with white, for instance a white shirt with a white knitted jacket, be sure that the shades of whites are identical or it will not look right. This is also true of black—there are many different shades of black and white.

As with men's shirts, a good alternative to white is pale blue or pink. Patterned fabrics add a more sporty touch to the outfit. However, traditional stripes and gingham are also acceptable in business, but dots and exotic floral patterns

Right:
The combination of a dark top and a dark skirt creates a very reserved and serious look. The crazy tights add a lively touch to the outfit (Falke).

Far right:
This Belvest ensemble consists of a simple white blouse and pale, knee-length skirt. It is very casual and summery but elegant as well.

may look too romantic in a formal office. Normally, straight pants or skirts worn with a patterned top will be perfectly all right in most companies.

Choose colors with care, avoiding very trendy or fashionable colors because they immediately date a garment. The same is true of obvious fashion details such as garish decorative buttons, rivets, zippers, fringes, and logos.

As well as being worn with a blazer or suit jacket, shirts and blouses can be worn with cardigans and sweaters. Depending on the company's dress code, an elegant knit wool or cashmere jacket also looks very good in the office. On the other hand, a sweater casually thrown over the shoulders will look better on more relaxed occasions.

If you buy your shirts and blouses in a shirt shop that formerly specialized in men's shirts, you will probably find that ladies' shirts and blouses are available with button cuffs or with French cuffs.

Button cuffs are more versatile and are suitable for both informal and formal occasions. They also make it easier to roll up the sleeves in summer. French cuffs are more formal and require cufflinks. You can either borrow some from a male member of your family or you can buy more decorative ladies' cufflinks at a jeweler's or from a department store. Another good alternative are fabric knot cufflinks that are available in all colors and therefore can be matched with the shirt, jacket or accessories. These fabric knot cufflinks are unisex, so you have to be careful that they do not end up in your partner's drawer.

Some shirtmakers will also make shirts to measure using the pattern of your choice. You can choose the fabric, the shape of the collar, the type of cuff, and the buttons. The shirtmaker will take care of the cut and the quality of the finish. Even if you are tempted to order a shirt different from anyone else's, be careful to avoid making the mistake of combining details that do not go together, such as a sporty button-down collar with French cuffs, or a lumberjack check fabric with a flowing tie-collar.

Blouse or light jacket? The answer to the question may depend on the weather.

The blazer

The classic, traditional navy blue lady's blazer with no decorative frills and no acknowledgment of fashion trends is one of the most timeless items of clothing in any woman's wardrobe. Combined with a pastel-colored shirt and a dark knee-length skirt or charcoal gray, straight-cut pants, it makes a correct formal outfit. But when it is worn with a sports shirt or T-shirt and beige cord velvet pants, khaki chinos or even jeans, it also works as a chic casual outfit. But even in more informal combinations, a blazer will always add a touch of soberness and no-nonsense. Its versatility means that most women have an all-purpose blazer in their wardrobe, which always comes in very useful whenever the situation requires it. There is no easier way of changing from looking "casual" to "casual but formal" than by putting on a blazer.

Although the classic blazer is often worn for formal occasions and at the office, it was originally a sports jacket. Its ancestors include the caraco jacket, the redingote and the lounge jacket. The caraco was a jacket, short at the front and longer at the back, with narrow, three-quarter sleeves, that was worn by horsewomen at the beginning of the 18th century. The redingote (the word is a French corruption of the English "riding-coat") was also a riding-coat, and the hip-length lounge jacket or sack coat also developed from jackets or coats worn by the upper classes when riding or participating in open-air activities. Even then it was quite fashionable to select a few items usually worn for outdoor leisure activities and integrate them into one's everyday wear in town. Thus at the end of the 18th century women would sometimes wear the latest chic sporty outfits even when not riding or taking part in sports activities. In the 19th and 20th century, these jackets changed continuously. Sometimes they were hip-length, sometimes they were waist-length, and at other moments they were even bolero-style. The classic blazer as we know it today became established in the early 1960s, but the popularity of

The term blazer does not only describe the blue classic jacket—it also applies to jackets such as this one by Daks with a check pattern.

With a custom-made blazer such as this model by London Savile Row's tailor Tobias, the buttons on the cuffs can be undone.

this sober, sensible jacket only burgeoned in the 1970s.

The double-breasted navy blazer with brass buttons is a variation on the single-breasted blazer. According to legend it was created in 1837. Shortly before a naval parade in honor of the recently crowned Queen Victoria, one of the captains inspected the men on his ship and was horrified at the shocking, disparate clothes of his crew. In order to introduce a little military uniformity he dressed the sailors in identical short navy blue jackets. To do justice to the festive nature of the occasion, shiny brass buttons were sewn onto the jackets. Queen Victoria is said to have been so enthralled by the result that she immediately ordered the rest of the navy to wear similar jackets. Whether the story is true or not, it is certain that the navy blazer is still very popular with women today. Its shiny buttons give it a more festive air than its sibling with horn buttons, and it can therefore be worn with a light colored skirt and flat shoes to produce a sporty yet elegant, feminine look. Double-breasted jackets look more bulky because of the double front, and they should therefore only be worn by tall, slender women. Those who find navy blazers a little too sober and dark may prefer a blazer-style sporty-casual tweed jacket that still looks very "dressy." The mottled tweed composed of many different colors has the advantage that it will match almost anything in the wardrobe.

Many women who prefer the classic, sporty look envy men for some of the items in their wardrobe, such as their beautiful, indestructible shirts, their comfortable welted shoes (in which he can be comfortable all day while she longs for the moment when she can finally remove her pumps), and last but not least, the excellently-made sports jackets. The manufacturers of these wonderful jackets are well aware of this and have in recent years included ladies' versions of these and other basics. In particular the three cult Neapolitan manufacturers Kiton, Attolini and Isaia, the most famous tailors in southern Italy,

have acquired many satisfied female customers as result. Established at the foot of Mount Vesuvius, these traditional dressmaking workshops design and produce timeless clothes made from the finest fabrics with soft, natural shoulders and without thick shoulder pads. They are as supple and comfortable as knitted jackets and will last forever because they are made with the greatest care, to a great extent by hand. Instead of being bored when you accompany your beloved partner as he shops for clothes, ask the store if they have a ladies' department that stocks the women's collections of these wonderful Italian designers. The relatively high prices of their clothes is well justified.

The double-breasted navy blue blazer is a traditional garment for both men and women. But the original blazer has itself inspired numerus outfits. Flying to the U.S. in 1994, Princess Diana wore a dark blue suit with a double-breasted jacket whose naval touch was pointed up by a nautical striped T-shirt.

Salvatore Ferragamo's collection shows that the jacket of a pantsuit can be casually fastened with a belt instead of buttons.

The pantsuit

When the social-democrat politician Lenelotte von Bothmer appeared at a sitting of Parliament wearing a pantsuit, her outfit caused quite a scandal. How long ago was that? No, not in the early 20th century, but in 1971. It is written in the Bible that women must not wear men's clothes nor men women's. This pronouncement was accepted and applied well into the 19th century, and this was sometimes imposed by the police because in many countries it was a punishable offence for women to appear in the street or in public wearing non-women's clothes. Yet in spite of these sanctions the history of women's emancipation is closely linked to the conquest of the male wardrobe.

When women were fighting for their rights and the male privileges they were denied, they preferred to do so in men's clothes. During the French Revolution women protested against their social and political discrimination and, like the men, they wore long riding-coats and the so-called Phrygian hats, the symbol of freedom at the time. After these subversive, revolutionary years, things returned to how they had been and fashion became gender-specific again. But a few women continued unwaveringly to wear men's clothes, such as the novelist George Sand (1804–76), who with her suits and cigars challenged the double standards of her time, and the celebrated actress Sarah Bernhardt (1844–1923), who can be seen in a few sepia photographs wearing men's clothes.

However, men's suits for women only became really fashionable in the 1920s when the two-piece or sometimes three-piece suit, with matching vest, became the standard uniform of female artists and the emancipated garçonnes as they were known at the time. In the evenings, insecure men also had to come to terms with the sight of women in dinner jackets. But it would be another 50 years before the pantsuit was accepted as an alternative to the conventional suit with skirt and jacket.

Today the pantsuit is unlikely to be linked with women's emancipation. It is widely popular with both working and non-working women because it is so practical and easy to wear. A pantsuit is chic and it does not date, it looks elegant, and if well-cut it can even improve the figure. In business, the pantsuit is seen as the counterpart of the male two-piece or three-piece suit, expressing competence and objectivity. In private life, it is ideal for both official formal occasions and more relaxed gatherings because it can always be dressed "up" or "down" with the appropriate accessories.

The most important garment worn with a pantsuit is a plain shirt or blouse. Depending on the cut the collar is worn under or over the lapels of the jacket. Those who prefer can also wear a low-cut, tight bodysuit or T-shirt that will also look very businesslike. If you think your neck looks a little bare, wear a little silk scarf. On the other hand, if you are going to wear your pantsuit to go shopping, wear a thin sweater instead of a shirt or blouse.

For parties after work, you can turn your business suit into a glamorous evening outfit by wearing the jacket completely buttoned up but with nothing underneath or left casually open over a sequined camisole. Put on a beautiful necklace, clasp a glamorous clutch bag under your arm and slip on some high heels—you will then be ready for an evening out, the opera or a concert.

Pantsuits are made by many designers and are available under many labels, or of course they may be made to measure by a tailor. They come in a wide range of colors and cuts, from very feminine, soft and flowing to business-like and rather masculine. Which type you finally go for is merely a matter of taste, but you should be wary of exaggeratedly masculine, angular designs since these might make you look like a caricature of the fight between sexes. In the same way, a pantsuit should not be worn with a tie, even in a business environment, even though designers are always fond of ties on the catwalk and they can be a versatile part of many outfits.

The Italian manufacturer Belvest, based in Piazzola sul Brenta, is known for its summer pantsuits such as the one shown above in light colored, striped cotton.

Working

Often it is difficult to find the right kind of clothes for work, and it is much less fun to think about what to wear for work than deciding what to wear to go out. Nevertheless, an appropriate, correct appearance should not be dismissed as irrelevant or unimportant. Often one works with people who do not know one very well, who can therefore only go by appearances. Or they may not be broad-minded enough to ignore blunders in the choice of dress. What is overdressed, under-dressed, and just right varies according to the type of work, the company, its dress code, and what is generally expected from a newcomer. But there are a few basic rules for guidance.

It is easiest for women working in a profession or job where they are expected to wear some kind of uniform. For instance, doctors and nurses will wear the appropriate hospital clothes—only the doctor with her own practice might be able to introduce a little fashion into her outfit.

The daily question "What shall I wear today?" is easily answered in the case of women soldiers and those with civilian uniforms or other standard clothing dictated by the job. Women working in an artistic or creative environment, or in the media are at the opposite end of the spectrum. Here women will go to meetings dressed in the latest outdoor fashion, super-trendy designer clothes, or casual jeans and sweatshirts. But what should women wear who work in companies that are between these two extremes, such as in an insurance company, in a bank or in an antique shop? What should an interpreter, a teacher, an exhibition organizer or a zoo director wear?

The general consensus is as follows. The business outfit should reflect the wearer's status and position—the higher these are, the more elegant, serious and classic she should be in her dress. The wardrobe of a woman in a managerial position should include dark skirt and jacket suits or pantsuits, blazers in muted colors, and sober shirts, all of the best quality, worn with a small number of high quality accessories. But a sober, classic appearance will not hurt even in the lower and middle echelons. By dressing in this way a woman indicates to those around her that she takes her work seriously and that she is a force to be reckoned with who will not let anyone take advantage of her.

In the past, women working in typically female occupations could wear more feminine clothes, while those in jobs traditionally held by men would wear more masculine garments. Now personal assistants and multilingual secretaries adopt a classic office look without frills, in the same way that many teachers, judges and politicians wear appropriate, serious clothes without necessarily concealing their femininity behind an excessively masculine appearance. It is also important that they should observe the dress code within their team. If you work in the most casual department of an insurance company, there is no point in going to work wearing a sober business suit. But however relaxed the atmosphere, it is best to avoid excessively casual clothes such as jeans, sneakers, baggy T-shirts, and so on. Well-cut beige pants, a pair of elegant flat loafers, and a sporty cotton button-down shirt look casual yet well-groomed.

Three classic, elegant outfits featuring the white blouse, but certainly not conservative ones. These extravagant models are by Emanuel Berg.

A suitable shirt for the office: perfect under a jacket but also sufficiently formal without one. But the cut, fit and finish must be of the highest quality.

Dress codes vary from field to field. This outfit would be too casual for a bank but sportswear basics such as this T-shirt and denim jacket would suit the world of media.

Business tips

- Make sure that your clothes are always clean and neat. Exceptions: an old but elegant handbag or a valuable heirloom are all right.

- Make sure that you yourself are clean and well-groomed from head to toe. Exceptions: none.

- Avoid excessively short skirts, necklines that are too low and clothes that are too tight.

- Remain true to your serious, sober business style even if you are tempted by new fashion trends.

- Keep your make-up as light and natural as possible.

- Always wear pantyhose at work—bare legs are definitely reserved for home. The same is true of bare shoulders.

- Only wear your more bulky jewelry outside the office.

- Shoes should be cleaned and polished. The heels should not be worn.

- A good quality handbag that matches the rest of the outfit is an indispensable accessory.

- Jingling earrings and clattering ethnic bracelets may add an exotic touch to your outfit but may be irritating for your colleagues.

- If your job includes carrying documents and work material, avoid large, clumsy attaché cases and buy a ladies' briefcase instead.

- Keep your business wardrobe as simple as possible, making sure that all parts can be "mixed and matched" with each other.

- Pattern or plain? Plain is much better. It looks more serious and it is easier to find matching accessories.

- The type and weight of fabric should be appropriate to the season. A warm tweed jacket looks as out of place in summer as a light linen suit at a Christmas party.

Pleasure and pain of shopping

For a long time before ready-to-wear clothes existed, both men and women went to a tailor or dressmaker when they needed a new outfit. The making of the clothes and their sale took place under the same roof, namely the workshop. When the first ready-to-wear collections came on the market in the early 19th century, these two areas became separated because the factories did not sell to individuals. But now the questions were how, where, and through what kind of outlet should these factory-produced clothes be sold to the public? They would not be sold through tailors or dressmakers since they would not want these cheaper, industrially-produced clothes to compete with their own. Consequently new shop concepts were invented, giving rise to the birth of the clothing store and also to the idea of the shopping expedition. As long ago as the end of the 18th century it had been possible to buy ready-to-wear clothes by mail order, but in 1824 the businessman Pierre Parissot decided that the goods should be presented "live" in order to encourage the customers to buy. Accordingly he founded the first ready-to-wear store, named "La Belle Jardinière." Later, the large department stores such as the famous Harrods in London, founded in 1861, had ready-to-wear departments.

Today the department store is still a good place for a leisurely shopping expedition. Many women appreciate the great choice offered by this ancient temple of consumerism that houses every kind of garment under one roof. These department stores include famous names such as Galerie Lafayette and Au Printemps in Paris,

Liberty's in London is the quintessential English department store: old-established, conscious of tradition, very British and beautifully arranged.

Harvey Nichols and Selfridges in London, the Italian chain La Rinascente, and Bergdorf Goodman and Macy's in New York. As well as offering luxury labels and brands, many also sell reasonably-priced basics marketed under their own label. The advantages of a department store are that you can go from sweaters to evening clothes, from suitcases to lipsticks, without getting your feet wet, and the in-store restaurant can provide a welcome interlude for exhausted shoppers. The downside is that the choice is often overwhelming, the presentation of goods may be confusing, and the service is not always very helpful.

Women who prefer a little less choice, some pre-selection and more personal service will be happier shopping in a boutique. Every boutique has its own style and the buyer chooses items from the fashion collections that reflect the style of their boutique. If you like the style of the boutique you will almost always find something that pleases you, and over the years a personal relationship will often develop between the sales assistant or owner and the client. You can always expect helpful advice in a good boutique and you will of course be able to browse, choose and try on clothes in peace. You should also feel that the assistant is honest with you and will not persuade you to buy something that does not fit, does not suit you, or is just too expensive. In a good boutique the staff will know the meaning of the word service; the services provided range from alteration services to the recommendation of a trustworthy dry cleaner or a reliable shoe-repairer. Ideally, a special request should be met with an attempt to satisfy it, not immediately rejected as impossible.

There are boutiques that are entirely dedicated to one label such as those of Louis Vuitton, Hermès, Gucci, Chanel, and so on. These boutiques attract attention with the fame and prestige of their name and the considerable investment made by the company concerned. This financial backing is reflected in wonderfully attractive presentation and imposing premises in the most expensive streets in the world. But do not be put off by the exclusive atmosphere of these shops—they are definitely worth a visit. Who knows, perhaps this is where you will find your dream outfit, possibly even at a reduced price! As far as the quality of the

service is concerned, the same rules apply here as in your favorite independent boutique.

Besides these three classic types of stores, there is of course a whole range of alternative shopping outlets where you can save a lot of money. But obviously you should not expect much knowledgeable advice in discount outlets, and you may have to try on the bargains you have picked up behind a temporary partition. The clothes may be original designer labels, although they are unlikely to be from the latest collections. There are also luxury secondhand shops where you could be lucky enough to track down a Kelly bag or some other cult object. Another resourceful idea is to mix "very expensive" and "very cheap" items. Whether a white cotton T-shirt has a designer name or a Hennes & Mauritz label is quite immaterial and it is therefore not worth spending large sums of money on such items. A smart shopper will only spend money on items that matter, meaning garments that fit perfectly and will last a long time, such as suits and pantsuits.

Burberry's new flagship store was opened in London's Bond Street in September 2000.

In the Paris headquarters of Hermès you can have a saddle made to order, and if you wish its color will match your favorite silk scarf.

Label mania and the cult of the brand

The characteristic horse-shoe shaped "A" of Aigner stands for high class leather goods and very chic, wearable designer fashion.

Known world-wide, much sought after, and unfortunately copied much too often: the Lacoste crocodile is one of the most famous textile logos.

Designer labels? Fashion maker? Rising brands? A lady is not normally interested in these things. She is rather conservative in matters of taste—conservative in a positive sense because she swears by old-fashioned concepts of quality and perfect finish, first-class fabric and timeless design. A flimsy shirt that costs a fortune and has only a designer label to justify it should definitely be ignored. A wise woman will buy from a wide range of outlets, both expensive and less expensive. English women in particular are very good at seeking out the best buys: stylish, well-made underwear from the middle-class chain-store Marks & Spencer may be worn under elegant made-to-measure clothes. But elegant women also have their cult labels. Of course these cult labels vary according to individual preference but there are a few that are without doubt considered superior to all others. These magical guarantors of beauty and exclusivity include houses such as Chanel and Hermès.

But what gives a label a cult status? Usually several factors contribute to creating this image, such as the long, uninterrupted success story of a house, the fact that their customers include generations of the rich and elegant, a certain innovative spirit that is reflected in "innovations" typical of the label, and an unmistakable symbolic character that is kept alive for future clients by a skillful promotion of the brand image. Frequently these fashion houses have launched a garment or product that has somehow acquired cult status and thus endowed the rest of the collection with this particular aura. We recognize these items as authentic, trailblazing, and the original product in their category. Thus the flagship of all silk scarves is the Hermès scarf, the archetype of two-tone ladies' shoes are Chanel pumps, the quintessential eternity ring is the Cartier Trinity, the mother of all polo shirts is the Lacoste shirt, the archetype of the waxed jacket is the Barbour, the original jeans are Levi 501s—the list goes on.

It is interesting to note that a few of these cult accessories are somehow associated with the "core brand" or "core competence" of the house. The entire Lacoste label including its very wide range of products is based on that simple piqué cotton T-shirt with which tennis champion René Lacoste revolutionized the sportswear industry after he retired from active

sport life. In the case of the legendary jeweler Cartier, it is the timeless jewelry designs that have immortalized the name, rather than the sidelines such as scarves, notebooks, ball-point pens, and perfumes that were introduced later. Gucci, originally a well-established saddler and bag manufacturer, is still more famous for its leather goods, such as the unmistakable Gucci loafers with mini-snaffles, than for its watches and ready-to-wear clothes. Other much sought-after goods become famous on their own strength, having distanced themselves from the original brand and its image by changing completely. Prada, for instance, was originally a Milan-based manufacturer of luxury bags and so it remains, but it is also widely acknowledged to be the inventor of the black nylon rucksack. Another example is Coco Chanel who was not a perfumer to start with, but her Chanel No 5 is one of the best known fragrances in the world.

Sought-after brands are expensive, and expensive brands are sought-after. Luxury branded products have been copied and cheap imitations have been launched on the market for a long time. From the point of view of the companies, fakes are a two-edged sword. On the one hand, they are a recognition of the company's high prestige, its powerful influence on fashion and style, and the vast demand for their products. On the other hand, brand piracy inevitably results in financial loss as well as discrediting the brand image by the creation of inferior look-alikes. Coco Chanel knew that she was constantly copied but that did not bother her; on the contrary, she saw it as a proof of success. Louis Vuitton, on the other hand, could not bear his creations being copied and he was the first to add a distinctive logo to his products. Today the numerous unconvincing fakes that can be found everywhere show how difficult it is to reproduce the LV monogram successfully. Yet the sight of a bad fake may even enhance the pleasure and excitement derived from the real thing by the owner of the genuine article bought for a vast sum of money. Only the genuine article has the magical aura of the cult object. But whatever the cult brand, one woman will enjoy playing the game while another will see no pleasure or point in it. Both are right.

The phrase "cult label" immediately conjures up the name of Louis Vuitton. The famous LV monogram was introduced in 1896 to protect the goods fromimitators. Before this it was the checked damier canvas, designed in 1888, that had been the trademark of the house. It was redesigned in the 1980s for the company's 100th anniversary.

№ 4

Smart casual and sportswear

The invention of leisure time

A lady of leisure? In the 18th century it is unlikely that the term would have been used or understood because a lady did not work anyway, or at least not in a particular occupation with fixed office hours. Consequently, there was no specific time when work was over and a more relaxed, casual outfit was required. The clothing worn was always that stipulated by the particular occasion, so a lady's daily routine was one of repeatedly changing from one set of clothes to another, even without considering the complicated styling requirements of grand social events. Nevertheless, even then there were hours in a lady's daily life that did not have quite so official a character, so at those times something a little more comfortable was permitted.

One of the early forerunners of leisure wear was the house dress. This was usually made from a simple, hard-wearing material, and as the name suggests the well-off lady would wear it at home, when she was overseeing the servants or dealing with suppliers at the back door. Admittedly the house dress was not well-suited for physical activities, but since the staff did the exhausting jobs, it was fine for simple practical matters. There was one early form of sportswear that already existed 200 years ago, the garments worn by ladies who enjoyed horseback riding. But it was not a relaxed costume; riding side-saddle was obligatory for ladies, riding habits reached down to the ankles, and of course a corset had to be worn underneath it.

As the driving force of the industrial revolution brought about changes in the 19th century, some innovations also occurred in ladies' fashion. Sport was suddenly seen as a stylish activity, and with it the clothing that was worn for it. A corresponding outfit was needed for each of these modern activities, but this was no problem since people at that time had plenty of practice in changing their clothes. Fortunately for the elegant city dweller, the pastime of horseback riding (anyway a domain of the rural upper classes because of the space it required) was supplemented with sports that could be pursued in town as well. Cycling, rowing, croquet, tennis, badminton, fencing, and ice skating all developed into the fashionable sports of this period. The capitals of Europe vied with each other in laying out parks and sports pavilions, so that everywhere ladies could take exercise and become fit, albeit still formally clad in blouse, skirt, coat, and hat. It would be some time before dress conventions relaxed in this area. Even in the early years of the 20th century, the female urge to be on the move was hindered rather than promoted by the completely impractical sports fashions then current, and a person had to be very enthusiastic about leisure exercise in order to undertake more than a short walk at a snail's pace in these bulky outfits.

The picture changed fundamentally in the 1920s. At last, more practical garments became generally accepted. The sportswoman was now allowed to take part in the widely popular game of tennis wearing a knee-length pleated skirt, a blouse, and a scarf wrapped round the head instead of struggling with the long skirt, cardigan, and the obligatory cartwheel-sized hat. For golfers, the first suits with knickerbockers appeared in the fashion journals, and female skaters, skiers and anglers could at least wear knee breeches, albeit these were usually worn with a "traditional" short skirt over it.

The decade of the 1930s was one of contrasts. While the bulk of the population lived in extreme poverty, the rich indulged themselves in a chic lifestyle of sophisticated elegance. Anyone who could afford it would travel according to season, between one fashionable vacation resort and another, spending the days shopping and the evenings at cocktail parties and elegant dinners. Tennis and skiing became the most important fashionable society sports, for which appropriate outfits were designed, more colorful and essentially more stylish than they had been even in the 1920s. Women wore pants more and more frequently, no longer only when actually taking part in their favorite sport, but sometimes also as components of their smart-casual wardrobe.

In the 1940s, every detail of life was affected by the war. The strict rationing of food and goods that restricted everyday life throughout Europe also had an effect on fashion. Pants were recognized as practical garments giving welcome protection from the cold. They also hid the coarse woolen stockings that were then worn, since fine silk stockings were virtually unobtainable. However, the 1940s were also

notable for the start of a remarkable development. Until then sport and leisure fashion had been seen as a single entity, but now they began to go their separate ways. As a result of this, sports fashion came to attend more and more strongly to practical requirements, while recreational or leisure fashion developed its own esthetic independent of sport.

The casual look of the today's lady had its origins mainly in the 1950s. After the trauma of World War II, people seized the chance to live normal lives once more. In the vanguard of those grasping this opportunity was the new jet set of movie stars, musicians, industrialists, playboys, and artists. What the select few wore in Portofino, Nice and Palm Beach was loyally reported in the media and eagerly copied by designers and tailors everywhere. Newspapers, fashion magazines, and weekly newsreels depicted a timeless, current style that included Capri pants, jeans, tightly-cut short-sleeved blouses, polo shirts, penny loafers, ballerinas, flip-flops, and cashmere sweaters. These elements are still to be found in almost every wardrobe today.

Swimming costumes worn by Californian beauties on Venice Beach in Los Angeles. Daring at the time, today some ladies would not hesitate to put them on for a shopping expedition into town.

Classic pullover

Pull-over with a round neck
People who wear round neck sweaters often wonder whether the collar of the shirt should be worn inside or outside. Traditionalists say inside, while fashion says outside—for the moment at least.

Sweater with roll neck collar
The roll neck sweater is not to everyone's taste. Many find it too constricting or too warm around the neck. But ladies who find it comfortable consider it a perfect compromise between smart-casual and formal wear.

V-neck pullover
The V-neck pullover is usually worn over a blouse, shirt or polo shirt, although it also looks very elegant worn on its own. In general, pullovers made of very fine wool usually look best worn on their own.

Polo neck pullover
Depending on the thickness of the yarn, polo neck pullovers may be worn as a light substitute for a T-shirt or to provide a thicker warm layer over a blouse or shirt.

Slipover
This is making a comeback! After an absence of over 20 years, the slipover, which many remember from their school days, has reappeared on the fashion runway.

Troyer pullover
This pullover with its zipper neck became part of a woman's classic wardrobe in the 1990s after the revival of the 1970s made it popular with the younger set.

Charmingly beautiful: pullovers

The subject "knitwear for ladies" ranges from the comfortable cardigan, worn when cozily reading by the fire, through the Irish Aran sweater that is ideal for gardening, to the awesomely expensive thin length of cashmere that may be draped carelessly over the shoulders when shopping in the Via della Spiga in Milan. Anglo-Saxon tradition and Italian style—both are possible, and countless fashion leaders have proved it. For example Lady Diana Spencer, who became Princess Diana, often appeared in a sweater in the early years of her public life, before she found the minimalist style that turned her into a fashion icon in the 1990s. As an authentic member of the upper classes, she presented all varieties of the "Sloane Ranger" look during the late 1970s and early 1980s. When working as a kindergarten teacher she wore various hand-knitted sweaters with slim, ankle-length jeans, in the city she might wear a wine-red reindeer-patterned cardigan over a frilly white blouse and a knee-length pinstriped skirt, while at the edge of the polo field she sported the legendary red sweater with a single black sheep among many white ones.

The opposite picture to the playful country concept of the young Princess Diana is found in the sophisticated minimalist look of Miuccia Prada, with her stylishly simple cashmere sweaters that wind elegantly around the shoulders or hips. All in all, Italian ladies are masters of the art of wearing a sweater without actually pulling it over. Many ladies have admired and emulated this Italian stylishness, including, for example, Katharine Hepburn, who in the last few decades of her life was hardly ever seen without a cashmere sweater. Her preferred Italian luxury brand is said to have been Avon Celli of Longastrino near Ferrara, but any Italian sweater of the luxury class would have added a well-measured touch of European flair to her American leisure outfit of polo shirt, slacks, and sneakers.

The sweater as a topic for the gossip columns or even as a cult object—this would have been unimaginable in the 19th century. When its successful story began, the sweater was worn for athletic activities. The healthy value of sweating had just been recognized by science and the sweater was used in a health program, the name of the garment actually coming from the verb "to sweat." The theory of the benefits of sweating was first advanced by Dr. Gustav Jaeger, a German professor of zoology and physiology from Stuttgart, and his book Die Normalkleidung als Gesundheitsschutz ("Rational clothing as health protection") rapidly became the Bible of the advanced woolen knitwear enthusiast. The work even inspired the Englishman Lewis Tomalin 1884 to open the first London specialist store for "Dr. Jaeger's Sanitary Woolen System." From this store the Jaeger fashion house later emerged, making clothes for ladies and gentlemen. It is still a place favored by the conservative English lady when shopping for clothes.

Since knitwear had proved to be practical for golf, riding, bicycling, and tennis, it soon became part of the weekend wardrobe. As in men's fashion, two different style directions developed from it: on the one hand the original practical sweaters from Great Britain, Scandinavia, and the Alps, and on the other hand the elegant model designs in classic cuts. The robust originals were retained largely for outdoor use, but urban weekends called for lighter pullovers with round or V-necks. The heavy Guernsey fisherman's sweater was in any case much too warm for wearing indoors. While British knitwear still enjoys great prestige, Italian brands have firmly established themselves in the luxury area. With only slight adaptation of traditional forms, the work of these manufacturers is often essentially more modern than the classics from the United Kingdom. This is also because of the color palette used. As well as navy, bottle-green, black, beige, red, and sky-blue, the Italian labels always include garments in the colors of the current season.

Peter Scott started producing high quality knitwear in 1878. Based in Hawick in Scotland, the company is world-famous.

The twinset

The twin set? You mean this somewhat bourgeois combination of pullover and cardigan, worn with the inevitable string of pearls, the favorite outfit of a lady of the old school? This is indeed true. But as well as that, the twin set was also the uniform of the sex bombs of the 1940 and 1950s—what better outfit could there be to display and publicize the bust measurements of Lana Turner, Jayne Mansfield or Marilyn Monroe? Since then it has been promoted every few years to the position of darling of the designers. It was celebrated most recently as a cool revival by various fashion labels in the late 1990s.

The classic lady actually values the twin set very highly. First of all it is very practical in that it is two garments in one, that can be combined together or worn separately. The twin set is also extremely versatile, since it is at home in all environments, from business to smart casual. With a narrow skirt and high heels, it becomes an outfit for the office, while with flannel Bermudas and penny loafers it creates the athletic college look, and with jeans it instantly fulfils the function of a weekend outfit. In short, the twin set is an all-purpose garment for all situations, and experienced travelers therefore always reserve a place for it in the suitcase.

Bourgeois or dramatic—that depends on the nuances. If the color, cut and details are not correct, the twin set can turn quickly into an image-killer. This does not mean that you must replace your entire wardrobe each season. Simply keep an eye on what you buy. The keyword is timelessness. This does not necessarily mean "classic," because unfortunately this term is often a polite way of saying "bourgeois," "unimaginative," and "antiquated." Timelessness rather means utmost simplicity, not overtly in fashion, in colors that are never unfashionable, and made of high-quality material. Only when these three criteria are fulfilled can you really expect that you will still be able to wear your twin set in five years.

So where does one buy such a knitted twin set for the long-term? With a little luck one will be found from a favorite fashion label, as long as the brand stands for pure design. Otherwise, they always appear in the collections of typical knitwear suppliers, that often feature twin sets as a standard next to the reliable pullover designs. In both cases, as a rule, you will find simple garments with a modern aura, with color and cut that are not reminiscent of ten years ago. In boutiques that sell the traditional ladies' assortment of separate skirts, frilly blouses, and gold-buttoned blazers, you would hardly expect to find an up-to-date interpretation of the twin set. Unless the Queen of England is your ideal as a fashion model, you would do better to go shopping in less old-fashioned establishments.

A Laura Ashley twinset immediately conveys the mood of an English country weekend.

The first knitted twinset is said to have been created by the designer Otto Weisz for the knitwear manufacturer Pringle of Scotland.

Pure luxury: cashmere

The Italian weaving mill Loro Piana is the largest buyer of raw cashmere in the world. A large part of it is used for precious cashmere knitwear.

The word cashmere even has the sound of oriental luxury: Does it not immediately suggest luxury sweaters, feather-light scarves, flattering stoles, and the finest materials? It is hard to believe that the fiber comes from an extremely shaggy goat, but that is precisely what cashmere is—goat hair, before the various stages of processing have taken place. Strictly speaking it is the soft down under-coat that grows hidden beneath the coarse top hair. Like a built-in downy undershirt, it protects the cashmere goat from the cold of Inner Mongolia, the region in which the animals supply the best quality fibers. Today only a small part of this sought-after raw material comes from Kashmir, the region from which the names for the goat, its hair, and the luxurious knitwear are derived.

The history of cashmere is long and rather mysterious. It is impossible to establish when the first hair was spun into yarn for knitting or weaving into fabrics, but it has been proven that the Romans already valued cashmere and made their finest garments from it. Sadly the history books do not explain how the great demand for this stylish export was met at that time. But it is known when the production of the fabric experienced its first great heyday: in the 16th century, when Muhammad Sahir Ud Din Babur established the empire of the great Moguls in the north of India. He promoted the weaving of cashmere on such a scale that it sometimes occupied as many as 60,000 workers. It is worth noting that today only carpets and embroideries are produced in this crisis-shaken region that is now divided between three countries—Pakistan, China, and India.

With the decline of the Roman Empire, cashmere yarn and fabric fell into oblivion in Europe. The delicate luxury was only rediscovered in the mid-18th century. It was the Mogul Aurangzeb, India's ruler at that time, who was the cause of this. He licensed Europeans to set up trading posts in his country, and this was how a French doctor came to the court of the oriental ruler along with a number of other adventurers. The records that the doctor took back home with him also contained reports of the strange goats he had seen, the first mention of cashmere after Europe's long abstinence from it. It was however, another Frenchman who caused the first European boom in cashmere, the Emperor Napoleon. During the Egyptian campaign of 1798, his soldiers carried off valuable cashmere scarves from the opposing Turks and gave them to their wives who remained at home. Naturally, other ladies were envious of these exotic presents and in no time the scarves became the most sought-after fashionable accessory. The second big cashmere craze also involved a Napoleon, on this occasion Napoleon III. His wife, the Empress Eugénie, was one of the most imitated leaders of fashion in the second half of the 19th century, and accordingly her preference for cashmere created a huge trend throughout the rest of Europe as well as in France. Queen Victoria played a similar role with the British to that of her French colleague, and since she was not only Queen of Great Britain and Ireland but had also been proclaimed Empress of India in 1877, a constant supply of cashmere goods from the colony

was secured. Whoever took pride in being fashionable imitated the queen, and London quickly blossomed to become the world center of the trade with its elegant stoles and scarves.

Until the early years of the 20th century, cashmere was primarily synonymous with woven fabric, but this was about to change. In the 1920s, the demand for high quality knitwear suddenly increased rapidly, and the soft but warm yarn established itself as a fine, luxurious alternative to the lamb's wool pullover. The Scottish textile industry played the leading role in this because it had the best trade relations with the countries from which the expensive raw material came. Knitted cashmere made in Scotland therefore soon became the most sought-after export and the number one souvenir for visitors to London. Shops in Burlington Arcade were stocked with piles of sweaters, cardigans, and of course, twin sets. The 20th-century enthusiasm for cashmere became muted for a time with the outbreak of the Korean War in 1950 because Europe was almost completely cut off from deliveries. After the end of the conflict in 1953 economic relations were renewed and the spinners, weavers, and knitters started working again with the same success. However, a truly consistent range of good quality knitwear only existed until the mid-1970s, and at the same time prices were constantly climbing.

British domination in the area of luxury knitwear remained undisputed until the 1960s. Then in the 1970s and 1980s it was strongly challenged by the Italian knitwear industry, which secured itself an ever-larger share of the main markets such as the United States, Germany, and France. In the 1990s some luxury brands of knitwear such as Aida Barni, Avon Celli, and Fedeli finally caught up with the British in matters of styling, the area in which the they had long been supreme. Then, at the start of the 21st century, the Scottish manufacturers began a clever counteroffensive, playing a trump card with new, more fashionable designs. Suddenly the classic labels such as Pringle, Corgi, and Peter Scott began to appeal strongly to young people again. Some ladies who had sometimes reached for Italian goods, now started buying British products once more. Italian women on the other hand, had no need to be convinced by this rejuvenation of the quality of Scottish knitwear, since they had actually always remained loyal to the Scottish labels.

When buying cashmere knitwear it always worth paying more because high quality cashmere keeps its shape better and tends to pill less.

How a soft dream is born

Cashmere exists in three forms, as a sweater, as a material (for an outfit, a jacket or a dress), and as a scarf. The sweater is knitwear, while material and scarves are fabric. The difference is quite simple. Knitting consists of interlocking stitches, while a fabric is the result of interweaving longitudinal and cross threads, known as weft and woof. In both cases, the starting point is a yarn. This is produced by taking fibers, in this case cashmere fibers, and twisting them together until they form a thread. The process of spinning is the first step on the way to the finished garment. Beautiful long fibers are used for particularly high quality yarns, while shorter fibers are spun to make less expensive yarns.

A cashmere sweater of medium quality may be produced by using the yarn immediately after the spinning process is completed, but for the best quality, the yarn must first be twisted further. Two or more yarns are twisted together in the same way as before so that the fibers are combined together. When two threads are combined in a yarn, the result is called two-ply cashmere, while four threads produce four-ply cashmere, and so on. The advantages of a multiple yarn are that it is more stable and elastic than a single thread. These qualities are also enjoyed in the resulting knitwear. The sweater will not become baggy, and the tiresome formation of little balls, known as pilling, is reduced. Pilling is caused by shorter fibers coming away from the yarn and matting together. Since two-ply or four-ply cashmere is made from long, fine fibers, pilling does not occur so easily.

Next comes the knitting. Normally garments are no longer knitted by hand on knitting needles since knitting machines now take care of the work. The origin of these time-saving, cost-saving devices goes back to the imaginative English priest William Lee, who invented the sock-knitting machine in the year 1589. The appliance delivered flat knitted material that could be sewn together to make a stocking, for example. However, Queen Elizabeth I banned this innovation out of consideration for the countless hand-knitters in her kingdom, and William Lee therefore had his mechanical knitting machine built in France. In Britain, the machine was only permitted from the mid-17th century onward. It provided serious competition to hand-knitting and very quickly dominated the industry. In the course of the 18th century the technology was constantly improved, and from 1769 seamless stockings could be knitted on the circular sock-knitting machine.

Whether made from cashmere, wool or cotton yarn, all knitwear is divided between the categories of "fully fashioned" and that cut from knitted fabric. "Fully fashioned" means that the shape of the garment, for example a sweater, is actually created during the knitting process, so the garment fits better and the seams are flat and unnoticeable. The disadvantage is the relatively high price. Cut knitwear is less expensive because it is more economical to make. The yarn is knitted flat and the individual parts of the garment are cut out from a length of material and sewn together. It should be pointed out that the work of luxury suppliers is exclusively "fully fashioned." However, knitting technology is only one factor that influences the quality; the other is the finishing operation. This is a carefully controlled process of repeatedly washing, drying, and ironing the knitted cashmere that gives it the desired qualities of softness, optimal stretching capability, and maximum durability. This process demands that the temperature and moisture should be adjusted individually according to the color and fiber quality. One mistake, and the dream of soft cashmere is finished. On the other hand, when perfectly executed, the highly sought-after luxury material will become a wonderful sweater that its owner will not want to take off from the moment it is first worn.

[1] It is a long way from central Mongolia to Genoa and from there to Annapurna in Prato.

[2] An object of desire: the fine fuzzy hair under the shaggy guard hair of the cashmere goat. Yield: under 7 oz per animal per year.

[3] The cashmere fibers must be as long and as fine as possible because it is used to spin very high quality two-ply yarn.

[4] The yarn is dyed at Annapurna only after it has been spun because the undyed fibers can be spun thinner.

[5] The best cashmere pullovers are produced on knitting machines that produce "fully fashioned" knitwear.

[6] No item is allowed to leave the Annapurna factory before being carefully checked for any defect.

Scotland and fashion

Anglomania, the boundless worship of the English style, is above all a male phenomenon. But often the classic lady also has a certain tendency toward the British, whether in the sense of a mid-morning cup of fine Darjeeling tea from Fortnum & Mason, or in the sense of fashion. In any case, many of the garments in her wardrobe are likely to have "made in the United Kingdom" on the label, including blouses or summer clothes in Liberty fabric, quilted and waxed jackets, and miscellaneous knitwear. But the clearest sign that a lady's heart beats for Great Britain is most clearly demonstrated by the Scottish kilt, the scarf with a tartan design, and every other textile in the colors of the clans.

The combination of the twin set and kilt (the latter ideally fastened with a large safety pin) is for many young ladies the quintessence of the completely old fashioned lady's style. It may be that this look has become so over the years, but it can easily be updated. In the end, it boils down to the cut and the styling, whether the unsophisticated plaid skirt turns out to be elegant or currently fashionable. The stylish Italians know this best, because clothes, skirts, scarves, and capes in the tartans of the Black Watch, Gordon, Royal Stewart, and other clans are among the indisputable basics for autumn and winter. Italian ladies in Milan particularly like to stock up on tartans at Guenzati in the via Mercanti, the Scottish specialist store founded in 1700 that is believed to be the oldest business in the capital city of Lombardy. Connoisseurs of the tartan scene declare that this traditional house near the cathedral has the best range of tartan fabrics on the European mainland, in the form of bales or as ready-made garments.

The fashion for all things Scottish was a side effect of the enthusiasm for the Highlands that Queen Victoria, the British monarch developed in the mid-19th century. The trigger was the purchase of the Scottish estate of Balmoral by her husband Prince Albert, who in 1853 laid the foundation stone of Balmoral Castle, the royal vacation residence. In this consistently well-groomed Scottish ambience, the queen could enjoy the romantic enthusiasm for the Highlands that soon also infected the rest of high society. Not surprisingly, this trend was also reflected in fashion. People throughout the island kingdom became unrestrainedly intoxicated by tartan, as did the women of mainland Europe and the United States. At that time, what was fashionable in Britain was swiftly imitated by the rest of the world. The tartan boom even managed the leap into the 20th century. Eventually, tartan skirts and scarves, wooly Shetland pullovers, and perfect Argyll socks were adopted by the fashionable sport of golf, which originated in Scotland, and consequently in the casual wear that was inspired by it. Recently, Burberry has impressively turned a tartan pattern that once eked out a low-key existence as the lining of conservative raincoats into a fashionable design that is now used in numerous garments and accessories.

The Scottish tartan beret is part of the standard range offered at Lock's, the famous London hat makers.

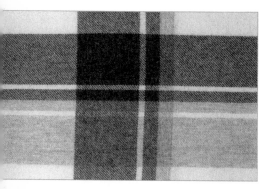

Tartan made in Bavaria: a classic plaid by the traditional German manufacturers Eagle Products.

Complete understatement: soft Italian cashmere socks with the traditional Argyll pattern.

This unassuming check pattern was originally used for the lining of trench coats. Today it is the world-famous trademark and key visual identity of Burberry's of London.

Chrysalis makes its field coats from brightly colored district checks derived from the tweeds, which were designed for the inhabitants and workers of Scottish landowners.

Traditional shoes for the Highlands. Tricker's of Northampton, supplier to the royal court, also makes ladies' versions of its sturdy highland brogues.

Scottish classics

Tartan kilt
For a long time the tartan kilt or skirt was the uniform of conventional anglophile women. But the transformation of the old-established, traditional house of Burberry into a hip fashion label has turned the kilt into a trendy garment for the young.

Tartan shawl
Whether made from lamb's wool or the finest cashmere, tartan shawls are unquestionably one of the indispensable classics of a woman's wardrobe. Very few women do not have at least one tartan scarf.

Argyll socks
Socks with the traditional Argyll design have been popular since the 1920s especially as sportswear. The geometric pattern is a traditional Scottish one that is also used for pullovers.

Ladies' brogues
Brogues are actually Scottish in origin and in the 19th century they were much appreciated by ladies as well as men. At first ladies' brogues were only made from fabric, but in the 1920s welted leather ladies' brogues made their first appearance, and they are still available today.

Scottish beret
The Scottish cap, also known as the Tam-o'-shanter, was once an important part of the Scottish highland dress. In the 19th century it became an everyday item that was especially popular as sportswear.

Shetland pullover
In Scotland, fabrics and knitwear are made from native fibers as well as from wool and cashmere imported from Australia, New Zealand and China. The sheep bred on the Shetland Islands produce a particular strong quality of wool.

Women going shooting

Unlike their male counterparts, who go hunting for pleasure and because it is a traditional sport, women are hardly ever seriously interested in hunting activities. Women shooters are still quite rare and the skillful handling of rifles and shotguns is still not considered a particular feminine quality. But those who enjoy lying in wait and being on the look-out will enjoy this activity. Are the pros and cons of hunting perhaps linked to fashion? Possibly—the question "What am I going to wear?" has probably deterred many a woman who might have been interested in hunting because she did not see herself wearing a Barbour or a tweed jacket, a Tyrolean jacket or a loden coat. Traditionally these are indeed the type of clothes that are worn when hunting, so women who usually wear Gucci, Jil Sander or Prada will hardly be fascinated by traditional hunting outfits. But a woman's preference for modern, fashionable clothes should not automatically make her reject hunting as a hobby, because there are other clothes she could wear.

When a European or American woman is invited to a British shooting party, she has two options. First: she can dress as she would at home. Second: she can follow the local custom—but this also means that she runs the risk of looking like a foreigner disguised as an Englishwoman. This can be avoided by looking through the gossip columns of English magazines. In them there are plenty of photographs that will prove a useful source of information about "shooting parties." The outfits worn by the female members of the parties can be used as a source of inspiration and guide for the visiting lady. The members of the British upper classes wear very varied kinds of outfits but nevertheless the photographs will give a good general idea of what to wear. Essential are a warm hat, anything from a knitted hat in the shape of a tea cozy to a picturesque slouch hat, fur hat or scarf, and a warm weatherproof jacket for protection from the rain, wind, and cold. The Barbour is still a very popular choice, the older and more battered the better; it is usually worn over a quilted jacket or vest. Others prefer a field coat, which is a short coat with a thick lining whose tweed fabric is made water-resistant by a waterproof membrane. Most women wear pants that, depending on the wearer's age, may be moleskin, cord or denim, and only very rarely tweed skirts. As far as footwear is concerned, green rubber boots are the most popular, either the basic model by Hunter or the classier winter version with leather lining and welted treaded sole.

The elegant yet vaguely absurd English shooting outfit expresses one thing above all: understatement. The fact that the clothes were once expensive is no longer obvious because of their age and the wear and tear that they have undergone. Naturally there are handmade tweed suits to be seen but these will not always have been made for the people now wearing them. Often they are heirlooms that are worn by the daughter or even granddaughter of the original owner. This respect for tradition is also found among the continental aristocracy. The middle classes, on the other hand, do not tend to recycle clothes in this way, and those who have made money with their own hands tend to buy their own hunting outfits. In mainland Europe, there are three stylistic factions: the anglophiles who have completely adopted the English style, the fans of the Bavarian-Austrian loden and folk costume look, and the young, unconventional women who combine American outdoor gear with elements of street and sportswear. Groups one and two buy their clothes from authentic hunting outfitters, while group three combines weather-resistant leisure wear or après-ski clothes with footwear suitable for hunting, including just one or two specifically hunting touches such as an "interesting" loden coat or tweed garment.

Snug, warm field coats by Chrysalis (here seen with matching hat and pants) protect the wearer from cold, wind, and rain.

The apparently striking multi-colored tweeds of traditional British shooting clothes come in a wide range of autumn colors providing perfect camouflage.

Casual pants

At first women wore shorts only for sports activities, but today they are entirely acceptable as leisurewear, provided the legs are elegant.

Capri pants are not worn only in Capri. These ones by the sportswear label McGregor are here seen on the Atlantic shore.

Pants were taboo for women until World War I, although earlier precursors of pants had existed in ancient times. Women in ancient Greece used to gather their clothes at knee-height with a ribbon, the so-called periskelis, while women in ancient Rome "controlled" their tunics with leg rings when they needed more freedom of movement. The Turkish pants that were introduced into Europe by Moorish women in the 14th century were very similar in concept. Because it was impossible to jump easily in floor-length garments, pilgrims often wore pants under their skirts in the 16th century. In the 18th century, women were allowed to wear wide knee-breeches for working. For everyday wear, pants were usually part of a woman's underwear. In the 19th century, they became known as pantaloons and were worn under calf-length shirt-dresses.

It was only in the 19th century that fashion began to make tentative moves toward pants as they are known today. The trigger for this was the awareness of the concept of fitness, because knee-length harem-pants were much more practical for horseback riding and cycling than a fluttering skirt. It followed that what was allowed in sport could not be completely wrong for everyday wear, an argument put forward by the American feminist Amelia Jenks Bloomer who propagated the idea of pants as a standard item of clothing for women. It is true that in saying this she was referring not to long men's pants but to voluminous Turkish pants, and the revolutionary concept of pants for women was toned down by the knee-length dress that was worn over the pants. Even so, this new look did not really catch on since the time was not yet ripe for women to wear pants. Bloomers survived, but in the form of specialized garments that were used by cyclists, and in children's clothing.

In the 1920s people's resistance to pants crumbled away. This was partly due to the current sports fashions, which were inspired by men's clothes, and World War I had also contributed to the relaxation of conventions. The traditional allocation of roles was severely shaken up between 1914 and 1918 when women suddenly, out of necessity, began to take an active part in public and professional life. When peace returned women were not prepared to give up their new-found freedom, and that also involved fashion. Clothes designers noticed that women wearing pants did not turn into men. The new fashion was here to stay. There were hardly any protests when more audacious women followed men in wearing Oxford bags, which were very wide, pleated-front pants in gray or white flannel.

Pants became really fashionable again in the 1950s, especially as casual and casual-smart wear. Among the best examples are Capri pants. These are said to have been invented by Emilio Pucci, the aristocratic fashion designer from Florence. According to the story, he began his career in 1947 by coincidence. When on a skiing holiday in Zermatt he helped out one of his acquaintances who had torn her clothes in a fall by giving her a sweater and ski pants that he had designed himself as an amateur. A correspondent of the fashion magazine *Harper's Bazaar* photographed Pucci's companion in her improvised outfit and the picture was published the United States in December 1948. The unusual skiing outfit from Europe greatly impressed the American public. As a result, Pucci's

outfit was copied by a department store and sold very successfully. Encouraged by this unexpected success, the Marchese opened his first shop in Capri, where his knee-length pants—which became known as Capri pants—launched his very successful career as a designer. The southern Italian island was an excellent choice because American high society had just begun to discover the delights of Italy. Pucci's Capri pants came in Capri blue, Emilio pink, Taormina yellow, and Agrigento green.

In the early 1960s, the waistband of Capri pants descended from the waist to the hips but the legs remained narrow. Because of the popularity of the French Riviera, this variation on Capri pants became known as St. Tropez pants. When skirt hems slowly moved upward on their way to becoming miniskirts, the popularity of the pant suit increased. It became a new "combination outfit" because the top could be worn without the pants as a short dress. The leg part was becoming increasingly flared from the knee down until reaching the legendary proportions of the 1970s. The illustrated magazines of the time clearly show how different pants had become from what they had been in the past. While flared pants were extremely popular with young women, the older generation appeared more reticent. Nevertheless, even elegant women began to wear a slightly toned-down version. In the late 1970s and early 1980s, new styles of casual pants were developed such as the carrot shaped pants, culottes or divided skirts, and Bermudas. Elegant women soon adopted these new styles but they rejected hot pants. In the mid 1980s, skinny-legged pants became the most popular casual wear. Available in various lengths and materials, especially in pale colors such as beige, off-white or white, they soon became the classic leisure wear of the 1990s.

The secret of a successful smart-casual look consists in looking relaxed, but not untidy. These chic three-quarter-length pants are the perfect solution.

Jeans

The attitude to jeans is mainly a reflection of age. Those born in the 1920s and 1930s will usually regard them with skepticism and see them at best as practical leisure wear. For the post-war generation jeans were the outfit of their youth in the wild 1960s, a symbol of rebellion and protest. Consequently women who wore jeans in those days find it difficult to see these indestructible pants as designer clothes, so they do not think it is worth paying a lot of money for them. It is those born in the 1960s who really experienced the transition of jeans from "scruffy" pants to elegant designer wear because they were able to follow these fundamental changes in their own changing perception of fashion. The protest pants of their childhood slowly developed into a prestige garment during their formative years in the 1980s. Women born in the 1970s and later only see jeans as a designer garment. But young people today no longer have to defend the jeans against disapproving parents and teachers, since they too have been wearing jeans since they were young.

Besides the subjective aspects, there are also the more objective reasons affecting the suitability of jeans. In this respect very little has changed since the 1950s since there are still many areas of life in which jeans are forbidden, even and especially in their country of origin. In the United States jeans are a very popular item of clothing partly because they are so inexpensive, but no successful woman would be seen dead wearing jeans in the office. In the U.S., leisure and casual wear are part of two

The German jeans label Mustang launched the first ladies' jeans in Europe in 1953. In 1955 its designers created cord jeans and in 1961 they developed stretch jeans.

completely different worlds that never mix. This has always been apparent in Hollywood movies of the 1950s an 1960s. In them we see Doris Day for instance in rolled-up jeans fishing for lobsters and shortly afterward as a smart, stylish lady in a suit, hat, and gloves. This irreconcilable contrast between the informality of jeans and sneakers on the one hand and the formality of the correct business suit on the other is present in American movies today. In Europe the boundary between what is worn on the weekend and at the office is much more blurred, but it still exists. No woman would wear jeans for an interview or for a presentation to colleagues or clients. Even in private life there are many occasions such as weddings, funerals or a formal evening occasion when even the most modern, fashionable woman would find jeans unacceptable.

The reason for this dichotomy can be traced back to the history of the garment. Jeans were originally work clothes, just as the coveralls still are today. A period of 50 years is not long enough to erase this fact from the collective memory. Nevertheless, there is no doubt that at some time in the future denim as a fabric will rise above its original station. In fact, before jeans there have been other clothes that have succeeded in rising from modest origins to the most select circles. The pullover is a perfect example: it used to belong to the working clothes of fishermen, farmers, and sailors until it was discovered as a sports outfit in the 19th century. Gradually, it developed from the rather inelegant garment of the Victorian era to the chic golfing outfit of the 1920s, finally ending up as a luxury garment produced in precious cashmere. The same could happen to jeans. You probably think this is impossible! Just have a look in your partner's wardrobe. The elegant corduroy pants hanging among the tweed jackets and suits were developed from the typical pants worn by laborers and artisans not long ago. What happened to corduroy could also happen to denim.

Jeans started life as cheap work pants. These humble origins long forgotten, jeans are now indispensable part of the leisure wardrobe.

Designer jeans by European labels such as Mustang, Joop or Bogner are often superior in cut and fit to the original jeans brands.

What kind of jeans suit a lady?

Women have three alternatives as far as jeans are concerned. First, there is the genuine classic by one of the original brands such as Levi's, Wrangler or Lee. Second, there are the designer jeans by Armani and other similar designers. Finally, there are European jeans labels such as Replay, Mustang, and Pepe. Traditionalists swear by U.S. jeans because they are the original article, based on the idea that "if jeans, then let them be the right ones." Especially as the manufacturers of these jeans will make sure that these classic models will always be available. Levi's will always make 501s.

Designer jeans are said to have the advantage of being better cut, and many women may therefore have a preference for one label or another. But if the jeans of a particular designer fit better than those by a woman's favorite designer, she will compromise. So a woman's wardrobe may contain jeans designed by Joop, Versace or Armani although she has never bought anything else by that designer. Indeed, it may be more stylish to combine a single item by a particular designer with a classic outfit than to be dressed from head to toe in that designer's clothes. Of course, designer jeans do not have the authenticity of the long-established brands, which is why jeans should be chosen with the greatest care to fit into a classic wardrobe.

The jeans produced by European manufacturers are something between the American originals and designer labels. Brands such as Replay, Mustang or Pepe do not aim to compete with prestige designer labels but rather with the old-established U.S. brands as far as quality and style is concerned. In fact, some European brands have already moved close to becoming classics such as the German Mustang jeans which have been around since 1948. European jeans usually aim to achieve a perfect fit and a more daring style. This may alarm some women, but many of the fashion-conscious appreciate the trendier style, and Italian manufacturers benefit greatly from women's preference for Italian designers and labels.

Pregnant and elegant

The fashion problems that accompany pregnancy are almost unavoidable, but they are successfully negotiated by most women. In the early stages, the little bulge is generally ignored and normal clothes continue to be worn. When this is no longer possible, they will wear slightly looser clothes that will accommodate their increasing girth. But eventually the time comes when their tummy becomes impossible to ignore or conceal. Even this will not drive a lady to put her entire wardrobe into mothballs for the next few months. It is more a question of combining maternity clothes as much as possible with everyday clothes to accommodate changing proportions.

This is very easy to achieve with leisure wear. For instance, you can wear special maternity pants with one of your partner's shirts and turn this into quite a nice outfit. Overalls are also very popular, while in summer loose dresses may be bought a couple of sizes larger or borrowed from a slightly larger friend. The problem of the business look is rather more difficult to solve. The jackets of pant suits and skirt-and-jacket combinations can be worn open for quite a while. But pants and skirts will have to be replaced much earlier in the pregnancy by equivalent maternity garments.

Many ladies put off buying maternity clothes for as long as possible. No doubt this is because of their proverbial sense of thrift— it appears to be a terrible waste of money to buy a whole wardrobe for only a few months since it will become entirely redundant at the end of the pregnancy, and in any case, maternity clothes are not particularly attractive. Also, many women refuse to turn pregnancy into something out of the ordinary by buying special maternity clothes. Expecting a child is a normal and very beautiful event, but it is not the only purpose in a woman's life, so motherhood is treated as much as possible as "business as usual." Women often display amazing inventiveness and imagination when dealing with the problem of what to wear during pregnancy. They borrow their partner's jeans, pants, sweaters, and sweatshirts, they even borrow their grandfather's coats and cardigans, and they dig out cashmere scarves, stoles, and pashminas they had completely forgotten about, using them to wrap around their belly to conceal its size.

Going through pregnancy in style is hard enough, but the months following the birth of the baby will also be quite difficult from a fashion point of view. Obviously a woman who can afford a nanny will find returning to a certain normality, including dress, much easier after the baby's birth. But most women will be caring for the baby on their own and they will have very little opportunity in the first few weeks or even months to find a few minutes to take care of themselves. This is largely because of the round-the-clock care needed by the baby, but it is also the result of a lack of motivation. The baby is often so much the center of everyone's interest that the young mother neglects herself and feels unnoticed, and wonders why she should bother with hair and clothes when family and friends are only interested in the new arrival. But even without a nanny, and regardless of how adorable the little one is, there should always be a certain fashion standard maintained. This is certainly something of which the elegant woman is well aware.

Because she hates to let herself go at any time, there is no danger she will go wrong on the fashion front. Instead of a T-shirt and leggings, she will wear leisurewear classics such as polo shirts, button-down shirts, men's shirts and the obligatory pullover. She will combine these with jeans, chinos, Capri pants or Bermudas, depending on the season, and on her feet she will wear sneakers, loafers, espadrilles or flip-flops. These are all things she would normally wear at the beach on the weekend or on an informal Sunday afternoon in winter. For going out for walks or shopping, the elegant mother prefers the smart casual look, and for her this is "business as usual." So taking care of how you look is not too much of a problem. You will have time for the equally important question: what should your baby wear?

Cate Blanchett, 8 months pregnant, wearing a gold-colored outfit and boots at the London Film Festival. The elegant collar and furry boa seem to reduce her belly.

With her husband, top model Cindy Crawford in a light, low-cut summer dress with a transparent effect on the arms and along the hem when seven months pregnant.

Erja Häkkinen watching a Formula 1 practice session when seven months pregnant. The bright, cheerful green dress and coat contrasts beautifully with her dark hair.

Heavily pregnant Yvonne Keating (with husband Ronan) wearing a red shirt with overlong sleeves, denim jacket, and feather necklace at the MTV Music Awards.

Queen Rania of Jordan a few weeks before giving birth. The matching orange earrings, "body," and buttonholes of her trendy denim coat add a perfect touch.

On an official engagement: the Infanta Cristina of Spain, six months pregnant, in an elegant dress with matching coat. The turned-up sleeves give it a more casual look.

Suzanne Lenglen was both a sporting and a model legend because her outfits—here seen at Wimbledon in 1921—were considered very audacious.

All in white?
Tennis fashion past and present

When the winner of the Ladies' Singles at Wimbledon accepts the cup from the Duchess of Kent, it is a meeting of classic English style and modern tennis fashion. The contrast between the Duchess's summer dress and the tennis player's skirt could hardly be more striking. Today it is hard to imagine that a 100 years ago a tennis player wearing a summer dress like the one worn by the Duchess could have taken part in the competition. A calf-length skirt and long sleeves were still the compulsory tennis outfit for women in 1905. But only a few decades earlier it was even worse, because women had to wear a floor-length, high-necked dress and also a corset. If a tennis player had worn a mini-skirt in 1877 she would have been arrested long before she ever made it to the court.

When tennis became the favorite upper-class sport, special sports fashions did not exist, so men and women would play in their normal everyday clothes. Although these clothes were completely unsuitable for tennis or any other sport, the development of appropriate clothes only occurred very slowly, and as usual, women's sportswear lagged far behind that designed for men. Was this a coincidence or was it intentional? There is no doubt that women were clearly at a greater disadvantage with their long skirts and large hats. It became easier to serve and return the ball in the calf-length skirt mentioned above, which was launched in 1905. Women had to wait until the 1920s for tennis fashion to make further progress. Then developments in tennis fashion were brought about by the female tennis stars of the day who were appearing in increasingly progressive outfits. A notable example was the eight-time Wimbledon winner Suzanne Lenglen who appeared in a pleated skirt that she boldly wore without a slip, with white knee-length socks and a headband that soon became her trademark. The most popular fabrics were knitwear and jersey, while toward the end of the decade other practical alternatives such as washable silk and light crêpe de Chine came into use.

At the beginning of the 1930s, skirt hems rose above the knee and the first divided skirts appeared on the tennis courts. Even more shocking than these innovations was the appearance of Mrs. Fearnley-Whittingstall without stockings at Wimbledon in 1931 while two years later Alice Marble played wearing short pants. This outfit caused less of a stir in America where women tennis players had already been wearing the practical combination of blouse and short pants for some time. As well as showing more leg, a greater area of bare flesh as a whole was exposed, and it had to be as tanned as possible. A pale complexion was completely unfashionable in the 1930s and anyone who wanted to look fit and athletic would spend many hours sunbathing. In the 1940s and 1950s a short-sleeved shirt and short pants became the generally accepted outfit for tennis players. Tennis outfits were now characterized by a certain uniformity, but women were able to add a touch of individuality by changing a few details. For instance, a player could replace the short pants by a short skirt with a pair of lacy panties that showed when she moved. First introduced at Wimbledon by Gussi Moran in 1949, this new look was designed by the Englishman Teddy Tinling who continued to develop interesting, innovative tennis outfits well into the 1970s. In the 1950s, short pants became increasingly short and mini-dresses became a fashionable alternative. When the mini-skirt made its appearance in the 1960s these tennis minidresses were hardly different from mainstream fashion.

Much has changed on the international tennis fashion scene, but what does the classically elegant woman wear today? In the 1960s, she had the choice between the practical dress from a traditional sports shop such as Lilywhite's in London, Abercrombie & Fitch in New York or Brigatti in Milan, and the expensive designer models by Patou, Chanel or Dior. Her decision depended on the state of her bank balance and her seriousness as a tennis player. The 1970s saw the launch of smart sport labels such as Lacoste, Fred Perry and Fila that are still popular today. Many women still swear by these brands and their reliable products. However, for style the fabric need not be the latest high-tech innovation and the shoes may well be from the season before last. White remains the favorite color in spite of attempts to introduce other colors. But although the elegant lady respects tradition, she is not ruled by it. If all her white polo shirts are in the wash, she will be quite happy to wear green, red, or blue or whatever she has in her closet.

The shirt with the alligator

By the 1990s, the boundaries between sportswear and casual wear were becoming more blurred than ever. Wearing sneakers and a cricket sweater to go to a museum or for a walk around town? No problem. But what is considered completely acceptable today would have been unthinkable in the first half of the 20th century when sportswear and everyday clothes were completely separate. One of the first items to cross this boundary was the Lacoste shirt. Since the 1950s, it has been worn not only on the tennis court but also as casual leisure wear.

René Lacoste was a French tennis legend in the 1920s and in this capacity he knew everything there was to know about the needs of tennis players. He developed this popular classic in 1927 as an alternative to the long-sleeved shirt. He had not originally thought of it as a commercial venture but simply as a beautiful, functional tennis shirt for himself. But there was such a demand for it that he began to produce the shirts commercially in 1933, at first selling them only in France but after the war exporting also to Italy, the U.S.A., and ultimately all over the world. The shirt with the crocodile became so successful that the company also developed a whole collection of basic garments. Lacoste chose the crocodile as a logo because the American press nicknamed him "Aligator" after he had won the Davis Cup.

During the 1970s the Lacoste shirt became synonymous with continental European casual chic, unaffected by current fashion and trends. In the 1980s it lost some of its prestige to Polo Ralph Lauren, but the spirited alligator was not going to be defeated that easily. In the 1990s, it acquired cult status among the trendy young who gave France's most famous sports label an unexpected boost in its old age, a success that still continues today.

The subject of the first advertisement for "véritables chemises Lacoste," ("genuine Lacoste shirts") is indeed a tennis player. but the text already hints at other areas where this practical shirt was worn: on the golf course and the beach.

The irrepressible Lacoste alligator is a democratic classic. The taxi driver may wear it as well as the lady sitting in the back on her way to Cartier. Regardless of how much it costs, it cannot be improved upon.

Tennis star René Lacoste (seen here wearing a sports jacket with a maximum version of the alligator) had originally created the piqué shirt in 1927 just for himself. Today, the little green reptile has friends all over the world.

Stylish beachwear

Stylish ladies by the sea—this immediately conjures up pictures of a nice afternoon somewhere at the shores of the Mediterranean. Think of a small group of friends strolling along the beach, one of them wearing a striped T-shirt, white shorts, and espadrilles, her sunglasses on top of her head; another in a black swimsuit, her hair covered with a bright head scarf, light canvas espadrilles on her feet; and the third one wearing a straw hat and a white man's shirt over her bikini, pale blue flip-flops in one hand, and a raffia beach-bag containing a bath towel, bottle of water, cigarettes, and newspaper in the other. Such a scene is typical of the French Riviera in the 1950s, St. Tropez in the 1960s, the Costa Smeralda in the 1970s, and Majorca at the beginning of the 21st century.

The classic beach look seems to be timeless although its roots can be traced back to the 1930s. It was further refined and internationalized in the Fifties. But beach fashion already existed in the mid-19th century when women ventured into the water in ankle-length or calf-length swimming costumes, not only out of modesty and misplaced prudery, but also because they wanted to protect their bodies from an unwanted tan. It was only in the 1920s that that the bronzed look became fashionable and was considered very modern. As result, bathing suits (still one-piece) began to show more flesh on the back and under the arms. The two-piece bathing suit, very similar to those still worn by women today, made its first appearance in the 1930s. It is true that it still did not allow an all-over tan, but it did expose considerably more skin to the sun. In 1946 the Frenchman Louis Réard reduced the two-piece bathing suit to its essentials, creating the swimsuit that we now know as the bikini. At first the one-piece bathing

Strappy tops are ideal for holidays because they can easily be combined with pants, skirts, sweaters, and jackets to create a wide range of looks.

Escada presents this luxury variation on the bikini—the perfect outfit for a private beach on the exclusive Costa Smeralda.

Walking on the promenade by the sea, women can wear less formal clothes than in town, for instance a strappy top and very short shorts.

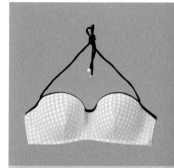

Topless or not?

The amount of skin exposed or covered by a woman depends on many factors. One of these is the location of the beach resort. Nudity is obviously taboo in very religious countries, and even in the United States "going topless" is not approved of, but on the beaches of the Riviera it is generally accepted. Even in southern Europe, sophisticated women should only remove their top (if at all) while sunbathing. When walking along the beach or having a drink at the bar, women should put their tops back on. Most women have a clear idea of what to wear when and where. What is acceptable on a private yacht and among close friends would be completely out of place on the Promenade des Anglais in Nice on the French Riviera.

suit was considered more ladylike and remained the favorite, but in the 1960s bikinis became more widely accepted. The first monokinis were launched in the 1970s, then being worn by only a few brave women. Since then almost everything is possible on many beaches.

Besides bathing suits and bikinis, beachwear also includes the clothes worn to go to the beach or pool and on short excursions inland. It is fashion tradition to be inspired by the clothes worn by the local population. This makes sense, since they know what is best for their climate. It is also a way for tourists to show their respect for regional customs, even when they are staying in a luxury hotel. Because the French Riviera was one of most the popular seaside vacation spots for sun-worshippers in the 1920s, these visitors found their inspiration in the clothes worn by the local fishermen and port workers. This made them feel part of the local scene, and it explains how millionaires and duchesses came to be dressed in striped T-shirts, berets, and canvas shoes, almost passing for natives as they drank pastis and smoked Gitanes cigarettes in the local cafés. In the 1940s and 1950s the Mediterranean

look acquired a few American style details, such as the simple seersucker dress from New Hampshire and the Hawaiian shirt from Honolulu.

Classic swimwear and beachwear would not be complete without summer shoes and accessories. These will probably include inexpensive items bought near the harbor and elegant articles from luxury boutiques on the promenade, as well other things already owned by the visitor. For instance, she may be wearing cheap espadrilles bought from a street-vendor, an expensive cotton sweater from the luxury shop in the hotel, and sunglasses she happened to find in the car because she had to rush to get to the airport on time. Expensive or not, simple or exotic, practical or luxurious—these contrasts give her outfit a particular charm. The style icons of the 20th century have always dressed in this way: Princess Caroline of Monaco would wear a simple sarong on the Côte d'Azur, Princess Diana was seen in shorts and Tod's with a Louis Vuitton bag in a marina on the Costa Smeralda, and Jacqueline Kennedy wore a sweater, white jeans, and light canvas shoes in Martha's Vineyard.

The lady on horseback

Women fall into two groups: those who are passionate about horses and those who are not interested at all. There is nothing in between. Indeed, passive interest in horseback riding is extremely rare because those who like horses usually like riding as well. It is true that in horseback-riding circles today, fun, performance, and the love of horses are paramount because the accomplished handling of horses is no longer the key qualification for entry into society. Even so, the upper classes still admire accomplished horsewomen. This is no coincidence because for a long time horseback riding was linked to the ownership of land and was therefore the prerogative of the landed gentry. In spite of the elitist nature of riding, the clothes worn by these blue-blooded amazons have influenced fashion at every social level. But first a specific riding outfit had to develop.

As late as the 17th century, women of high standing would only attend official events, such as processions, on horseback. On such an occasion a woman would of course wear courtly festive attire, and because the horse would only move at walking pace during these processions, the impracticality of her clothing did not bother her. At other times women wore the same type of clothes when on horseback as they wore during the day or for traveling. It was only when horseback riding developed into a popular social pastime that a specific riding outfit came into existence. In the early 18th century it consisted of a riding jacket, vest, long skirt and tricorn hat. At the end of the 18th century, the tricorn hat was replaced by the cylindrical top hat. The skirt had to be adapted to the lady's asymmetric side-saddle position that prevented it falling evenly. In order to achieve the desired look, the fabric was cut longer on one side, and when walking this longer side was turned up and secured with buttons. Apart from a few minor changes, this riding outfit remained unchanged throughout the 19th century. It was also the inspiration for the most important and innovative concept in ladies' fashion in the 20th century: the suit.

By about 1900 the skirt had become just a decorative facade, because the horsewoman wore pants and boots underneath it. After World War I most women had given up riding side-saddle, which made the so-called "amazon dress" redundant, and this led to the modern riding look as we know it today. Although the modern riding habit no longer includes any features of today's fashion, it is nevertheless very elegant: white shirt, silk scarf, fitted tweed jacket, tight-fitting pants, and riding boots. Heroines of countless films have been seen wearing these or very similar outfits. Pullovers, quilted down vests, and leggings are worn for everyday purposes, while the more formal habit is reserved for riding competitions and fox hunting. There are still a few elegant ladies who will wear a tailor-made tweed jacket for their morning ride in London's Hyde Park, but generally the choice of clothes is determined by practical considerations.

As well as inspiring the development of the suit, the riding habit has also influenced other parts of women's wardrobes. The most important examples are the riding coat, the jacket with a center vent and slanting pockets, the white blouse, the quilted jacket, and jodhpur boots. The bridle has also been a valuable source of inspiration for accessories and jewelry—the reins have become belts, the snaffle bit has become a shoe decoration, and the stirrup has been reduced to miniature scale and turned into clip earrings. The collections designed by Hermès and Gucci would have been much less interesting without horses.

Even if you do not go horseback riding yourself, you need not give up on the equestrian look because your sportswear will include many clothes and accessories from this world.

Fashion and accessories from the world of horseback riding

The number of silk scarves with horse motifs is impossible to count because almost every fashion label decorates its scarves with horses, riders, stirrups, or snaffle bits.

Jodhpur boots were originally worn by polo players as a shorter replacement for high boots. Today they are worn as smart leisure shoes by elegant anglophile women.

The traditional riding coat is made from rubberized cotton. To ensure that the protective tails did not flap, they were tied to the lower leg.

A well-cut hacking jacket is an indispensable garment, even if never used for horseback riding. (The name comes from the verb "to hack," meaning to ride at an ordinary pace on roads rather than cross-country, or racing.)

As leather specialists par excellence, bag-makers and saddlers also make belts and other accessories. The brass parts are inspired by the bridle and other harness fittings as a reminder of the world of horses.

The Italian luxury saddler Gucci was the first to decorate his loafers with a brass mini-snaffle, thus creating a classic shoe model that is still copied today.

The English Tattersall check was originally designed for horse blankets and was later used for riding clothes. It is now often used for shirts and waistcoats as well as lining for jackets and coats.

On the slopes and afterward

Of the many popular sports of the 19th century, there are very few that have lost little of their exclusive aura even though they became widely practiced sports in the 20th century. Skiing is undoubtedly one of these. This may be because from their invention in about 1890 until the ski boom of the 1970s, winter sports vacations remained the prerogative of the upper classes. The vacations of ordinary people were seldom long enough to go as far as the Alps, and the cost of the journey to the mountains plus the equipment necessary for such a trip was far too expensive for most. Once skiing became less expensive and more widely accessible to all, it nonetheless retained its image of exclusivity because high society was able to withdraw into "splendid isolation" in spite the arrival of the masses. They gathered in Klosters, Zermatt, and Kitzbuhel where the high hotel prices protected them from the nuisance of the "hoi polloi."

From the sport's earliest beginnings, ladies' skiing outfits reflected the sports fashion of the decade. At the end of the 19th century, the first women skiers wore long skirts on the slopes because special skiing clothing had not yet been developed. Shortly before World War I, the first knee-breeches appeared on the slopes, but they were still often concealed by a skirt. In the 1920s, this was no longer necessary and pants could be worn without having to be concealed. They were cut wide and gathered around the ankles so that they looked like long knickerbockers. These wide breeches were replaced in the 1930s by tapered pants, which were much better from an aerodynamic point of view. These new skiing pants were tightly held in place by a strap that went under the sole of the foot or boot. The outfit was completed by an anorak made of water-repellent cotton

Ski fashion is more than just sportswear. The choice of a particular look is also a fashion statement.

gabardine. In the 1950s, ski overalls made from elastic fibers made their appearance on the slopes. In the 1960s they became even more windproof and water-resistant as a result of the development of more sophisticated synthetic fabrics. Ski boots were now made of plastic rather than leather and the laces were replaced by buckles, which were more practical.

Going on a ski trip involves not only the actual sport of skiing but also the events that occur after skiing, generally known as après-ski. The clothes worn for après-ski are an interesting variation on the smart casual theme. A complete chapter would be needed to discuss all the aspects of this special category of the smart casual look, but the main features are the following: 1) Current leisure chic. 2) Typical accessories from the particular ski region. 3) Special fashion trends from the skier's own country of origin, for instance, a down parka and cowboy hat in Aspen, or a loden Tyrolean jacket and Tod's boots in Klosters. The classical lady is slightly more reserved in her dress but takes a few more liberties than she would in the city or on vacation on the Riviera. She will steer clear of the over-the-top look sported by the jet set—Versace sunglasses, white fur coat and silver moon-boots are not her thing. For sitting on the terrace of her chalet, she will choose a timeless, classic weekend look such as a cashmere sweater, a pearl necklace and a down jacket by Moncler.

Where would skiing be without après-ski? The lifestyle label Bogner also has a wide range of perfect outfits for that time of day.

Bogner – Sportswear made in Germany

An imaginative designer and perfect model: Maria Bogner presents her famous tapered ski-pants.

German fashion labels with a world reputation? Bogner is undoubtedly one of the first that would come to mind. The company was founded in 1932 and owes much to the great design talent of Maria Lux, the fiancée, and later the wife, of sports fashion entrepreneur and skier Willy Bogner. She designed the outfits for the German ski team in the 1936 Olympic Games and Bogner still supplies the outfits of all the teams of the German Ski Association. In 1948 Maria Bogner launched her first post-war models and completely revolutionized ski fashion with her legendary tapered ski pants made from stretchy fabric. She herself was often the model in fashion shows and publicity photographs, but international high society too was frequently photographed in the sexy, streamlined look that also proved to be very effective publicity. It was little wonder that the brand became increasingly successful. In 1950 Maria Bogner presented her first men's collection and the label quickly became a worldwide success for men's skiwear. In 1955 her Tip-Top ski hats with the Bogner B on the zipper became a bestseller, and in 1956 she designed an aerodynamic outfit for the United States ladies' national ski team. The company continued to expand—when it started in 1947 it had 25 seamstresses, and by 1960 it already employed 500.

Meanwhile Willy Bogner, Jr. also made a name for himself as a skier, film-maker and fashion photographer while at the same time preparing himself to join the family business. In 1972 he married the Brazilian model Sônia Ribero and in 1973 they both moved to the U.S. in order to make Bogner even more successful there. In the meantime, his parents opened a succession of Bogner boutiques, now selling fashion wear and accessories for all types of sport. In the 1980s and 1990s Bogner became known as a first-class sportswear specialist, comparable to the greatest names in the field such as Polo Ralph Lauren and Armani. In 1992, Sonia Bogner launched a designer collection under her own name that further extended the range offered by the Bogner label.

Sportswear made in Germany: Maria Bogner began conquering the U.S. market with her ski fashion as early as the 1950s.

The Ivy League look

The button-down shirt is an indispensable part of the sporty East Coast look. Women wear this unisex classic with chinos or short pants, with a pullover and a blazer.

Straight-cut cotton gabardine slacks are an important foundation stone of the smart casual wardrobe between spring and fall. Khaki, white. and navy are the most traditional colors.

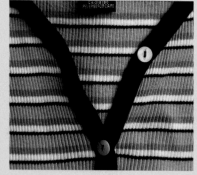

Plain, crew-neck cotton pullovers in a wide range of colors can be found in most women's closets and drawers because with their fresh colors they combine beautifully with light-colored chinos and button-down shirts.

As well as checks, wide or (as here) narrow horizontal stripes are among the most popular patterns of the east coast leisure look. They combine beautifully with almost everything in the wardrobe.

The Ivy League look also includes very stylish outfits for fall and winter. The light summer chinos are replaced by thick twill trousers while a snug lamb's wool pullover replaces the light cotton one.

The polo shirt is an indispensable, versatile item in a woman's summer wardrobe. Under a blue blazer it can be worn in the office; with light-colored chinos it is a perfect town outfit; and on the beach it gives protection from too much sun.

The discreet charm of the polo player

The range of leisure wear is amazingly wide, but most garments seem to be variations on the particular basic concepts that were developed between the 1920s and the 1950s. Thus, Mediterranean fishermen inspired the fashion for Capri pants, striped T-shirts, and espadrilles, while the English landed gentry with its country charm influenced the clothes worn for uncomplicated weekend elegance. But the United States also provided an important source of inspiration, the main one being the neat, casual look of the American East Coast. This consisted of simple dresses, shirts, skirts, and pants, in summer made from cotton, linen or silk, and in autumn made from warmer cotton and linen fabrics, wool, and cashmere. Another source of inspiration was the sportswear worn by students at private schools and the elite Ivy League colleges, such as blazers, polo shirts, hooded shirts, jeans, short pants, and sneakers. Both these categories of basics were completed by a hand-knitted sweater,

Not without my polo player. In the 1980s Ralph Lauren's polo shirt became the symbol of the elitist Ivy League look.

country-style belt, and flat shoes. Women sporting this type of look presented themselves as spontaneous, clean, sporty, and tanned, with wind-tousled hair as if she had just arrived back from a long walk with the children and the dog.

Ralph Lauren did not invent this style but he perfected and reinterpreted it. Born the son of a Russian immigrant in the Bronx in New York in 1939, Lauren grew up in modest circumstances. He did not become acquainted with the traditional East Coast style, which he subsequently made famous all over the world, at home or on vacation in New Hampshire, but he studied it as a young man in the store windows of traditional gentleman's outfitters such as Brooks Brothers and J. Press. These legendary gentleman's outfitters dressed prosperous New Yorkers in gray flannel business suits, and regimental ties for the office, and in navy blazers, khaki chinos, button-down shirts, and loafers for the weekend. To go to the shore his wife would wear a plain seersucker dress or a checked blouse, light-colored slacks, and white canvas sneakers. Ralph Lauren's skill lay in his ability to "pep up" this rather plain look: he added elements of the "college" look, a touch of Wild West Romanticism, and a little English country style, completing the look with a dose of 1930s Hollywood chic.

Ralph Lauren's mix was perfect and his approach proved very successful, first in the U.S. and starting in the 1980s, also in Europe. Because Ralph Lauren's classic mix included something for everyone, from practical unisex basics to country-style wrap-around skirts with Navajo prints to the sophisticated elegance of evening dresses. However, the hot favorites have always included his sportswear with the distinctive polo player: chinos and Bermudas, jeans and denim skirts, corduroy and flannel pants, navy blazers, blousons and cable knit sweaters, navy, pink, violet and bottle green polo shirts, button-down shirts in thick twill, soft cotton flannel shirts, and stone-washed denim. In other words, his clothes included everything an economics or law student needed to imagine herself at Harvard or on the beach at Montauk. That Polo Ralph Lauren was actually a designer label, many clients didn't fully realize. And so it became the favorite brand for all women who usually dislike designer fashion.

When it comes to sportswear with East Coast flair, there are alternatives to the label with the polo player. For instance, McGregor also has a wide range of classic basics.

Bavarian and Austrian folk costumes are very versatile. A straight-cut jacket of pure new wool tweed by Schneider looks just as good with an elegant velvet skirt as it does with jeans.

Not fashion, but stylish tradition

Dirndl skirt, Tyrolean jacket, loden coat—these are not to everyone's taste. But there is no doubt that since the mid-19th century traditional folk costumes have played a major part in classic leisure and sportswear. The romantic image of these traditional garments does not appeal to everyone, but the history of clothes such as this dates back to the 15th century, while the authentic clothes that inspired many national costumes goes even further back.

The rise of traditional costume from popular to fashionable dress started when Europe discovered the Alps as a geographic region, a vacation destination, a lifestyle concept and a designer trend. Suddenly, the entire world wanted to travel, ski, row on mountain lakes, or shoot chamois, always dressed in the right clothes, of course. So what better than to wear the same clothes as the local inhabitants? Obviously, this would not be in the plain rural style but reinterpreted in a more sophisticated version for city dwellers. The Alpine influence was at its most obvious in the recently invented ladies' suit. Made from Loden fabric with green or red trim, stag horn buttons and matching accessories, the traveling outfit became a suitable outfit for the cool summer temperatures in the mountains. It was also at about the same time, that is, in about 1870, that the dirndl was invented. This was not actually a real traditional garment but more a fashionable adaptation of the country-style skirt worn in Bavaria and Austria. The dirndl soon became synonymous with life in the Alps: a favorite dress worn in operettas, musicals, and movies as part of mountain scenery, and an absolute must-have for ladies on a Heidi trip.

World War I heralded a temporary end to the European boom of national costumes, at least outside Germany and Austria. After 1914 no woman in France or England wanted to be dressed like the wife of a Prussian officer when she went hiking in the mountains. But in the 1920s and early 1930s the international image of the Alpine national costume experienced a new revival and women could be seen once again wearing loden clothes. Thus Marlene Dietrich's daughter, Maria Riva, describes in her biography of her mother how the star went to Salzburg during a trip to Europe in 1930, to visit the traditional costume outfitter Lanz to order a complete outfit. She also remarks that the Hollywood star looked like "a distinguished Austrian mayor's wife" in her green loden jacket, short black waistcoat with silver buttons, and velvet hat. However, she adds that the shopping expeditions to Salzburg ended when Hitler occupied Austria. It was at that time that the dirndl was put back in moth balls.

But not long after 1945 it reappeared once more, not least because many American soldiers were as taken by this romantic traditional costume as they were by Salzburg's architectural treasures. In this way the "Austrian look" and "Bavarian style" became popular again throughout the world in the 1950s.

In the wild 1960s the fashion for traditional costume became politically charged again. Progressive contemporaries no longer considered the dirndl, loden jacket, and Tyrolean hat as a harmless fashion statement or an expression of a regional lifestyle, but as the epitome of narrow-mindedness. This meant that until the 1970s this traditional dress was no longer worn by self-respecting women outside Bavaria and Austria. The exceptions were members of the German and Austrian aristocracy who since the 19th century had always been very fond of the Alpine look. They refused to give up their favorite outfit because of some liberal bourgeois finding fault with it. Indeed, they considered traditional costume a fundamental part of their wardrobe. The return of this traditional Alpine costume is due to the non-political yuppies who saw it as part of general fashion, or more precisely as leisure wear that combined beautifully with English sportswear.

Pure understatement: a traditional loden jacket with the addition of cashmere.

Manufaktur Habsburg

Stylish traditional costume is very hard to find. Even the more prestigious labels in Germany and Austria often sell watered-down, kitsch versions, which they describe rather meaninglessly as "country-house" style. This is why many discriminating ladies and costume connoisseurs buy their Alpine wardrobe from Manufaktur Habsburg in Salzburg. The company's name is meant verbatim because it hand-tailors fine hunting clothes and formal dress in the style of the Austro-Hungarian Empire. In spite of its traditional image, it was only founded in 1992. Nevertheless the company has already achieved cult status among the fans of the aristocratic Alpine look. Being both timeless and contemporary, the coats, suits, jackets, and hunting outfits produced by Manufaktur Habsburg combine easily with other styles of clothes. In addition, in spite the image of authenticity, the clothes have an international dimension that means that they can be worn in Milan, New York, and Paris as well as in Munich.

№ 5

Art of the outer garment: coats and jackets

Coats and jackets

The coat is a real newcomer in the woman's wardrobe because until the late 19th century women preferred to wear capes. This was because the clothes worn then would have been difficult to wear under a coat. However, as sports activities became more popular, day dresses became less bulky so that women could wear coats and demand for them rose rapidly. Because fashion still dictated that clothes should vary according to the occasion, a wide range of different coat models were developed. In addition, the new mobility made possible by bicycles, automobiles, railroads, and ocean liners required different models with different finishes to resist wind, dust, rain or soot. The newspapers of the early 20th century were full of advertisements for practical yet elegant coats. The suppliers of this new type of garment recorded a steadily growing demand, and coat departments in large stores became increasingly important.

Around 1900, traveling in the new, modern means of transportation was still rather uncomfortable, so that to survive an automobile journey an ankle length, double-breasted coat with a high collar was necessary. But as cars became more weather-resistant in the 1920s and 1930s, travel clothes became lighter. At the same time, the growing number of working women also needed practical and thick coats that could be worn to go to the office. This led to the development of a few basic forms that still exist today and are endlessly varied by designers, such as the trench coat, the knee-length swing coat, and double-breasted wool coat with or without a belt.

Because the ladies' coat developed relatively late and was therefore unable to fall back on traditional examples, its designers turned to the classics in men's fashion for inspiration, at least as far as daywear was concerned. Consequently a woman's wardrobe may contain a number of well-known, traditional designs with this inspiration, ranging from the chesterfield coat with velvet collar to the sporty polo coat with patch pockets. On the other hand, fashion designers created very feminine silhouettes for evening wear, and the fashion for fur developed its own interpretation of the coat. After World War II, haute couture also began to concentrate on coat design, which now had to reflect the fashion of the day. The coat's length had to follow that of the dress or skirt, as a result of which coats became very short in the 1960s, when designers created simple but very elegant coats.

In the field of leisure, jackets and parkas sometimes came to replace more conventional coats. These garments that were originally designed to be worn when going on country walks, shooting or skiing were often also worn as daywear. But it was only after about fifty years that the sports top came to be accepted as a valid substitute for the coat, when waxed cotton jackets and quilted jackets, including leather and sheepskin versions, became trendy accessories in the 1980s. In the 1990s, down-filled coats and jackets were created, resulting in feather-light but very warm vests, parkas, and coats becoming the new favorites. But women who were not enamored of the "Michelin man" look did not have to freeze because the slim coats of the 1960s and 1970s made a comeback— they looked very good with tight tops and hipster-trousers. Today, classic coats, jackets, and parkas are all equally popular, and the ways of wearing them are manifold. For instance, a slim beige cashmere coat may be teamed with jeans and flat shoes or a parka with a business suit.

Unlike the situation in 1900, lady drivers today no longer need to be wrapped in thick clothes to keep them warm – thanks to air-conditioning and heating.

Many women who are fond of anything "country-style" feel happier in a Barbour jacket than in a luxury cashmere coat.

Types of coat

A-line coat

Double-breasted blazer coat

Polo coat

The A-line coat, in this case by Brioni Donna, is the perfect coat to wear with flared skirts that would not fit under a straight-cut coat. But because few women wear full or flared skirts very often, the elegant A-line coat is becoming increasingly rare; it would look much too wide over a slim, straight shift dress or narrow trousers. Not being based on a man's coat, the A-line coat is very feminine and its details such as the collar, lapels, pockets, and buttons are much more imaginative. The collar and fabric tend to be strongly influenced by the current fashion, because such coats are often designed for a special collection. However, it is possible to find a relatively timeless A-line coat that will work well for many years. It is best to choose a plain, neutral color such as beige or black. A long black A-line coat also has the advantage that it can be worn over an evening-dress.

The blazer coat is double-breasted and has pointed lapels (here Les Copains has added some fur). It takes its name from the similarly cut, double-breasted men's blazer. Theoretically, the blazer coat can be any length, but it is usually just above the knee or calf-length. It should not be much shorter because the long, pointed lapels that create the characteristic low-cut neck need a certain length to ensure a certain visual balance. If the blazer coat is too short, the proportions will be all wrong. The number of buttons may vary, but usually there are three pairs of buttons: two pairs for fastening and one for decoration. Although the blazer coat is closely related to men's fashion, the ladies' version often has no pockets but it sometimes has the traditional hip-height flap pockets. Like the men's blazer, the blazer coat is usually navy blue. With its gilt buttons it is a traditional classic coat that could also be rather unkindly described as conservative.

At first sight the polo coat seems to be closely related to the blazer coat, but on closer inspection the only similarity is the double-breasted front. The lapels, buttons and pockets are completely different. The lapels of the polo coat are similar to those of the single-breasted lounge jacket but they are not as pointed. There are more buttons on the polo coat than on the blazer coat, usually three pairs of buttons that fasten. The polo coat has strong sports connections, having been worn in the 1920s and 1930s by college students and spectators at horse races. The coat has patch pockets, but the ladies' version of the polo coat usually has no breast pocket, first because there is no need for one, and second, because it does not do the female figure any favors. The real polo coat is very long and the traditional colors are camel, sand, and dark blue. Usually there is no belt but often there is a half-belt at the back. Apart from the classic model there are many fashionable variations on the polo coat, like this one by Belvest shown here, which differ from the original in the number of buttons, the length, the slope of the pockets, and the color.

Single-breasted coat

There are many variations on the single-breasted coat, but there is no precise definition for the various models as there is in men's fashion. The best way to differentiate between them is according to the characteristics of each individual version: length, number of buttons, type of fastener, pockets (welted or patch) and collar (velvet-covered or plain). In addition, the fabric itself can make the same model look completely different. Thus a knee-length coat with fly front and slanting pockets in dark gray worsted wool will look very elegant and sophisticated, while in brown herringbone tweed it will look more like a country outfit. A black velvet collar adds a stylish touch. According to legend, this was how the English aristocracy expressed its sympathy with the French aristocracy executed during the French Revolution in the late 18th century. Today the velvet collar is merely a stylistic detail that may be in any color. The straight sober model shown is by Loro Piana and does not feature a velvet collar.

Raglan coat

The term raglan coat usually conjures up pictures of a knee-length, single-breasted wool or gabardine coat. But the only unique distinctive feature of a raglan coat is the special cut of the sleeves and shoulders. Unlike the polo coat, for instance, that has set-in sleeves, the shoulders and sleeves form a unit so that it could be said that the sleeves practically begin at the collar. There are one-piece and two-piece raglan sleeves. The one-piece raglan sleeve lies very flat on the shoulder while the two-piece version sticks out a little across the shoulders because of the seam. The version preferred is partly a matter of taste and partly a question of what kind of clothes are worn underneath. The two-piece raglan sleeve is better if the coat is worn over a blazer or a jacket, but when the coat is just worn over a sweater, the one-piece sleeve is more elegant and it hangs better. A raglan coat is a rather sporty garment and even in a dark color it is not ideal as a classic business coat. It is more suitable for smart casual occasions, leisure outings and country weekends.

Loden coat

Opinions are divided about the loden coat. Some find it old-fashioned, bourgeois, and boring, while others consider it an indispensable, authentic classic. Fans of the thick green woolen fabric are found throughout Europe, where the loden coat is an important item in many women's wardrobes. Although the term "loden" only refers to the cloth from which it is made and not to a particular style, the loden coat is frequently long, with a shoulder cape and an inverted pleat. The men's and ladies' versions differ only in the position of the buttons, which are always sewn on the left side in the ladies' version. Some of the pictures by the English photographer Jayne Fincher demonstrate that the loden coat was worn by some of the best-dressed women of the 20th century as the perfect protection against cold and rain. One picture, dating from 1980, shows Lady Diana Spencer before her marriage to Prince Charles wearing a loden coat over a long dress and gold evening shoes as she leaves the Ritz.

What kind of coat do you need?

How many coats does a woman need? In the 1950s, a woman needed at least five coats : a winter coat, a coat for spring and fall, a summer coat, a raincoat, and an evening coat. The emphasis is on the words "at least" because any one who could afford it owned these coats in several colors, styles and fabrics. As a result wardrobes were full of coats because every season women bought new clothes that needed new matching coats.

The modern woman has fewer coats although she would prefer to have more. But because she often wears jackets it makes no sense to have a special coat for every occasion and certainly not for every recreational activity. Nevertheless, a well-equipped wardrobe should contain—apart from changing fashion trends and personal preferences—at least the following kinds of coats: a dark wool coat for business that can also be worn in the evening, a second, this time brown, wool coat that can be used for the office, smart casual and relaxed weekends, and a light raincoat for rainy weather.

What about the length? Ever since skirts became knee-length in the 1920s, ankle-length coats have not been necessary. They come back into fashion now and again but they do not play a major part in the classic wardrobe. But although ankles no longer need to be covered, the coat must always be longer than the skirt to prevent the creation of an unintentional layered look. The most suitable and versatile is the fairly straight, below-the-knee-length coat, but the very straight version of the mini era and short coat of the 1990s are also very popular. Women who wear trousers have more choice so far as length is concerned, in that they can follow the fashion or their own taste.

Coats are the most versatile items in a wardrobe because they have to go with almost everything. Those who only wear red or who never venture out in anything but black will naturally need a red or black coat. Everyone else will prefer a neutral shade such as a beautiful beige or a light charcoal. Patterns should be used with caution unless they are the traditional, classic ones, and even these cannot be wholeheartedly recommended. Although patterns such as herringbone, dog's tooth check and pepita have been popular for decades, like all patterns they restrict the possibilities of combination. Structured fabrics are an alternative for those who want to avoid plain fabrics. These provide a more interesting surface texture but do not distract with loud patterns or too many colors.

The gray coat worn for business purposes or going out in the evening may be single or double-breasted, but the single-breasted coat is slightly preferable. First, it also looks very good when it is left open, unfastened. Second, it has a straighter, cleaner line. Third, for the last 80 years it has been more popular than the double-breasted version. The second wool coat, the brown one, should differ from the gray one in style as well as color while still being formal. For instance, it might have a different length, wider lapels, and a belt, and it might perhaps be double-breasted. It should be more than just "the same but in brown." A good choice would be a polo coat, a blazer coat or a designer classic such as the 101801 by Max Mara. These coats can be worn both to work or on smart casual occasions. Beige or camel shades look particularly good with a gray flannel suit. These coats are also ideal for all those "semi-official" occasions where a jacket might look to sporty.

In spite of its name, the raincoat is also worn when it is not raining. Since it is made of light cotton gabardine, linen, silk or a modern synthetic fiber fabric instead of warm wool, it is also an ideal spring and summer coat. For the last 100 years the typical colors for raincoats have been neutral ones such as sand, off-white or khaki that go with almost any color. As far as the cut is concerned there is the choice between the classic trench coat that in recent years has also become available in a slim-fitting version, and the so-called slip-on.

To celebrate its 50th anniversary, the fashion label Max Mara presented a special reinterpretation of the legendary 101801 coat. This jubilee model was a great success among the label's enthusiasts.

A light trench coat is the perfect garment for spring and summer, providing protection against wind and rain, without being too heavy.

Stylish in the rain

There are few garments whose function is as clearly defined as the raincoat. Naturally, it should also be elegant, but its main function is to protect the wearer from the rain. Since the beginning of the history of fashion, the development of a fabric that meets these requirements has been an important challenge in temperate climates with relatively high rainfall. For a long time this search remained unsuccessful because natural, water-resistant fibers are rare and processing them is difficult, if not impossible. Leather, for instance, was too heavy to be cut into a really "wearable" ladies' cape, and who would want to wear a massively heavy leather coat that could only be worn when traveling in a coach? Oilskins, fabrics impregnated with wax or varnish, were also far from suitable for the elegant ladies' fashion because they were too coarse and unsightly as well as also being too heavy. Consequently, until the 19th century women had to make do with woolen capes and shawls to protect them from straying rain drops, while they used elegant umbrellas to shield them from the heaviest rain—if indeed they dared to venture out at all when it rained. In fact, elegant women of leisure had only to face the elements when traveling, since shopping for daily provisions was done by servants.

It is no coincidence that the first light, attractive, water-repellent fabric was developed at the time of the new mobility brought about by the railroads and the automobile. The solution came about with the development of gabardine, a twill

The anglophile woman often prefers a Barbour jacket to the ultra-light high-tech materials now available to protect her from wind and rain.

fabric woven with a special impregnated yarn that was developed by Thomas Burberry in the 1870s. At first he used linen fibers, but later turned to cheaper cotton fibers. This water-repellent fabric was first used for making sports, hunting, and outdoor wear. However, in 1900 Thomas Burberry had the brilliant idea of using this new water-repellent fabric to make raincoats. Like men, women soon learned to appreciate the benefits of the new fabric, because when lined with wool or fur, gabardine could also be used for warm winter coats as well as protecting from the wind and rain.

Compared with the modern, high-tech synthetic fibers of today, it is difficult to understand the enthusiasm of people in the late 19th and early 20th centuries for gabardine. But remembering the alternatives available at the time, it is less surprising that people were so excited about this new fabric. These alternatives included the so-called Macintosh, a coat made from rubberized cotton that kept the wearer very dry but was very heavy and exuded a strong smell of rubber. Another alternative was the waxed cotton as used in Barbour jackets. As far as water-repellent properties were concerned, it was undoubtedly more effective than gabardine, but it was hardly suitable as a fabric for an elegant town coat, besides the fact that it smelled strongly of wax.

The rapid progress in the development of synthetic fibers and fabrics led to a completely new generation of raincoats after World War II. They were received with as much excitement as Burberry gabardine had been in the past because nylon, PVC, and the like were considered modern, practical, and chic. These synthetic fabrics were sold to the public as pioneering innovations. This trend reached a temporary high point in the 1960s when many women identified shiny plastic coats as the height of fashion. In the 1970s and 1980s women rediscovered natural fibers such as cotton, wool, silk, and linen with the result that plastic and other synthetic coats were relegated to the back of the closet.

In the late 1980s and 1990s there was a quantum leap forward in waterproof clothing. Brand new chemical fibers and even more effective waterproofing methods gave designers a new-found freedom in designing raincoats. Because

As this Burberry advertisement shows, raincoats before World War I were still ankle-length, reflecting the skirt hem length current at the time.

it was no longer necessary to resort to rubberizing, waxing, and synthetic coating, rainwear could now be made from almost any kind of material. In addition, the technical possibility now existed of making the surface of any fabric waterproof by coating it with a special membrane, without interfering with the "breathability" of the fabric. This achievement marked the birth of breathable fabrics.

It therefore seemed likely that traditional raincoats would soon disappear. But as often happens in the history of fashion, things turned out quite differently. The retro fashion brought the shiny plastic raincoat of the 1960s and 1970s back onto the fashion scene, the Barbour jacket made a fashion comeback, and even the Macintosh that seemed to have been completely forgotten returned to the runway. It seemed that people no longer trusted rainwear that did not look like rainwear.

The concept of the trench coat is always being reinterpreted by fashion labels. This model from the Mustang collection has a surprisingly classic look.

Fur: a hairy topic

As recently as the 19th century almost any furry four-legged animal was considered a potential garment by the fur lovers of the time. Today's animal lovers and environmentalists can hardly believe the variety of creatures that used to be turned into coats, collars, hats and muffs. In those days, only the rich could afford precious furs, meaning the furs of animals that looked beautiful and expensive without much processing. The majority of the population had to put up with ordinary furs of more modest origin that required a lot of "making good" before being half-way acceptable. But apart from the esthetic and fashion drawbacks, fur enthusiasts today would have serious ethical misgivings about wearing the fur of an ape or a squirrel or the skin of a mute swan—not to mention the associations that a skunk coat might imply.

There are three sources for both precious and ordinary furs: nature, fur farming, and the food industry. In the 19th century, nature (which really meant the animals living in the wild killed by trappers) was the main source of fur. Today the major sources are fur farms and the food industry, which together represent almost 85% of the fur supply.

Fur farms supply furs such as mink, fox, coypu, raccoon, polecat, and chinchilla, while the food industry supplies lambskin, goatskin, calf, and rabbit fur. Hunting contributes only 16% of the total furs processed. Out of this only a very small proportion, just 0.2%, is caught in the wild by trappers looking for wild animals such as beavers, lynxes, squirrels, sables and seals. The remaining 15.8% is caught in cultivated areas where the number of animals is controlled through shooting, because musk deer, raccoons, coypu, red foxes, wild rabbits, and coyotes could cause a lot of damage to the environment there. This is the justification presented by the hunters.

The furrier is the person who makes fur garments from the raw materials, fleeces or skins. Only the finished garment is called fur, and the skin or fleece undergoes several more or less lengthy processes before it is turned into a coat, jacket or cape. The various processes depend on the type and origin of the skins and what is expected of the finished garment. Before the skins arrive in the furrier's workshop, they have usually already been washed, salted, dried, then washed and dried again.

The skins, which are still hard, are then dressed by tumbling or light trampling depending on the delicacy of the hairs. When tumbled or milled, the moistened skins are coated with hot fat and kneaded in a machine. The skins of wild animals must also be tanned to prevent the skin fibers from sticking together, which would result in rotting.

Precious furs are not usually dyed because they are most beautiful in their natural condition. Until World War II the demand for fur greatly exceeded the supply, so lesser quality skins were used whose appearance could be enhanced by dyeing. Dyeing also became quite common when black and dark brown furs became fashionable, since these colors hardly ever occur in nature.

One way of dyeing fur is by immersion. The main disadvantage of this method is that both the fur and the leather are dyed, so that even the layman can immediately recognize the deception. The other method is known as surface dyeing. As the term implies, only the fur itself is dyed and not the underside so that only the hairs take on the desired color while the leather underneath retains its natural color. With this technique it is very much harder to determine whether a fur is as precious as it appears to be. After dyeing, the fur is washed one more time and shorn, after which it is ready for the next stages.

Like other garments, furs can also be bought off the rack. But a lady who wants a perfectly made, well-fitting item should have it made-to-measure by the furrier. As usual, the cost is greater but so is the satisfaction given by the result.

Above left:
Fur is still very fashionable in haute couture, as is shown by Balmain's inclusion of silver fox hats and stoles in its 2001 winter collection.

The luxury label Loro Piana presents a discreet variation on the theme of the fur coat: it is the lining of this jacket that uses snug, cozy fur.

Above:
After a few seasons of relative absence on the catwalks, fur has made a fashion comeback even among the young. The most popular are light models such as this mink coat by Torrente.

Furs yesterday and today

The traditional house of Roeckl, often decorates its gloves with precious fur. Here the gloves are adorned with a fluffy arctic fox rim that matches the hat.

Bear
Bear skins were mainly used as rugs and coverings because of their size and coarse, shaggy hairs. Only the black bear provided a fur soft enough to be suitable for accessories and clothes. Raccoon fur was much sought-after because of its water-repellent properties and was therefore an ideal protection against bad weather.

Badger
Traditionally, the hard, coarse hair of the European badger was used to make rugs and brushes. Its American cousin had softer fur that could therefore be used for clothes.

Birds
It is hard to believe but true that in the past even bird skin covered with delicate down was highly prized. The most popular were eider ducks, geese, gulls, swans, and grebes. Because of their extreme delicacy, bird skins were mostly used for luxury evening wear.

Cats, large and small
Changing tastes in fashion have affected the popularity of different types of fur at particular times. Thus, during the 1920s the skins of tigers, lions, and leopards were very fashionable as wall hangings and rugs, and wild cat fur such as ocelot was particularly sought-after in the 1950s. The fur of smaller wild cats and house cats has also been used for making clothes, mostly as imitations of precious fur.

Fox
There are foxes everywhere in the world, the main difference between them being the color. Generally, foxes from the more northern regions produce the best quality fur. Blue foxes have been farmed for many years. Fox fur is mainly used as trim.

Hoofed animals
Hoofed animals whose skin is used as fur include sheep, goats, horses, and cattle. The most important skins are those of the broadtail sheep known as Persian lamb, Astrakhan, or karakul. In the past horsehide and goatskins were also used but today these furs are very uncommon.

Insect eaters
It is hard to imagine that not so very long ago moles were hunted for their velvety fur, which was widely popular.

Marsupial
Almost all marsupials were appreciated for their fur: kangaroo, wombat, wallaby, and dasyure. Today, only opossum fur is used and most of this comes from New Zealand where the opossum has become a real pest. The fur is therefore simply a byproduct of the legal culling of the animals. Opossum fur is mainly used as trim.

Marten
Martens can be found almost everywhere in the world. They are now bred on a large scale in the

United States, Canada, Scandinavia, and Russia. The most sought-after members of the large marten family are the sable, ermine, and mink which produce the most precious and most expensive fur. The stone marten, polecat, weasel, and wolverine have also been popular in the past.

Monkey
In the past this was a very popular type of fur but today it is quite unthinkable, as well as being illegal. The furs came mainly from species of African monkeys, including the Abyssinian monkey and the gray monkey.

Otter
Otter fur was used mainly for coats or collars. In the past the sea otter was particularly appreciated because of its very fine fur.

Rodents
Because of their relatively small size, the skins of rodents are generally used as a lining, but because of their softness they are also chosen as the basic fur for imitations. The best-known are beaver, muskrat, coypu, chinchilla, hamster, squirrel, and rabbit. In the past the fur of the snow hare and marmot were also used.

Seal
Fur seals and common seals used to be extremely popular until the media publicized the killing of baby seals in the 1980s. Today, only the fur of adult seals is used.

Skunk
The North American skunk is the best known, very popular because of its jet-black fur. The unpleasant smell it emits to discourage its enemies did not deter the trappers.

Wolf
Wolves used to be hunted on all continents because they were considered enemies of both men and of domestic animals. Wolfskin is hard and stiff and can therefore only be used as fur to a very limited extent. In the early 20th century it was often treated and used as fur collars. Today, the fur of the coyote, the North American prairie wolf, is still commonly used.

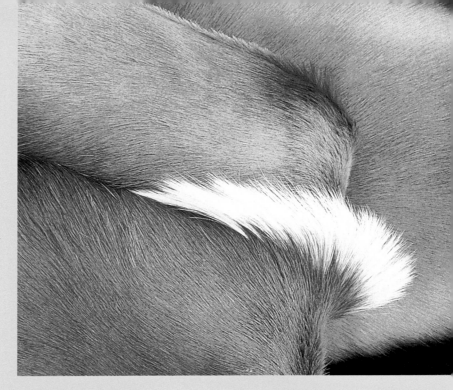

Antelope fur is used to make expensive jackets, and the German luxury label Aigner also uses it to make soft handbags.

The mink stole became a status symbol in the 1950s. This contemporary variation has a pocket for a cellphone.

Classic jackets

Barbour jacket

There are many waxed jackets but only one genuine Barbour. Its fans will wear it on all kinds of occasions and it will often last a lifetime. After a while they develop a kind of patina that enhances its value to the owner rather than diminishing it. It is said that some women will drive a few times over a newly acquired Barbour with their cross-country vehicle to give it a certain vintage character. There is a wide range of models but the most popular are the Beaufort and Bedale. The jacket's practical side vents also make it an ideal garment for horseback-riding. There are now more colors than in the past but the traditional and most popular color is still sage green.

Woolrich Arctic Parka

Italian fashion connoisseurs are particularly good at combining sports classics with business and leisure wear. For instance, the Arctic Parka produced by Woolrich has remained unchanged since it was first launched on the market in 1962 by John Rich and Bros of Pennsylvania. The sportswear company had been founded in 1830 but the Europeans only developed a taste for this garment in the 1980s. This was due to the Bolognese "brand discoverer" and importer Andrea Cane, who had already introduced the Barbour and the Husky to Italy where they had quickly become cult garments. Some may wonder why anyone would want to wear such a polar jacket in Italy, but the reason will be apparent on making a visit to Venice in January or to Milan in late autumn. It can be extremely cold in winter and a thick jacket with a down filling is the perfect garment for going to work or to the market, not to mention chatting with your friends on an open cafe terrace.

Husky

The British ironically describe the Husky as the "Range Rover you can wear." The comparison is quite apposite because, like the Range Rover, this quilted jacket with the dog on the label is quite inseparable from the image of British country life. The Husky was originally invented by American-born Stephen Guylas in Tostock in Suffolk in the early 1960s. At first it was only a vest but this was soon followed by a version with sleeves because of the great demand. In the 1970s it quickly developed into the uniform of the so-called Sloane Rangers, the young middle class English men and women whose dress style was copied in the 1980s by many yuppies all over the country. The great success of the Husky, which also spread throughout Europe, is really quite astounding. After all, it was a garment made of ordinary nylon. But because this very fact made it very easy to care for, its discreet plastic charm was never seen as a disadvantage. Originally, the Husky was only available in light green and navy but in the 1980s it also became available in other colors. Strong, bright colors were popular for a while especially with Italian women. In the 1990s the Husky's popularity diminished dramatically, although it is still worn quite a lot in Mediterranean countries. Barbour, the specialists for wax cotton, carry a quilted jacket in their collection.

Moncler

When elegant women in Paris go window-shopping in winter they often wrap up in a luxury down-filled jacket by Moncler. Unlike the American or English versions, the French version has a particular après-ski elegance so that it combines perfectly with a Hermès handbag and cashmere sweater. This sophisticated look is partly the result of the excellent range of colors that always includes elegant basics such as camel and black.

Chrysalis field coat

These rain-resistant field coats were originally only worn on shooting parties in Britain but they were soon seen in shop windows on the European mainland. The cut and arrangement of the pockets of these thick tweed jackets are reminiscent of a longer version of a Barbour jacket, but the quilted lining and woolly outer fabric make it more comfortable and supple. The field coat has an interlining made of a patented membrane and the cloth is treated with Teflon, giving it excellent water-repellent properties so that it can be worn in heavy rain and snow. Women who are keen on clothes in the English style have a particular liking for field coats because their pleasant warm tweed colors will match perfectly with the rest of their English-style wardrobe. These weekend country clothes may be bought at the traditional London-based field sports outfitters such as Holland & Holland, Purdey, and Farlow, and at their European counterparts. It does not matter where they are bought because all the shops that offer the original product are supplied by the English manufacturer Chrysalis Clothes which is based in Corby in the Midlands of England.

Woolrich down waist-coat

Do elegant women wear down vests? Absolutely. Traditionalists who find this difficult to accept have only to think of the Queen who is often seen wearing a down vest, often by the English cult label Puffa. The sleeveless down jacket is now the standard garment of all horseback-riders because it is warm without restricting the rider's movements in the saddle. But even spectators at equestrian events have become aware of its benefits. In fact, the boom in down-filled vests and jackets was not triggered by an equestrian fashion trend but rather by street and sportswear, which in the last decade have influenced almost all areas of fashion. The down-filled vest was welcomed enthusiastically by women with a traditional, classic image because this practical garment combines beautifully with the timeless, elegant, casual look. Younger women even wear it with their business clothes, for instance a black Woolrich waistcoat over a camel-colored sweater, with a gray pinstripe skirt and black boots.

Lady in leather

Belvest showed a reversible short coat in sheepskin very reminiscent of the 1970s in its fall/winter 2001/02 collection.

To go with its "tweed" tights, Falke proposed a knitted jacket, embellished with exotic leather in its 2001 winter collection.

The leather jacket was a rare occurrence until the 1990s. Naturally there were the very "unladylike" women clad in black leather who came from various backgrounds: Hell's Angels on one hand, and decent housewives wearing cheap leather jackets and fakes often sold in flea markets on the other—not to mention the creative, ultra-hip fashion victims in obligatory designer black. But more traditional women were slightly suspicious of black and felt more confident with brown, and even then only in combination with smart casual wear with a masculine look. For instance, a brown leather buckskin blouson over a blue cashmere sweater, scarf, jeans and Burlington socks was very popular in the 1980s among young women for driving around in their convertibles. The more adventurous preferred Chevignon-style leather jackets. Similar to college blousons, these jackets were made from different colored leather and fabric, often decorated with stitching. These jackets, worn with denim shirts, jeans, and cowboy boots were indispensable ingredients of the yuppie power-casual look.

That leather jackets are more often associated with leisure and sports and less so with classic ladies' wear is no coincidence. Throughout the history of fashion women have worn cloaks or capes to go out into the street, these only being replaced by coats in the late 19th century. Jackets as outer garments were not part of their wardrobe at the time. It was only at the beginning of the 20th century, when women became involved in activities usually reserved for men that required practical protective clothing, that women were finally seen in leather jackets—at the wheel of a car, on a motorbike, or in the cockpit of a plane. From the beginning leather jackets were associated with mobility and modern life, and anyone who considered themselves avant-garde wore leather, like for instance the American Nancy Cunard, the Cunard shipping line heiress, who in the 1920s led a bohemian life as a poet and publisher in Paris. In the 1930s Amelia Earhart, famous for her solo airplane crossing of the Atlantic—the first Atlantic crossing by a female pilot—also started a trend with her leather aviation wear.

After World War II, the fashion industry discovered youth as a target group, and this led to the development of a wide range of casual wear for teenagers. The leather blousons and jackets were an amazing success with both sexes. In the 1950s and 1960s leather became even more popular because it symbolized youthful opposition to the fashion conventions of adults. What started as an anti-style ended up as a mainstream one in the 1970s. Now widely accepted socially, leather clothes became less interesting to fashion gurus. The punk movement turned the leather jacket back into a symbol of protest, but this look was also seized by fashion designers who diluted it and toned it down, thus making it wearable by all.

In the late 1980s, the fashion for leather slowly disappeared from the windows of luxury boutiques but not from department and discount stores. As a result leather coats, jackets, skirts, trousers and blazers were thrown out of the sophisticated woman's wardrobe or handed down to her daughters. They loved their mother's old clothes, and in the 1990s they discovered the 1970s again, including leather garments. This retro trend was also reflected in the luxury fashion sector, where it has led to the comeback of nappa, ostrich, glacé, calf, and deer leather, so that at the beginning of the 21st century women could enjoy new contemporary, wearable leather clothes made of beautiful leather.

The advertising campaign promoting Revlon's Colorstay Liquid Lip shows country singer Shania Twain looking sexy and self-confident in a leather outfit.

Classic casual coats

Duffle coat

The duffle coat became known in World War II as an army coat, but its history goes much further back. According to the history of fashion there are two forerunners to today's duffle coat: first, the medieval monk's cowl, and second, the 19th-century Polish jacket. Later the duffle coat was also worn by women in the 1940s and 1950s when the British army cleared its stores and sold its surplus equipment to the civilian public. Faithful to the Biblical saying, "A prophet is not without honor except in his own country," the duffle coat achieved cult status not in its country of origin but in France. There in the 1950s it became the uniform of jazz lovers who followed the example of prominent artists and intellectuals. The duffle coat, the symbol of existentialism, went to ground in the 1970s until it was rediscovered by the Italians, where this thick woolen coat was ideal for the harsh winters of

northern Italy. In addition, the fact that it was English was an important feature in the eyes of Italians who are extremely anglophile in all matters of fashion. But in Milan, Florence, and Rome the classic colors of beige and navy were soon complemented by a whole range of crazy colors. In the 1980s, when yuppies began to be interested in Italian fashion, they too discovered the multicolored duffle coats. However, this coat was not condemned to cult status but was accepted as a unisex basic in women's wardrobes. This is why it still appears regularly in the collections of fashion houses, which continue to produce elegant cashmere variations on the old duffle coat theme. In practice, women usually prefer English originals by Gloverall because authenticity and functionality are more important to them than image.

The denim jacket

In the 1990s several items of clothing, originally associated only with the young (including street wear, club wear and sportswear) have become so-called classics, for instance, the denim jacket. Other items such as the previously completely "unacceptable" flip-flops and sneakers will be mentioned in the next chapter. In the 1970s, the denim jacket was still a symbol of adolescent protest, the older and more faded the better, patched and even with the sleeves cut off, and it was worn with the intention of annoying parents. Any girl who actually dared to appear at her confirmation or a graduation party dressed in denim instead of a frilly dress was sure to be greeted with long faces. But today? Now there is nothing more ordinary than the denim jacket. Both society ladies and students wear it to go shopping, often combining it with a Hermès bag and JP Tod's loafers or with a bowling bag and Puma sneakers. It is debatable how long this fashion will last—no-one would be surprised if it stopped tomorrow. But the complete disappearance of the denim jacket is not in sight yet, because it has been shown in the past that once an item of clothing or accessory is really "in," it will never disappear completely. It will recede into the background but it will still be worn, an observation that will reassure all fans of the denim jacket.

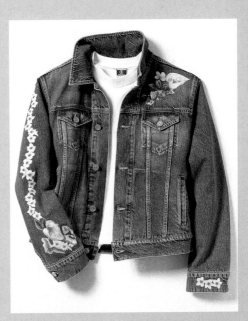

Jeans have been socially acceptable for women for quite a long time but denim jackets only became accepted in the 1990s.

Reefer or pea jacket

Many women found it amusing when in the early 21st century the reefer jacket was introduced as a new trend in coats. She will have remembered this navy blue, double breasted jacket that had been available for many years in small nautical shops. But in spite of its marine appearance it is not certain that its origins are naval. The history of fashion mentions the 14th-century reefer or pea jacket as a possible forerunner, but the short Arab coat is only distantly linked to the reefer jacket of today. It is possible that it has descended from the jacket worn by the British Navy, which is also recognized as the origin of the blazer. Much more important than its history is the question of when a reefer jacket should be worn. It is the ideal garment for leisure wear and smart casual occasions, its mid-thigh length making it ideal for such purposes. But it can also be worn to go to the office because the dark color and straight cut give it a certain uniform-like soberness.

№ 6

Shoes

Delectable shoes
worn by elegant women

The British designer Emma Hope designs shoes that make every woman feel like a queen. But feet, too, have rights, which is why the motto "Regalia for feet" appears on the label.

A perfect appearance starts with the right hairstyle and ends, quite logically, with good, well-polished shoes, suitable for the occasion. Naturally, what lies between also matters. But compared to the large surface area of the outer clothing, the relatively small areas of hair and feet play a very important part in a woman's general appearance. The dreaded "bad hair day" can ruin a beautiful outfit as much as unsuitable shoes. It is therefore well worth while paying particular attention to the head and feet. But while women usually do not change their hairstyle very often, shoes are the variable element in the fashion equation that can change every day. Shoes can add a special touch to an outfit; they must suit the occasion and express the mood.

There are very few women who find buying shoes boring and even fewer who are immune to the magical attraction of elegant pumps or strappy sandals that can transform anyone into a divine creature. Admittedly no-one can run in these adorable shoes, but that does not matter. Who has not bought a pair of irresistibly beautiful shoes simply because they were so lovely, although they probably ended up at the back of the closet because they were not wearable? It is probably because footwear is much more than just an item of practical use that reason often goes right out of the window in a shoe store and practical considerations are pushed to one side with a credit card.

Precious shoes embroidered with gold or crimson motifs used to indicate the social status of a person. In ancient Rome, the wearing of shoes indicated freedom because slaves had to go barefoot. Worn in the manner of an amulet or good-luck charm, shoes were believed to protect the wearer from evil; the custom of keeping a baby's first shoes as a souvenir is reminiscent of this.

Last but not least, shoes are a symbol of eroticism. Shoes represent everything that is feminine and the foot everything that is masculine—there is no need to explain the symbolic meaning of putting on a shoe any further. In this context, the bridal shoe symbolized the virginity of the bride and the custom of drinking champagne from the loved one's shoe, admittedly after several bottles had already been consumed, is still not entirely defunct. Perhaps all this information is still stored in the recesses of our collective memory, but in any event it is certain that shoes fulfill all kinds of functions besides that of keeping our feet warm, comfortable, and dry throughout the day.

Anyone might succumb now and then to the attraction and fascination of a pair of shoes, but most ladies can generally resist the urge. The millionaire's wife who keeps her shoe collection in a walk-in closet the size of an apartment is no more a role model than the Hollywood star who buys a shoe design in all the colors available simply because this or that designer has become a "must have" overnight. But without being a slave to shoe fashion or being driven by the urge to buy everything that catches the eye, the elegant woman will still enjoy the new developments and trends in the world of shoe fashion. She is always looking for that little something that attracted her to the shoes she already has: quality, timelessness, and always a certain degree of comfort.

Admittedly she is quite capable of spending a long evening in high heels, but for everyday wear she prefers comfortable shoes that will not hurt her feet and spoil the day as a result. It is true that the elegant woman is a rather conservative shoe buyer because she is not influenced by every fashion trend. Nevertheless that does not mean that she will disregard good quality and stylish innovations.

If the new season includes nothing acceptable to her she will simply fall back on her own collection of classics that includes models for every situation, ranging from plain black pumps for formal occasions to more dainty strappy sandals for summer parties with friends. Her collection will also include a large number of casual shoes, a custom that goes much further back than the 1990s when smart sportswear became acceptable as everyday wear. Even in the 1920s women had discovered the charm of practical, and at the same time, chic sports shoes that have inspired and influenced fashion since then. In the 1920s and 1930s two-tone spectator shoes were as fashionable as sneakers are today, while in the 1980s Jodhpur boots and boat shoes became the height of fashion. These types of shoes are not appropriate for all occasions and it is obvious they cannot be worn with a little black dress. But they are becoming increasingly acceptable in the world of business, especially in fields like the media and advertising as well as in companies specializing in leisure and lifestyle. Hence, a wine merchant is more likely to wear moccasins or sneakers than pumps to meet her clients. This is also true of the interior architect and antique dealer. Nevertheless sports and leisure shoes are still taboo in many conservative companies and traditional professions.

Slingbacks

In principle, slingbacks or sling pumps are not a category in their own right but a variation on normal pumps. The difference from the basic model lies in the open heel, secured by a strap. This apparently small difference between the conventional, completely closed pumps and the open slingbacks has opened up an entirely new stylistic dimension, the partially-bared foot having a sexy connotation without being too daring for evening wear since the toe part remains covered. But while slingbacks are ideal as elegant going-out shoes they can also be worn at the office, as long as the office does not require strictly formal dress. Obviously they tend to be worn only when the weather is sunny and warm, because the open heel makes them more of a summer shoe.

Pumps

Pumps are the quintessential ladies' shoe, although when they first appeared in the 16th century they had been created especially for men. Basic pumps were widely cut and flat, the thin sole making them suitable only for parquet and marble floors, carpets, and rugs, the floor coverings usually associated with courts, hence the name "court shoes," the alternative English name for pumps. In the 18th century, pumps were made with a thicker sole and sturdy heels so that they could also be worn outdoors. It was also at this time that women discovered pumps for their own use. In the course of the 19th century the heel became increasingly high, eventually reaching its peak in the 20th century. The typical heel for pumps is not the stiletto but the more elegant and practical intermediate form between the flat ballerina shoe and the stiletto.

Shoes for the city

Ballerina shoes

The name "ballerina" clearly reveals the origin of this flat traditional shoe based on the ballet shoe. In the 1950s, the style was made famous by Audrey Hepburn who influenced an entire generation with her love for almost completely flat shoes. The true ballerina shoe is made of fabric, reflecting its origins, and the difference from ballet shoes lies in the sole, which was reinforced to make it strong enough to wear outdoors. Because ballerina shoes can also be considered sports shoes, they are ideal for smart casual wear, and in black velvet or silk they can even be worn in the evening. On the other hand they are rarely worn for going to work. But women who like ballerina shoes need not switch to high heels, because there are also variations on the ballerina shoe with low heels that look like elegant pumps.

High heels

Are stiletto heels really right for the elegant woman? Absolutely, when she wants to show her sexy side. Women have been able to wear high heels since the 1950s, when stiletto shoes first appeared on the runway. The identity of the first manufacturer is not known, but whoever had the idea of enhancing the elegance of pumps by adding a heel was a genius. By the late 1950s practically all women were wearing high heels—in spite of all the warnings about the dangers of slipping and falling, not to mention the damage to floors, everyone loved high heels. However, stiletto heels were soon forbidden in many offices and public buildings because of the damage caused by the points. During the 1960s, the block heel came into fashion, and parquet floors, linoleum, and oriental rugs were safe from stiletto heels for a time. But in the late 1970s, high heels made a comeback, and in the 1980s high heels experienced a second boom as the perfect accompaniment to the broad-shouldered power look of the yuppie era.

Mules

Mules were elegant house shoes worn at certain times of the day. Decorated with marabou feathers, they were the standard footwear for all Hollywood divas of the 1940s and 1950s. The elegant woman had little use for these frivolous shoes because she did not see herself as a vamp, nor did she like the idea of dancing all night in such wobbly shoes. But in the 1990s the opinion of mules changed completely because designers had rediscovered and re-interpreted it. Unlike the earlier models, the new mules were fitted with a low but elegantly curved heel. The new popularity of the open shoe was soon spotted by the manufacturers of casual shoes and soon there were heel-less casual shoes for every situation and social occasion, from business to evening wear and smart casual.

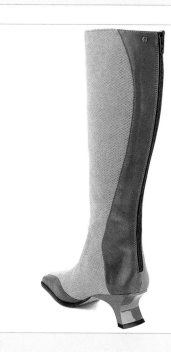

Sandals

Fashionable sandals have very little in common with the sandals worn by the health-conscious—they are more like an "open" version of pumps or high heels with straps or very little upper leather. The construction of the basic sandal is as old as civilization: a sole that is secured to the foot with straps. Elegant women in Egypt were wearing papyrus sandals by 3500 B.C. while in ancient Rome wealthy women wore expensive sandals lavishly decorated with gold leaf. These are just two examples of the amazing variety of sandals found throughout the world. Yet, according to the history of fashion, sandals more or less disappeared after A.D. 1000. It was only in the 20th century, in the 1920s to be exact, that sandals were rediscovered as elegant footwear that is here to stay. The basic idea of securing a sole to the foot as simply as possible, in a manner that also looks attractive, has not altered much through the centuries. The only significant change is in the materials that are now available to shoe designers.

Boots

Most trends come and go in cycles of twenty years, a rule of thumb that has recently proved true of ladies' boots. Having first became popular in the 1830s, in the 20th century boots made a triumphal return in the mini-skirt era and the hippy years of the 1970s, when mini-skirts became longer once more, and they were revived again in the 1990s. Boots varied in height from knee-high to thigh-high according to the skirt length. Knee-high boots were also indispensable with the culottes or divided skirts that were very popular in the late 1970s. These knee-high boots were also available with high heels. Then this look disappeared from the runway to the great regret of many women because, in addition to their horse-riding associations, well-made leather boots were very popular with their combination of warmth and elegance, making them ideal for wearing in cold weather. It is therefore not surprising that women enthusiastically welcomed the return of boots as fashionable footwear in the 1990s.

Mary Janes

Mary Janes are actually children's shoes but their very distinctive shape with flat soles, cross strap and rounded toes has continued to influence designers since the 1960s. Opinions are divided about Mary Janes, but the women who like them are those who prefer flat shoes. But they should be elegant interpretations of the original version because square heels and excessively, wide, rounded toes are rarely becoming. Mary Janes are often made to look like pumps with more pointed toes and a higher heel, but this is rather different from the original. Wearers who appreciate the comfort of wide, flat shoes will prefer the original.

The great shoe designers

There are shoe makers—and there are the great designer shoemakers of the 20th century. Even the least vain women cannot remain unmoved by the sometimes dainty and elegant, sometimes provocative creations that bear a promising signature on the insole. With shoe lovers the name of the master is often synonymous with the product. Every woman would love to have at least one pair of sublime Ferragamos or divine Manolos and would swoon at the creations by Robert Clergerie, Emma Hope, Patrick Cox or Charles Jourdan. Let us now look at some of the gods of the shoe Olympus.

Salvatore Ferragamo

Salvatore Ferragamo was born into a poor southern Italian family in 1898. When he died in 1960 he was rich and famous as result of his craftsmanship. He opened his first shoe store at the tender age of thirteen, at sixteen he traveled to the United States. He worked with unceasing diligence and great creativity in Hollywood to become shoemaker to the stars, and in 1927 he returned to Italy as a self-made man. During the 1930s and 1940s Ferragamo created shoes for the glamorous rich of Europe, constantly surprising women with his new design ideas. In 1935, he launched the wedge heel and in 1938 the platform shoe. His amazing imagination enabled him to overcome the shortage of raw materials during and after World War II, and he made a virtue of necessity by using completely new materials. Salvatore Ferragamo understood his craft and he firmly believed that form should never be at the expense of function. Comfort was always the first requisite. This approach was greatly appreciated by countless VIP ladies, one of the most famous being Audrey Hepburn. In 1954, she traveled to Florence to be measured for shoes in Ferragamo's workshop in the Palazzo Spini Feroni. These first shoes were followed by many other creations until her death in 1993. From 1960 onward, Ferragamo shoes were designed by his daughter Fiamma.

Roger Vivier

There is hardly a Christian Dior enthusiast who does not own at least one pair of shoes by Roger Vivier. Born in 1907, he first trained as a sculptor. Vivier's career started in 1937 when he designed shoes for well-known labels such as I. Miller, Delman, Bally or Rayne. Then for ten years from 1953, he designed shoes to go with the creations of the most famous of all haute couture houses, Christian Dior, and these really made him famous. His designs were innovative in every respect but he always attached great importance to the shape of the heel. The names of the Vivier's various creations are as familiar to shoe lovers as the names of Dior's collections are to haute couture fans: they include Comma, Choc, Louis, Prisme, and Escargot. The list of Vivier's clients includes the rich and famous from all sectors of public life, such as Queen Elizabeth II (who wore one of Vivier's creations for her coronation), the Duchess of Windsor, and Catherine Deneuve, the undisputed divas of the French cinema.

Manolo Blahnik

Manolo Blahnik was born in the Canary Islands in 1942, the son of Czech-Spanish parents. According to legend, he learned the art of shoemaking from his mother. He went to Switzerland to study literature and architecture and later became a stage designer. Shoe design was at this point still a hobby. It is said that it was Diana Vreeland, editor of Vogue, who persuaded him to concentrate exclusively on shoe design. He opened his first store in London in 1973 and soon afterward his shoes could be seen on the runways of leading fashion designers. Blahnik describes himself as the master of the scissors, which accurately expresses his approach to design. It is true to say that his shoes are reduced to a minimum, and the result is always the height of elegance. These exclusive creations are manufactured in Italy and the shoes are rare and sought-after because the factory can only produce limited quantities. The prosperous devotees of Manolo Blahnik's shoes such as Paloma Picasso, Bianca Jagger, and Madonna often order by telephone, frequently by the dozen without even having seen the collection.

Jimmy Choo

Jimmy Choo was born in Malaysia and he started his career as a shoe designer in 1986. At first it was on a very small scale and very exclusive, with two pairs of handmade shoes a day. His filigree designs soon made him the darling of English society. The address of his workshop would have probably remained a well-guarded secret had Princess Diana's shoes not attracted the attention of the press. Suddenly Choo's shoes were considered very trendy, and, to the great distress of his clients, demand far exceeded supply. In 1996, he formed a partnership with the American Tamara Yearday who transformed the name Jimmy Choo into a world-famous label. What actually happened was that Yearday, the wealthy daughter of an entrepreneur (her father was a co-founder of the Vidal Sassoon hairdressing chain), made the shy artist an offer that he could not refuse. Besides introducing a large cash injection, Yearday was enthusiastic about the product and the brand, and she had excellent contacts with the fashion press. The modest beginnings in east London were quickly forgotten as Jimmy Choo boutiques rapidly opened in the most exclusive shopping streets throughout the world. These cater for shoe-crazy women with money, many of them movie stars such as Jodie Foster, Cameron Diaz, Cate Blanchett, Kim Basinger, and Minnie Driver. Together Tamara Yearday and Jimmy Choo have built up the brand into a worldwide success. Off-the-rack shoes are looked after by Tamara Yearday and Sandra Choi, the brand's creative director, while Jimmy Choo oversees the handmade department.

Christian Louboutin

It is possible to argue indefinitely about who should be included in the list of the greatest shoemakers of the 20th century and who should not. But there is no doubt that the first great star of the 21st century is Christian Louboutin. This leading Paris shoe designer is celebrated for his very contemporary fashion concept that makes the shoe the center of the wearer's image and independent from the outfit. As the designer says, "Louboutin shoes will look good both with jeans and with an evening dress." His creativity and highly original ideas have made him the absolute darling of the fashion world in the course of just a few years and his clients include many of the great and famous. There is no doubt that having famous clients such as Catherine Deneuve and Princess Caroline of Monaco is like a knightly accolade because both are known for their excellent fashion sense. Being style icons for millions of magazine readers, these two famous women have undoubtedly contributed to making the Louboutin boutique a local attraction in Paris. The designer says that his earliest inspiration for his own shoe design was the sign in a Paris museum forbidding the wearing of stiletto heels. Later, he also found himself inspired by the shoes worn by chorus girls, whose slingbacks and mules, combined with near-naked bodies, had a fantastically intense effect. Christian Louboutin learned the practical side of his craft from masters such as Charles Jourdan, Maud Frizon, Chanel, and Yves Saint Laurent—designing he had already mastered. Members of the privileged circle of Louboutin clients need no longer travel to his Paris boutique because these highly sought-after creations are now also available in New York

Emma Hope

Emma Hope's irresistible brocade mules have been a hit with women in London since the mid-1980s. Season after season since then, Emma Hope has regaled women with her new, original creations made from a variety of materials such as Nappa leather, suede, velvet, silk and even precious brocade. Emma Hope completed her education at Cordwainers College in 1984 and has since opened three boutiques of her own. In addition, she has also won five Design Council Awards. Emma Hope Shoes are distinctive with their clean lines, stylish look and perfect craftsmanship. A large proportion of her collections is produced in Florence. Besides designing shoes under her own label, Emma Hope has also designed shoes for Anna Sui, Nicole Farhi, Paul Smith and several other fashion designers.

Roger Vivier with one of his creations.

Manolo Blahnik in Madrid, May 2001.

Jimmy Choo with shoe designs by students.

Salvatore Ferragamo with Audrey Hepburn in 1954.

How ladies' shoes are made

Several manufacturing techniques are used in making shoes, ranging from the very expensive to the very simple, from the hand-crafted to the machine-made. Ladies' fashion shoes are usually cemented. Men who are interested in well-made shoes usually react with a wry smile to the mention of cementing, because they will accept nothing less than welted shoes that are sewn together. This technique of cementing is used for filigree pumps and other elegant models because the very thin soles and slender shape makes it very difficult to use a welt. This does not mean that there are no welted pumps, but they are extremely rare and very expensive.

The slender silhouette of the shoe is one of several reasons for using glue instead of a welted construction. Fashion shoes are only worn for a relatively short time so a hard-wearing construction is not really necessary. In addition, the orthopedic advantages of welted shoes are rather diminished by the basically uncomfortable shape of pumps and stilettos, so there is no real reason not to attach the sole with glue. Cementing only involves the sole, at least in the case of high quality models. The manufacture of the upper part of the shoe may be as expensive as that of a welted shoe, and it may be even be more complicated because of the very fine materials used.

The heart and starting-point of the shoe is the last. This is a special foot-shaped mold made of wood or synthetic material. Shoe factories have lasts for every model, every height of heel, and of course in many sizes. The number of lasts held depends on the manufacturing methods and capacity of the company. For each client, the craftsman shoemaker who makes every shoe individually only needs one last for each model and heel shape. Large factories, on the other hand, will need dozens or even hundreds of lasts if they mass produce shoes. Makers of made-to-measure shoes will have an individual, personal last for each client, while manufacturers of mass-produced shoes use the wide range of sizes and models that are pro-duced by specialist last manufacturers such as Fagus, a traditional company based near Hanover, Germany.

When creating a new shoe, the designer is first guided by his idea. Translating the vision into reality on the last plays no part at the start of the creative process. Nevertheless, the designer will look at the last shapes available on the market because they reflect the long-term trends. These changing trends could be reflected, for instance, in the shape of the toe cap, which may be round, square, or pointed. Inspired by this, the designer prepares the first sketches, which at the end of the first stage are translated into an accurate drawing. This design is then transferred onto a last and a two-dimensional pattern of the upper is created from it. This is what is known as the model pattern.

Now the upper leather is selected and cut out. With quality shoes, this is still done by hand, since the separate parts of the model pattern must be positioned on the leather with the greatest care. This is first to avoid any faults in the leather itself and secondly to take account of the stretching direction of the leather. The front piece, that is, the part for the toes and the instep, must be cut longitudinally, and the side pieces at an angle. This is very important so that the shoe can move with the foot without losing its shape. The parts are always cut in pairs and from the same piece of leather to ensure that the left and right shoes look exactly the same.

The next stage is the preparation of the leather. Marks are made on the leather to indicate to the stitcher where the individual pieces should be joined together. If the design calls for it, any openwork is punched out and the edges finished, for instance by pinking or by adding piping, and if necessary re-dyed. In order to prevent unsightly bulges forming at the seams where the leather is double, the edges are scarfed, that is, thinned along the edges. In the past this used to be done by hand but this process is now carried out by machine. The pieces are then sewn together. The finished upper is then joined to the lining, at first only along the sides because otherwise it would not be possible to add the reinforcements at the toes and heel. The eyelets, if any, are added at the very end.

Up to now the leather object has very little in common with a shoe but this will change at the next stage because now the last comes into play. Because the insole will later be put in the shoe, it is first attached to the underside of the last. Then the body of the shoe is slipped onto the last, the projecting edges being turned over the underside of the insole and secured. Before mechanization was introduced, the shoemaker had to mold the body of the shoe around the last. This operation used to require great strength and skill, but today this stage is mechanized and takes only a few seconds. The shoe is now almost finished. Only the outer sole and the heel are missing. Before these are added, a metal reinforcement is added from the heel to the ball of the foot to prevent the shoe from snapping or bending in the middle. Then the outer sole can be cemented on and the heel attached. Very high heels have a metal core so that they can survive the great strain they are under when walked on. The final task is the cleaning stage when the shoes are cleaned and polished. They are then sent to the dispatch department where they are given a final check before being packed and sent off. Soon afterwards they will be in the stores where they will tempt shoe lovers everywhere.

The leather is selected in the storeroom, which is kept at a relative humidity of 65%.

Cutting the uppers. It is vital that the leather of both shoes should look identical.

The soles are punched from sheets of hard tanned leather using a punching machine.

Inevitably some wastage of the leather cannot be avoided in punching out the soles.

The base of the shoe is spread with glue. The sole is glued on and left for 20 minutes to dry.

The heel is screwed onto the shoe and the fixing is then reinforced with nails.

A cushioned inner sole is fixed inside the shoe to prevent any contact with the heel fixing.

The completed shoe is carefully cleaned to remove all traces of glue and dust.

Up to 130 different operations are involved in each pair of shoes that is manufactured by Peter Kaiser. Established in 1838, it is Germany's oldest shoe factory.

The materials from which dream shoes are made

In the history of footwear, people have used almost any available material to make shoes. These include sandals made from papyrus, bark, hemp or flax, boots from animal skins, wooden clogs, elegant slippers made of velvet and brocade, and modern footwear made from various synthetic materials. But the most important and most popular raw material used to make shoes is still leather in its numerous varieties.

Calfskin

Calfskin, also known as calf or box calf, is the most valued type of cowhide because the skins of young animals make a particularly soft, supple, fine leather that is free of grain defects. Calf's leather is a byproduct of slaughterhouses, which is why it is relatively inexpensive. If vegetarians were to become the majority at some time, the calf's leather that is readily available today would soon become a rare, exotic commodity.

Cowhide

Cowhide is the skin of mature bovine animals. It is much tougher and thicker than calfskin, just as beefsteak is less tender than veal fillet. Consequently ladies' shoes are seldom made of cowhide, which is normally used to make country shoes and sturdy boots.

Horse leather

Horse leather only began to be used to make ladies' shoes in the 1980s when manufacturers of men's welted shoes also started to produce shoes for women. Like cowhide, horse leather is obviously a byproduct because horses are not bred for their skin. Horse leather became much more expensive when draft horses and working horses were replaced by automobiles and machines.

Pigskin

Pigskin is used mainly to make gloves, for which the skin of the South American water hog is usually preferred. But the ordinary domestic pig also produces leather with an interesting structure, mostly used for shoes.

Antelope leather

The leather from antelopes, chamois, deer, and other cloven-hoofed animals are all classed together under the generic term buckskin. This is mostly used to make sports loafers and sneakers.

Goatskin

Goatskin is traditionally used to make gloves and also luxury shoes. It is especially popular as velour leather, often combined with smooth leather.

Crocodile

Exotic leathers such as crocodile have a similar image problem to fur. But in the end there is no difference whether it is the skin of a calf, a crocodile or an alligator. Anyone who does not reject leather as a matter of principle can also enjoy crocodile skin shoes, provided that the skin is from farmed crocodile and not from a protected species in the wild. The price of crocodile leather depends on which part of the animal it comes from. Considerably less expensive than real crocodile are imitations made from embossed cowhide or calfskin.

Lizard

Lizard skin or snakeskin is not always popular with women. Most women only remember its existence when it comes back into fashion. Before these thin skins can be made into shoes, they are stuck onto calfskin because they are not sturdy enough on their own.

Ostrich

Ostrich skin is not one of the most popular types of leather, but the exclusive status of ostrich makes it all the more sought after. With its characteristic thickened sections, ostrich only became known to the general public in the late 1990s when shoe designers used it for sneakers and loafers. However, what looks like ostrich is often imitation since real ostrich skin is quite expensive.

Suede leather

Suede leather has a rough top surface that is in fact the underside of the skin, which is used inside out. In fact, any leather could be used as suede although usually the lesser qualities of leather are preferred for this "inside out" treatment. The logic is that it would be a waste to conceal a perfect outer surface inside a shoe. In addition, sports shoes made of suede often do not need to be lined because the smooth outside is sufficiently soft and comfortable.

Nubuck

At first glance Nubuck looks like suede leather but there is a substantial difference. In the case of Nubuck it is not the underside of the leather that is used outside; it is instead the outer surface itself that is roughened. Nubuck looks and feels different from suede; it is smoother and firmer.

Patent leather

Patent leather has a hard, highly glossy surface created by lacquer. It is not made from the highest quality leather because it would be a waste to conceal the surface of a beautiful hide under a layer of lacquer. Patent leather has a place in the shoe closet because pumps, ballerina shoes and sneakers in patent leather are real classics.

Fish skin

It may be hard to believe but shoes can also be made from fish skin. It is true that the average shoe manufacturer would seldom make pumps from the skin of a carp or a ray, but it is not so unusual for shoe designers to use such exotic materials. Made-to-measure shoes are also sometimes made from these interesting materials. Being very thin, fish skins are glued onto stronger kinds of leather to give the necessary strength before being made into shoes.

Nappa

Nappa leather is mainly used to make bags and leather jackets as well as boots and shoes. It takes its name from the city of Napa, California, where it was first made, and it refers to the manufacturing process rather than to a particular kind of leather. This technique involves the processing of soft, scarred leather that is "unskived," meaning that the skin is not cut into thin layers beforehand. The result is a dyed-through, washable material that is ideal for high boots.

Fabric

Fabric is a very traditional material for ladies' shoes. Indeed, until the late 19th century upperclass women wore fabric shoes almost exclusively. That these delicate shoes were quite unsuited for walking on rough pavements or along a sandy country lane was unimportant because women mostly stayed indoors. Even today, fabric is still a popular alternative to leather, especially for elegant pumps or mules that now have a sturdy enough sole to walk outside. Women who prefer not to polish shoes will be better off with fabric shoes. But stains and dirt from the street are more troublesome with fabric shoes than with leather ones.

Horse leather is expensive which is why it is only used on sturdy, longlasting welted shoes.

The right shoes for the right outfit

Men have an easy task: their shoes are brown or black and if the colors match, the rest is easy. Women have a slightly harder task in getting the combination right, or so it appears at first glance because there are so many types of shoes and colors. To try and achieve a perfect match between the color and model of the shoes and the rest of the outfit is an almost hopeless task. In fact, this is unnecessary because there is an easy ground rule that should overrule any complicated system of combinations: the color, material and style of the shoe should match the clothes, accessories, and circumstances. But even this simple ground rule leaves one vital question unanswered: what matches and what does not?

It does not matter whether you first choose a skirt, dress, sweater or trousers from the closet and then select matching shoes, or whether you choose the shoes first and then pick the clothes. The main requirement is that they go together. Whether the effect is striking or subdued depends on whether the shoes and clothes contrast with each other or are in harmony. Red shoes and a red dress would produce a perfectly harmonious result while a white, green or black dress with red shoes would produce an interesting contrast.

While the color of the shoes may contrast with that of the clothes, the handbag should be the same color as the shoes—"should" because there are some exceptions, but on the whole it is a sound basic rule. For instance, if you wear red pumps you should have a red bag. So far so good! But does this mean that you should always buy matching shoes and bag? Not at all, because shoes and bag should only be similar in color and material, not absolutely identical. For instance, you could easily wear wine-red velvet mules with a Bordeaux red leather bag. This means that you can also successfully combine bag and shoes made of different materials and slightly differ-

ent shades and still achieve an excellent result. Matching the individual parts of the outfit is one thing, but matching the clothes and shoes to the occasion is another. The apple-green slingbacks may look wonderful with the light green beaded silk bag, but they will not be appropriate for the business meeting with your besuited colleagues at the office. An etiquette book is not needed to figure this out, common sense should be quite enough. Common sense is always the best guide when it comes to dress sense. For instance, loud, brightly colored shoes are as unsuitable in the office and on festive or serious occasions, as patterned leather shoes or sneakers. Women who work in conservative professions should display some restraint, while those working in creative jobs can afford to be more relaxed in their approach. This is not a license to dress in anything you like, but in a colorful, smart-casual way.

It is not only the color of the shoes that may be dictated by etiquette, for the shape and type are important too. In spite of the relaxation in dress codes, the rule about open toes and slingbacks not being "respectable" is still valid. So in theory mules would not be the right shoes to wear with a business outfit because they expose the naked heel. According to traditional conventions, slingbacks with open toes also show too much skin. However, pumps that are not too low-cut will be acceptable to even the strictest guardians of convention. As far as evening wear is concerned, it is the occasion that determines whether these restrictions apply or not. The shoes worn at a relaxed party attended mainly by young people will naturally be more revealing than shoes worn to the opera. Last but not least, it also depends on how presentable your feet are. However, here too it is a matter of common sense, because shoe fashions are constantly creating new boundaries with their fashion trends. Whether women also want to wear their new mules in the office is really up to them. In the end, rules are made to be broken—but only if it is done with style.

A perfect combination in a Falke advertisement. The way the exotic leather picks up the color of the coat is particularly sophisticated.

The VIPs of the shoe closet

Like clothes, shoes also include some famous classics that are immediately recognizable. Many of these classics have a long history in the course of which they have changed very little, at most only in minor details in order to reflect contemporary taste. Although copied thousands of times, the "real thing" is still at the top of every shoe lover's wish list, even though they are more expensive. One of the legendary classics that every woman would probably like to own are the two-tone Chanel pumps. These made their debut on the world fashion stage in 1957, three years after Coco Chanel, then aged 70, had re-opened her couture house. At an age when even the most creative designers are planning their retirement, this legendary fashion grande dame launched her famous Chanel suit. She asked the shoe designer Raymond Massaro to design matching two-tone shoes that first came on the market as relatively low-heeled slingbacks. The color scheme was extremely refined because not only was it reminiscent of the sporty look of spectator shoes—Coco Chanel's favorite shoes during the 1920s and 1930s—but the black toe caps made the feet look smaller and more slender. The light-colored heel, back and sides of the shoes had the visual effect of lengthening the legs. Today this model is still produced in numerous versions with different heel heights, from stiletto to ballerina shoe. But whatever kind you own, they are still as wearable today as they were in 1957.

Another star of the shoe closet are the Vara pumps created by the house of Ferragamo, the most successful ladies' shoes of all times. They were designed by Fiamma Ferragamo, the eldest daughter of the legendary shoe designer Salvatore Ferragamo, who took over the running of the company after the death of the famous shoemaker in 1960. She ran it very successfully together with her mother and five sisters, making it what it is today: a fashion house offering a total look from head to toe. The talented Fiamma designed the Vara in the late 1970s. The basic idea was to create shoes that were elegant and timeless but also easy to wear. Consequently, the Vara was given the narrow shape of classic pumps, although not as close-fitting, and a low heel. The rep bow secured by a gold buckle gave them the special touch that turned them into status symbols. This decorative element continued the tradition of pumps as reinterpretations of ball shoes, giving the Vara their special touch, just as the snaffle bit did for Gucci loafers.

Thus we arrive at a real VIP shoe that was the quintessential casual society footwear in the 1970s and 1980s: the Gucci moccasin with the unmistakable snaffle bit as decoration. The original model was a unisex flat loafer that was available in a wide range of colors and types of leather. Interestingly, this classic shoe was not designed by an actual shoe maker but by a leather specialist. The company was founded in Florence in 1904 by Guccio Gucci and specialized in saddlery. In the 1960s, this Italian counterpart of Hermès in France became the darling of the international jet set, whose members would stop over in Italy to buy Gucci suitcases, travel bags, handbags, leather accessories, shoes, and silk scarves. The Gucci designs were immediately identifiable through the green-red-green house colors that were present as a ribbon on most accessories, and from 1960 the snaffle bit on the loafers had also become a key motif. The decorative element, reminiscent of saddlery and therefore of the origins of the company, was later used on pumps and elegant models of ladies' shoes. The original Gucci loafers still remain as flat moccasins.

Top right: The celebrated Vara by Ferragamo is an elegant combination of high-heeled pumps and flat ballerina shoes.

Right: The two-tone look has been the distinctive trademark of Chanel shoes since 1957. This one is a variation with laces.

Far right: In the pre-Tod's era, Gucci loafers were the smart leisure footwear of the international jet set.

Leisure classics

Ladies' leisure shoes are relatively recent protagonists in the history of fashion. First people had to make time for leisure and then they had to discover activities to fill these leisure hours in an interesting and amusing way. The development of shoes in which women could run began in the late 19th century. At the time emancipated women wore the so-called "trotteurs," ankle-high lace-up boots or walking shoes with a wide, low, heel, inspired by the male sports shoe. These comfortable walking shoes were used for cycling and playing tennis. Women who wanted to go on walking holidays could buy special ladies' hiking shoes.

But the true century of leisure was undoubtedly the 20th century. Besides walking shoes, women now also began to wear moccasins and loafers. In addition, the world of leisure fashion began to be invaded by real sports shoes. It is true that in 1868 the inventor Heinrich Franck had already developed a forerunner to the sneaker, made of leather and fabric, but specialized sports shoe manufacturers did not emerge until the early 20th century. These included the Converse company (the famous All Star dates from 1917) and the international brand Adidas, which Adi and Rudi Dassler founded in 1923. Since the 1970s sports shoes have been an integral part of everyday life. Casual shoes have been part of fashion for a long time, and there are now very chic sneakers that would not look out of place combined with the most expensive casual weekend look.

It is important that even leisure shoes should match one's outfit. The rule of thumb is that the more formal the look, the less casual the shoes should be. The most suitable are the classic models in muted colors. White tennis shoes and bright sneakers look better with sportswear of the same kind. Leisure shoes usually look heavier than pumps and other similar footwear. This optical effect should be reflected in the clothes, which should balance the shoes by being made from rather thick, possibly patterned fabric. Or the contrast can be deliberately emphasize by wearing heavy boots with a light summer dress as young women sometimes do.

The penny loafer made its first appearance in the U.S.A. in the 1930s but it only became really popular as ladies' shoes in the 1950s. Schoolgirls and students used to slip a cent or penny under the strap, which is what gave the shoes their nickname. They are an indispensable accessory in the classic American East Coast look of chinos, polo shirt and cotton pullover as well as in the college look.

Women often like to borrow items from their partner's wardrobe. One of the best examples are the sturdy lace-up boots whose design is inspired by the boots worn by lumberjacks and people who live in the country in North America. The boots followed deck shoes to Europe because manufacturers of deck shoes also offered boots with soles with heavy treads. One of the best-known brands is Timberland, which has became the symbol of American off-road footwear—although it is usually worn in the city.

Canvas sneakers with rubber soles were invented in the late 19th century but their use only became general in 1917, at first only in America under the Keds label. Today in the United States Keds have become synonymous with inexpensive canvas shoes and have remained very popular. In southern Europe, light sneakers are often worn instead of summer shoes or beach sandals. They only became a trendy leisure accessory in 1980s when the Italians launched Superga, their interpretation of the sneaker or plimsoll. But these models all have the same disadvantage, whether expensive or not: feet get very hot in them.

Deck shoes have been around for decades, quietly carrying out their duties on deck, until they suddenly came into the limelight in the early 1980s. The original was the Topsider by Sperry. Timberland's "Classic Boat" is another well-known classic. Women fell in love with the sailing shoe because it combined comfort with the elitism associated with yachting. Although moccasins and expensive sneakers have now replaced deck shoes, they still have their fans.

Rubber boots

Could anyone imagine Simone Veil, the elegant former president of the European parliament, walking through muddy fields wearing rubber boots? Hardly. On the other hand, one could certainly picture the Duchess of Kent in this situation, because like many upper-class English women, she looks just as much at home in jeans, a sweater and rubber boots for a weekend in the country as in an evening dress and a tiara. But the green rubber boots that the British almost lovingly call "wellies," short for Wellington boots, are not only worn in the country. Indeed, it is not an unusual sight to see people wearing green wellies when it rains in west London neighborhoods such as Chelsea. Nevertheless, gardens, fields, and country lanes remain the true stomping grounds of Wellington boots. The entrance hall of an English country house would be quite unthinkable without its characteristic array of wellies, as typical as the Range Rover parked outside the house. Besides being invaluable when taking part in field sports, walking in the fields or shopping at the market, rubber boots are also useful when going out in the evening, enabling the wearer to walk through puddles, mud, and wet grass without damaging their elegant footwear. So in Great Britain people are not surprised to see female guests arrive at a dinner party wearing wellies that they then remove and replace with their pumps.

The city dwellers of mainland Europe, on the other hand, could hardly behave in this manner, because when they go out in the evening in bad weather they call a taxi that takes them directly from their home to their destination. Rubber boots with an evening dress? Unthinkable. But country dwellers from Stockholm to Palermo will understand British women's love for green wellies much better, not only because of the general similarity in the infrastructure, but also because of the widespread anglophile tendency of country society. For the same reason, all the other components of English bad-weather

At Christmas time, the famous green wellies from Hunter's are also available in festive colors. Season's greetings!

gear, especially the Barbour jacket, are also very popular. Having said this, when going for a walk in the rain in a park in Paris, Milan or Zurich, ladies display a little more elegance than their British cousins. Wearing wellies for a walk in the Bois de Boulogne is undoubtedly acceptable, but they are likely to be an elegant leather-lined version by a well-known French hunting outfitter, or even by Hermès. Similarly, in Italy in the fall, bright yellow rubber boots on the dripping wet asphalt of the Via della Spiga add the right touch of color to a dark blue Barbour jacket, and thus justifies the investment in every respect.

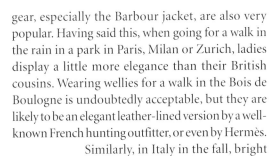

The best rubber boots

Le Chameau
As well as being the home of outstanding wine and exquisite food, France also has an excellent reputation for its high quality rubber boots. Based in Normandy, Le Chameau has been producing boots by hand since 1927. These are made from natural rubber, leather, and cotton jersey.

Hunter
Hunter is the symbol of the British rubber boot par excellence and it has been produced by the Gates Rubber Company in Scotland since 1856. The brand owes its legendary fame to the high quality of manufacture and finish, and to the excellent fit of the product.

Superga
Rubber boots from Italy? Of course, because the weather in northern Italy is much wetter than visitors might expect after visiting there in the summer. The sporty collections offered by Superga clearly demonstrate that function and elegance are not mutually exclusive in waterproof footwear.

Aigle
France may be a republic but its bourgeoisie still knows how to live stylishly in the country. When hunting or walking in the gardens of the elegant chateaux, rubber boots by Aigle are the indispensable accompaniment to the Loden coat by Mettez.

Nokia
Most people associate Nokia exclusively with cellular telephones. But in Finland, women also know the company as a manufacturer of sturdy rubber boots that protect the feet from the cold and snow while also keeping them very warm.

Handmade rubber boots

Those who have not inherited their rubber boots or simply found them in the cellar of the country house they have just bought (in Great Britain these are two quite typical ways of acquiring rubber boots) often wonder about the high price asked for new ones. Few people realize that the best rubber boots are still made by hand. As in the case of leather shoes, a last—in this case boot-shaped—is needed to make a rubber boot. The boot is built up from the inside out, layer by layer around the last. In standard models the inner sole is placed first on the boot last, followed by the fabric or leather lining and finally by the individual parts of the latex rubber outer shell.

When the boot has been completely assembled, it is warmed in order to make all the seams water-resistant and harder-wearing. Inevitably the process is an expensive one but this is reflected in the long life that may be expected of a pair of boots made in this way.

Welted shoes for ladies

The founders of the Crockett & Jones shoe factory: Sir James Crockett (left) and Charles Jones. Today the company is still owned by the Jones family.

At Crockett & Jones the upper leather is still cut out as it was at the beginning of the 20th century: namely by hand.

How can a businesswoman concentrate on work when her feet hurt? Her male colleagues are much better off in their welted Oxfords or brogues because they are comfortable and healthy for the feet as well as elegant. But what can the woman do except suffer in silence if dainty pumps are the only shoes that looks right with her business suit? Fortunately, with smart casual wear there are alternatives to the elegant but uncomfortable pumps, the most traditional being hand-crafted welted shoes. The models in question are clearly inspired by men's shoes but several manufacturers offer more than just a reduced, female version of men's brogues. These hand-crafted shoes have all the advantages of their male counterparts. The layer of cork placed under the insole soon takes on the shape of the foot so that the shoes can be worn for a long time without discomfort. Meanwhile the upper supports the foot firmly because it is stitched to the insole and the welt.

England is still one of the best sources of welted shoes. The best-known manufacturers are in Northampton, the center of the English shoe industry. Crockett & Jones was founded in 1879 and it is one of the few manufacturers that have always made ladies' shoes as well as men's. The collection includes over 25 models in black and various shades of brown. Women who love the

Many anglophiles would not know where they would be without their tassel loafers, because they are as well suited to jeans or corduroy pants as to pleated skirts or kilts.

The "Yarmouth" is a classic summer shoe in the U.S.A. and Europe, very popular with doctors as an alternative that is preferred to Birkenstocks by some.

English look will find oxfords, loafers and ankle boots with the most evocative names for almost every occasion.

For instance, Heyford black lace-up shoes would look great with gray flannel trousers and blazers, and Naseby brown tassel loafers would go very well with straight cotton trousers and a pale blue button-down shirt. In addition to producing welted shoes for business and leisure purposes, Crockett & Jones also offers something for special situations. For instance, horsewomen will find ankle-length riding boots here, and doctors will be attracted by white Nubuk lace-ups such as the Yarmouth.

The "Heyford" shoe from Crockett & Jones is a typical Derby, recognizable by the open lacing with which the sides are drawn over the tongue.

The custom-made shoe

Until World War I it was customary for wealthy women to have most of their shoes custom made, although small factories were already producing good quality shoes in the late 19th century. Shoe workshops produced a wide range of footwear including fine pumps, sturdy lace-ups, boots, and various types of sports shoes. Today very few women have their shoes made to measure. This is partly due to the fact that it is now possible to buy shoes of outstanding quality by famous designers in ordinary shoe stores, and partly because rapidly changing fashion trends make it easier to buy "off-the-rack" shoes. Very few women would be prepared to invest in custome-made shoes that would most likely be outmoded after only two seasons. Those who still like to indulge in custom-made shoes usually choose classic models, inspired by men's shoes, such as penny loafers and tassel loafers, Derbys, monkstraps, or brogues.

The time between ordering and delivery of custom-made shoes is the same in all great houses, whether it be in London, Paris, Rome or Vienna. Before the last-maker even looks at the client's feet and measures them, he discusses the design with her. Whether lace-ups or mules, it is more than a matter of taste so far as he is concerned because each model needs a slightly different last. Then the feet are measured, separately and very carefully. Nobody's feet are ever exactly the same size and build, and unlike factory-made shoes the master shoemaker can take these small differences into account, thus increasing the wearer's comfort. First, he draws an outline of the feet. To do this, the client places her feet on a piece of paper and the last-maker outlines the feet with a pencil held perpendicularly. He marks possible problem areas, for instance sensitive spots, on the drawing with hatchings and short notes. He then determines other parameters such as the plantar arch, the height of the instep, the position of the ankle, and so on. Some makers also take impressions of the foot on carbon paper in order to determine the stepping surface. The last can now be built on the basis of all these data. It is an accurate wooden representation of the feet around which the shoe is built. The first attempt is only provisional because new clients usually get a test shoe, made of leather. Only when this prototype has met all the requirements of both parties does the work on the actual shoes start.

The bespoke shoemaker Lobb of London also makes ladies' shoes. Its sturdy brogues and classic loafers are particularly popular.

A holiday for the feet

Moccasins? Espadrilles? Loafers? Ballerina shoes? The "Bethan" summer, beach, and holiday shoe by Clarks is a little bit of everything.

Beautiful shoes are uncomfortable and comfortable shoes are not beautiful—that is the experience of most women throughout almost the whole history of fashion. In the Middle Ages men and women of the aristocracy had to put up with the discomforts of pointed shoes. Knights wore such elongated, pointed shoes that the points had to be bent upward and attached to the shins. The lady of the castle wore slightly shorter shoes that nevertheless often caught in the hem of her dress, especially if she was hurrying to a tournament or to meet her minnesinger.

In the 16th century shoe fashion moved away from the unisex concept and developed separate men's and ladies' shoes. But this development backfired for women, since the first true ladies' shoe was the "chopine," a platform sandal with a height of two feet. That no one could run in these shoes did not affect their popularity. When walking the lady would lean on her male companion (who was secure in his men's shoes) or her maid (who would have been wearing sturdy but practical leather boots).

The Clarks "Natalie" lace-up moccasin may not be as elegant as pumps but it is much more comfortable. It particularly popular with young ladies.

Trends came and went but feet remained sore. At the end of the 19th century, the newspapers were full of advertisements for foot preparations of all kinds, miracles cures for corns, calluses, blisters, pressure points, deformed toes, and so on. In reality, not much has changed since those days. Every drugstore and supermarket stocks a vast range of creams, sprays, tinctures, and special bandages to alleviate sore feet.

Women's desire for comfortable, warm shoes that could be worn in the house while going about their chores goes back a long time. Since the 15th century slippers or mules that were cozy, and easy to put on have been worn as house shoes. Originally from Persia, these simple forms of footwear soon spread through Italy to France and Germany. The slipper or mule was a "sensible" unspectacular shoe that was more suited for wearing at home than at court.

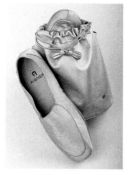

Who would want to wear toweling slippers in a hotel? These ballerina travel shoes are much better for the purpose.

The long tradition of the house shoe has survived. Almost every woman has a pair of old slippers near the front door that she looks forward to wearing when she comes home in the evening. What type of slipper she prefers is naturally a matter of taste. As children many women had to wear dreadful (and even then uncool) children's slippers, the most horrible being the unsightly slippe-r-socks, so that slippers of every kind have become unpopular. But even slipper-haters have their favorites for relaxing in, such as a pair of Donna Karan plastic sandals from last summer, old worn Tod's loafers, or frayed espadrilles from a summer holiday in Sardinia many years ago.

The main thing is that they should not look like slippers.

These light raffia sandals, mules and loafers by Gabriela Ligenza are perfect for hot summer days. Raffia is the fiber obtained from the raffia palm or palm tree.

Velvet slippers

While your partner tries on the tenth pair of welted shoes at Edward Green or Church's in Burlington Arcade in London, try and make good use of your time instead of getting bored. For instance, you could go and buy a pair of slippers at Berk's, a few yards away. There is no doubt that you will be the object of much envy. The easiest choice is a pair of plain velvet slippers that are available in a wide range of colors. But those who prefer more decorative footwear could choose an embroidered design. If you do not like any of the 20 motifs that include crowns, unicorns, pheasants, stylized flowers, hearts, fish, foxes, ducks, and leopards, you can always order a special motif. In principle, the store will embroider anything that the client would like. Coats of arms and initials are particularly popular. Naturally, such special orders have their price and they are really too good for wearing only in the house.

Flip-flops

Flip-flops are pure minimalism—anything less and it would be called walking barefoot. They are said to have been invented in the 1940s by US soldiers on active service in the Pacific. Since then they have become the most popular beach, holiday, and garden shoe in the English-speaking world. For many years European women disliked flip-flops because they considered them not very elegant and more suitable for surfers and beach volleyball players. But in the late 1990s these rubber sandals became a common sight in the elegant seaside resorts along the Mediterranean as well as in city centers from Stockholm to Lisbon. Working women who spend all the day in their pumps are very happy about this because they appreciate these comfortable yet modern shoes for wearing in their leisure time.

Espadrilles

The espadrille is the perfect example of how women combine simplicity with elegance—indeed it is hard to imagine anything simpler than a shoe made from raffia and linen. Even so, sophisticated women will wear espadrilles at Mediterranean seaside resorts with the same grace and elegance as the most luxurious mules. Espadrilles were discovered in Spain in the 1920s by the earliest sun-worshipers. They wore them with shorts and T-shirts or elegant cotton trousers. Espadrilles also looked very good with the Capri pants of the 1950s and 1960s. In spite of their Mediterranean connections, espadrilles are actually landlubbers because water can be fatal to their soles made of plant fibers. But their low cost compensates for this deficiency because you can easily buy a new pair for little more than loose change.

Clogs

An elegant woman in clogs? Yes, for gardening or going to the market on Saturday. It is certainly possible that a sophisticated woman might take off her elegant shoes and put on some clogs to do some gardening, especially in northern Europe. She will probably change into old clothes to weed the vegetable garden and cycle to the bakery to buy bread. Clogs became fashionable for a short while in the 1970s, but the flower-power version with red patent leather decorated with flowers held no appeal for the more sophisticated woman. She does not see clogs as a fashion accessory, but more as useful footwear. This is why she always chooses an original model, like the Dutch "Klompenmaker" Oerlemans

Modern classics: J. P. Tod's

There are inventions that after a short while we believe we could not live without. What we did before they existed is barely conceivable. In the 1980s, this was the case with the Walkman and in the 1990s, with the cell phone. However, this phenomenon is not exclusively restricted to electronics; it also occurs in the world of fashion. The best example are the moccasins with the little bumps on the sole, better known as Tod's. At the end of the 1980s, they appeared in magazines, having become the trendy "in" shoes

of the rich and famous. By the following decade they had established themselves as the chic leisure shoe of the sophisticated woman.

Tod's were not a really new concept when Diego Della Valle launched them in 1979. Their moccasin construction was a traditional one, the upper part reminiscent of the penny loafer. Even the sole with bumps was not new, having already been used in automobile driver's shoes in the 1960s and 1970s. But Tod's were not supposed to be just the latest creation, but rather the product of a tradition-rich brand. First, because the English name with initials before it, along with the presentation of the script and logo suggest authenticity. Second, because of the pictorial motifs of the advertisements showed stars of the 1950s and 1960s. The fact that the actors on the posters did not wear Tod's but merely similar loafers did not seem to matter. The advertising campaign created a particular image and inspired confidence. How and why did not matter to Tod's fans.

But it was not only advertising that caused Tod's to be accepted as a brand by discriminating clients. The inexorable triumphant progress was also helped by Diego Della Valle's clever public relations strategy. According to legend, he would give his precious moccasins free to VIPs and famous people who were then photographed wearing Tod's by the paparazzi. Whether this is true or not no one knows for certain, but it certainly resulted in extra publicity because this story was told over and over again. In any case Diego Della Valle succeeded in establishing a completely unknown product of no more than average quality as a very successful "must-have" item. Admittedly, this did not happen overnight but it took less than ten years, and it has become permanent because Tod's success has not abated. Tod's loafers have piled up in women's cupboards: in brown, black, white, red, yellow and green, in smooth leather, velour or exotic leather, with a heel or with a completely flat leather sole.

As well as varying his successful approach, Diego Della Valle has constantly added new models. As a result, there are now Tod's loafers for every season and almost every leisure activity. Women will even wear the original Tod's in the office and in the evening—after all this is the right time for the black patent leather model. Yet these exclusive loafers remain associated with a casual image, as illustrated by Princess Diana on a visit to Angola in January 1997 during her campaign against land mines.

With his famous loafers Diego Della Valle has succeeded in achieving what many fashion designers strive in vein to achieve: the creation of a classic.

Each shoe is given its final finish by repeated applications of different-colored wax polishes, followed by polishing. This stage is carried out by hand.

The wide range of colors makes it possible to have a matching pair of Tod's loafers for every outfit.

Sneakers with style

Andrea and Giuseppe Santoni make sure that every shoe produced in their factory meets the highest standards of quality. This is true not only of their classic models but also of the sneakers in their Club collection.

Only the Italians could come up with such an idea: take ordinary sneakers, replace the plastic and nylon with leather and natural rubber, and instead of joining the materials together with glue, use needle and thread as would be done with traditional footwear. The result is a perfect synthesis of the sneaker and the elegant loafer. Santoni, a family-run company situated in the heart of Italy, did precisely this to produce the hand-crafted sneakers of the Club collection. Produced in the Marches, the center of Italy's shoe-manufacturing industry, these sneakers only resemble ordinary ones in superficial appearance and performance. The differences lie in the luxurious details: first-quality leather, cut and polished by hand, a breathable leather inner sole, and natural rubber outer soles. The use of such fine materials for casual shoes may seem a little over the top. But it is this combination of first-class materials and lavish finish that explains the high prices of these luxury loafers. The Santoni philosophy is to pay as much attention as possible to each item produced. This uncompromising attitude is quite unusual today

Many ladies carry a pair of Santoni sneakers in their bag, to take the pressure off their feet when they are aching from their high heels!

and has almost completely disappeared outside Italy. The quality-obsessed cobblers in Corridonia do not care about this, the high standards of workmanship are kept up by everyone in the factory.

Although luxury sneakers are an Italian invention, their history started in America in the late 1970s when fitness almost became a civic duty among the rich and famous. The body-conscious woman would put on a T-shirt, sweatpants and running shoes to go running in her local park early in the morning before changing into a business suit and pumps to go to the office. Because high heels are not particularly suited to the sidewalks of Wall Street, more and more women go to work wearing their business suit and running shoes. It is only when they arrive at the office that they put on the "right" shoes. Then because the real yuppie woman only has a short break for lunch, she changes back again into her sneakers to get a snack to eat from a deli or salad bar.

This pragmatic changing of shoes by American women has always been observed with interest and amusement by tourists from Europe in New York, since elegant women in Milan, Paris or Munich would never dream of spoiling their chic ensemble of suit and pumps by wearing completely unsuitable running shoes. Then having made the effort to choose her outfit and shoes with the greatest care, she believes that taxi-drivers, newspaper vendors and waiters in cafés have as much right as her colleagues to see the result of her efforts. Nevertheless, European women cannot deny that soft-soled sneakers are much more comfortable than pumps. Unfortunately, they do not look right with a suit or a dress. When the dress code became increasingly relaxed in the 1990s and the smart casual look became acceptable in many work areas, sneakers made their appearance. With a white shirt, cashmere sweater, and Armani jeans, conventional sports shoes would have looked completely out of place, but the luxury leather version looks absolutely perfect.

The skills acquired in the manufacturing of traditional, hand-made welted shoes are applied to the making of luxurious Santoni sneakers.

With new colors and innovative finishes, Santoni satisfies the increasing demand for elegant, comfortable shoes by launching new lines of sneakers every season.

Nº 7

Accessories

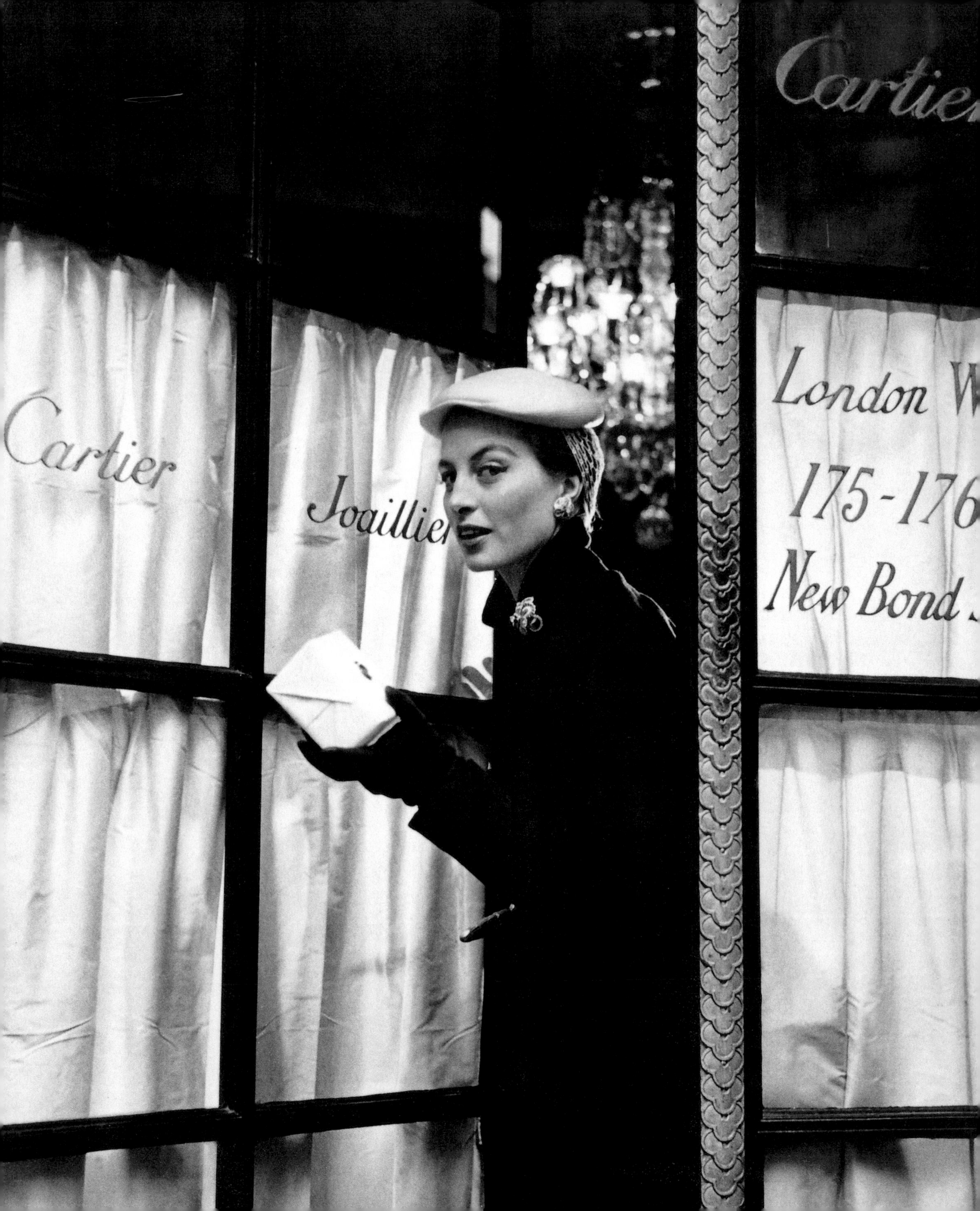
Cartier
Cartier
Joaillier
London W
175-176
New Bond

Optional: Accessories

The word "accessory" is derived from the Latin *accessio*, which means an addition, an appendage, or anything that is added to something else. The small and apparently unimportant additions to an outfit are more than just little extras. You can look at any chapter in the long history of fashion and you will always notice that the supposed second fiddle in fact dominates the fashion scene. Indeed, accessories add style, symbolism, status, power, and a certain presence to an outfit. In the 15th century women wore long dresses. The only changes in the dress of a noblewoman were the different decorative elements worn with the dress and the conical headdress that today we might associate more with a cardboard cone of candy than an important status symbol. Even nuns' habits were worn with accessories such as the cap or bonnet, the veil, and the cross. During the rococo period fans were one of the most important accessories because without them the seductive coquetry with which they were used would not have been possible. Even in the 1950s women would only go out if they were correctly and "respectably" dressed, which meant a perfectly assorted combination of hat, bag, gloves, and umbrella.

What was compulsory in the past is today a matter of choice, or rather a question of fashion, personal taste, circumstances—and sometimes also money. There is a wide choice of accessories, but the absence of some that were once important is no longer omission and should be seen instead as "purism." Nevertheless, accessories still exert a powerful attraction on most women. So the question arises, what goes with what and which accessories are suitable for which occasion? A purse that does not match or an unsightly hat or a scarf whose color does not go with the shirt can ruin the most beautiful outfit, while on the other hand a lovely brooch can really add a touch of elegance to a simple blazer.

Many modern women have a rather pragmatic accessory philosophy that could be described as "less is more." It is true that there are some women, especially the more eccentric ones, whose trademark is to combine as many elements as possible and still succeed in creating a good, interesting, and above all, distinctive personal style. But the majority of women still lean toward the "less is more" philosophy. This policy of "reduction to the essentials" can be summed up in a single sentence: it is better to buy a small number of items of very high quality than many of lesser quality. A lady does not care if fashion victims consider her unimaginative because she has had her old Birkin bag for years.

Sophisticated women have a weakness for luxury accessories even though they are rather matter-of-fact and not obsessed with clothes. Even their eyes light up when they see a red Cartier jewel case under the Christmas tree or an orange Hermès gift box next to their birthday cake. Who would not be happy to receive such beautiful gifts? But sophisticated women do not appreciate these luxury products for the brand name so much as because they admire their design, authenticity and value. The leading manufacturers of luxury accessories have always satisfied these three requirements, although the price is invariably high. But accumulating a collection of "fine accessories" without spending a fortune on them is an art that the elegant lady has developed: in her professional life she still appreciates the little silk scarf that was given to her when leaving school, the Kelly bag that she was given by her mother-in-law, the diamond she inherited, and the leather suitcases she bought many years ago at a reduced price when a famous leather shop closed down.

Silk scarves, umbrellas, purses, suitcases, sunglasses, and writing instruments—every detail of her appearance has been chosen with great care. However, she always has a favorite among her accessories, and this is the much loved jewelry, because it reflects her personality more than any other. In this case the monetary value plays a secondary part. She would like it because it is beautiful and because of all the memories it represents. Whether it is a simple cameo, a pearl necklace given to her by her grandmother or one specially made for her by Cartier, it does not matter. The sophisticated lady loves jewelry, she knows what she likes and she wears it with pride—whether it is costume jewelry or a precious piece with rare gemstones.

The Cartier boutique in London's New Bond Street has been a popular shopping address for British women since it was founded in 1909.

Handbags

The Paris manufacture Louis Vuitton makes handbags and small leather goods with the same care and attention as its famous luggage.

The purse is by far the most feminine of all accessories—it is unthinkable that men might go about their business with a Kelly bag or go out in the evening with an elegant little bag decorated with paste jewelry. How this taboo came about is not easy to explain, particularly since by contrast there is nothing wrong with a female executive going to the office with an attaché case or briefcase. From the point of view of the history of fashion, the purse is not an exclusive female prerogative. Until well into the 16th century, both men and women used to wear small pouches hung from the belt in which to keep a few belongings and some money. These pouches were identical in style for men and women, the ladies' version being perhaps slightly more decorated.

These pouches soon disappeared from view in women's fashion because they became "under-pockets" tied round the waist under the skirt. It was only in the late 18th century that the Pompadour, a direct precursor of the ladies' purse as it is known today, made its appearance. Unlike the previous unisex models, these richly decorated silk pouches were no longer tied around the waist but the custom was to hold them gracefully in the hand.

Early 19th-century fashion also contributed to the spread and popularity of this new ladies' accessory because the flowing Empire shirt dresses had no belt to which pouches could be attached. The purses of that period were known as "reticules," a term derived from the Latin reticulum meaning "small net." The reticule was a fairly small bag made of netting, beading or brocade and secured with a drawstring. Because the bag was small and therefore rather inconspicuous, it was frequently adorned with very decorative straps. The tradition of the small reticule continues in the modern evening bag with its long shoulder-length strap and small capacity.

In the course of the 19th century the range of purses widened and the first leather bags and wicker variations made their appearance.

Precious ladies' toilet box of platinum, gold and diamonds, produced by Cartier New York, in 1924, 3⅓ inches high.

"Mesh bag" by Cartier, 1906. The clasp, mesh, and chain are made from gold, embellished with emeralds and diamonds.

Chinese lacquer toilet box of gold, platinum, precious stones, and enamel. Cartier Paris, 1928.

Evening bag with platinum clasp, coral, and precious stones. Cartier New York, 1957.

Chatelaines also became popular, small bags with a handle made of chain links that could be held in the hand or hung from the handle of an umbrella. When wealthy women traveled, for instance in a stagecoach or by train, which was considered very modern at the time, she used a special travel bag. These bags soon developed into the slightly smaller but still roomy and practical bag so beloved by women today.

At the beginning of the 20th century the purse became the most important ladies' accessory and the essential finishing touch to an outfit. From then on, the well-dressed women had to be sure that her clothes and purse matched perfectly together. But the agony of choosing a purse was fortunately soon alleviated by designers who developed ranges of bags that went perfectly with the collections of the fashion houses. In doing so, fashion designers came into direct competition with saddlers and purse makers who until then had been the main source of supply of leather goods.

While the reticule, the chatelaine, and the like had been restricted to the more prosperous, the 20th-century handbag was used by every class of society. Money did not matter since a decent purse could be bought quite cheaply. But as always when a previously elitist product is popularized, it usually leads to the creation of very expensive versions of the product. The rich and famous always want to distinguish themselves from everyone else. This select circle also drew up a set of conventions that was difficult for low earners to follow, such as the requirement that the purse should always match the rest of the outfit perfectly, a code that was still valid in the 1950s.

In essence this formula is still current today, but because the well-dressed woman of the 1950s also had to wear a hat and gloves, and because she changed several times during the day, she needed a much larger collection of bags. Today life is much easier in this respect since the number of events that require a particular type of bag is much smaller. Also the concept of "what is suitable" is much more relaxed nowadays. This makes women's lives much easier because she no longer needs 20 models but just two or three, which can therefore be a little more expensive—in other words elegant, timeless classics that will combine perfectly with a formal suit as well as with smart casual wear.

Handbags for elegant women

Hermès

The Kelly bag was first launched in 1930 by Hermès and it was only given its present name in 1957 with the official approval of Princess Grace of Monaco. The former movie star Grace Kelly had made the bag famous throughout the world in the 1950s.

Hermès

Many women dream of having a purse named after them. This secret wish came true for Jane Birkin in the shape of a bag that in the meantime has become almost more famous than its godmother.

Goldpfeil

In the 1930s, Offenbach, near Frankfurt, was a world center of leather and bag manufacturers. Goldpfeil is the last surviving German manufacturer to continue this tradition of first-class craftsmanship.

Aigner

Purses are the specialty of Aigner Munich because the founder of the company, Etienne Aigner, had already made a name for himself in Paris as a leading handbag designer in the 1930s.

Lamarthe

The francophile lady will find that the purses produced by Lamarthe (founded in 1930) fulfil everything that she desires from a bag: contemporary, understated elegance combined with first-class craftsmanship.

Ferragamo

The house of Salvatore Ferragamo is universally known for its shoes, but it also produces a comprehensive range of accessories including purses, which have a very good reputation.

Cartier

Today, the legendary house of Cartier is no longer famous only for its jewelry. It is also celebrated for its leather accessories and purses that are now considered almost as precious as its jewelry and watches.

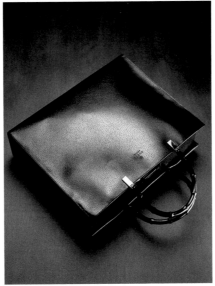

Borbonese

In the 1970s most elegant women in Italy could be seen sporting a Borbonese bag with its distinctive bird's eye effect leather. Today the brand has made a triumphant comeback thanks to designer Alessandro Dell'Acqua.

Gucci

The most famous Gucci purse is the model with the bamboo handle created in 1957. Besides this model, the Italian luxury goods manufacturer has produced many other classics since its foundation in 1904.

Chanel

This bag with its characteristic quilted motif and golden shoulder-chain was designed by Coco Chanel in 1955. It is a classic that is still produced—and widely copied.

Top secret?
A look inside a handbag

A purse's contents could include a cellphone, purse, lipstick, appointment calendar, Band-Aids, sewing kit, Walkman, pocketknife, make-up bag, headache tablets, eyedrops, and contact lens case. What a woman has in her purse is normally one of those well-guarded secrets, and which of these items are indispensable is a question of personal taste. In the past, the early huntresses and gatherers would carry berries and small animals back to their caves in their pouches, while medieval ladies carried an alms purse containing a few coins for the collection plate at church. In the 16th century, middle-class women displayed their wealth by wearing a leather pouch attached to a belt around their waist, from which other useful utensils hung such as a prayer book, scissors, and cutlery. In the late 18th century, women needed an elegant fabric bag in which they stored their embroidery and crochet work when going to ladies' circles. In contrast, the reticule of the early 19th century was so tiny that it could barely contain a small pocket handkerchief. Today the contents of a purse are a very personal matter, ranging from the organized chaos of half the household to a minimalist content consisting merely of credit cards and keys. Strangely enough, the contents of a woman's purse have always been a subject of male speculation, although it rarely contains anything very exciting. The fact is that women would keep their secret lover's visiting card anywhere but in their purse, and the contraceptive pills that most men are convinced women always carry around with them are usually kept in the bathroom or bedside table.

In reality, it is more than likely that only quite ordinary things would be found, similar to those you would find in a man's briefcase. The only difference is that the "clobber" in a woman's bag usually consists of more attractive things, including some that are frankly useless. Anything that has found its way in a woman's handbag is very unlikely ever to find its way out of it again.

1 Coin purse
The coin purse is an important accessory that is normally used several times a day. In order to minimize the pain of paying, it is important to choose a very beautiful design such as this elegant example in red leather.

2 Wallet
Personal documents such as driver's license and I.D. cards may not fit in a coin purse, so women may also have a wallet where they keep these documents along with their paper money.

3 Key ring
Men often ruin the pockets of their jackets and trousers with rattling keys, while women prefer to keep them safely in their purse, probably on a beautiful key ring with an elegant tag such as this.

4 Cellphone
How ever did people manage without a cellphone? Today, every purse contains one, unless it is kept in a jacket or pants pocket. Happily, tiny, elegantly designed models are now available.

5 Glasses case
At some stage in life many will encounter the moment when they can no longer hold the newspaper far enough away. An elegant glasses case may compensate a little for the inconvenience of having to wear glasses.

6 Pillbox
A small pillbox need not necessarily contain medicinal pills or tablets. It can also be used to contain little sweets, for instance. It is important that the lid should close tightly to keep out fluff and humidity.

7 Make-up box with mirror
A little mirror is indispensable for a final check before an important date or just to check on one's make-up during the day. So one will almost always be found in most women's purses. More extensive touching-up of make-up should be done in a powder room or similar facility.

8 Cigarette lighter
Non-smokers often envy their tobacco friends' elegant lighters, which are like miniature works of art. This is why most people are reluctant to keep them in a protective leather case, although such containers are available.

9 Pen case
Fountain pens can sometimes leak because of changes in pressure, for instance in an airplane, and extreme warmth can also make them leak. Luxury pens may also be fragile, so for all these reasons a pen case is a good investment.

1

2

3

4

5

6

7

8

9

Business accessories

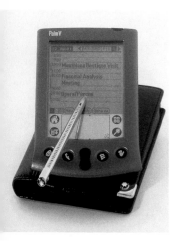

Palmtop case
Progress always leads to the development of new accessories. One such example is the palmtop case that has been added to the range of leather goods now available in luxury boutiques. There is no doubt that the style-conscious woman will reject the imitation leather case that is supplied for the palmtop but will treat herself to a real leather case.

In the 1950s, there was a clear distinction between leather goods for women and those for men: briefcases were for men and purses were for women. This strict distinction between well-defined sexual roles fortunately no longer exists and women are now fully involved in business and politics. In other words: briefcases, appointment calendars and laptop cases are now also used by women. To ensure that these business accessories satisfy all the requirements of their owner they should be thoroughly examined before they are purchased. Is the quality of the leather satisfactory? What is the finish like—will it last for years or will it be a write-off after the first business trip? Does the color match that of your business outfits? How is the inside arranged? Are there any compartments, and will you find them useful? Is there an extra pocket for small personal items? Besides the practical aspects of price, quality and function, there is a completely different criterion that should also be met, namely elegance. It is excellent news that women have made a lot of progress as far as emancipation is concerned, but these achievements do not mean that women should buy a heavy, clumsy briefcase, the most masculine organizer model in the range, or an unwieldy attaché case simply to make a point. Business accessories must suit the user and maintain a harmonious balance. Invest in an elegant ladies' briefcase and organize the contents on the basis of "less is more."

Laptop case
The digital age has not completely done away with pen and paper, as was originally predicted, but the laptop has undoubtedly replaced the typewriter, fax machine, files, and address book. In order to ensure that this mobile communication center does not get damaged during long business trips, it needs a sturdy case. This accessory must also be well designed to maintain the user's overall stylish image. The nylon case from the computer store should only be used in case of emergency.

Briefcase

Opinions are divided on the subject of briefcases. Some women swear by the angular men's model in order to prove a masculine ability to assert themselves in business, while others prefer a ladies' model that is more elegant but does not hold as much.

Portfolio

The best compromise between the sturdy men's briefcase and the rather more elegant ladies' version is the portfolio. It is slimmer and thinner than a briefcase and is therefore more suitable for the elegant business woman. The limited room inside leads to a better organization of the contents, which in turn reduces the quantity of unnecessary items carried around.

Organizer

Some may say that the palmtop is vastly superior to the classic ring-binder organizer. Nevertheless many businesswomen could not imagine life without their beloved leather organizers. This is not simply out of habit. An organizer combines an appointment calendar, address book, loose leaves for notes, a section with slots for visiting cards and credit cards, and a place to keep a pen. At the same time it is more practical and quicker to use than its digital rival.

Brief case with carrying straps

A brief case with carrying straps has definite advantages: the hands are free so that you can carry a "normal" handbag as well and still use the cellphone with your other hand. But it is also true that the shoulder strap can treat the coat or jacket harshly and when heavily loaded the case will knock against your hip at every step.

Attaché case

The attaché case is the symbol of male managerial glory. Women use attaché cases for different reasons. Many do so without a thought and just use what their colleagues are using. Others use one deliberately because it emphasizes their "toughness," while others use one almost as a joke. Indeed a square attaché case carried by a very elegant lady creates a contrast with a wink.

CD-ROM case or floppy disk holder

What use is a very fast laptop when the crucial information is not available or you are not connected to the internet? Floppy disks and other means of storage need to be as mobile as their user. That is why special disk cases have long been part of the frequent traveler's standard equipment. It is possible to buy ones that match the attaché case or purse.

Creating a handbag

Aigner Munich is one of the few German fashion labels that have become world famous. The founder of the company, Etienne Aigner, was born in Hungary in 1904 and he become famous in Paris in the 1930s for the bags he designed for well-known haute couture houses. In 1950 he presented his first collection in New York under his own name, and in 1965 the label with the horseshoe moved to Munich. Since 1972 all Aigner bags have been manufactured in the company's own factory in Tuscany. There are many stages in the production process, from the initial stage of design to the final stage of quality control, which completely justifies the investment.

Every stage of manufacture requires an excellent eye, experience and meticulous care, because even the smallest imperfections would be obvious in the finished product. Like all leading brands, Aigner relies on highly skilled craftsmen for the manufacturing of its handbags. No machine or computer could ever match their skill and dexterity.

Before commencing the actual design of a bag, designer-in-chief Madeleine Häse will examine the current trends in leather qualities. When choosing the type of leather she will also take into consideration the colors and fabrics used in the Aigner fashion collections because the bags must go with the clothes.

The quality of the finished product is to a high degree determined by the texture of the skins. Aigner Munich uses mostly materials from Italy and France and pays great attention to the proper keeping of the animals and environmentally-friendly manufacturing processes.

Even in the age of Computer Aided Design (CAD), designers still rely on their pencil and paper. Before producing detailed drawings on the computer, Madeleine Häse sketches her ideas on paper with a pencil and coloring pencils.

In the same way that the building engineer transforms the architect's drawings into reality, the cutter produces the pattern based on the designer's sketches. This will be used to make the first sample bag.

Each piece is cut out separately by hand. To do this the cutter uses patterns made from the initial drawing. When the design is converted into a three-dimensional sample, it must be checked to see whether it is suitable for series production.

A tense moment for all designers: what does the design look like when converted into a three-dimensional object? Madeleine Häse studies each version very carefully while the sample maker explains the practical aspects of the manufacturing process.

When the designer has approved a design, the final sample bag is assembled for production in the factory. This prototype must be perfect in every detail because it will be used as a model for the entire collection. The cut edges of the leather are dyed by hand.

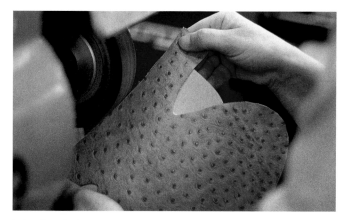

Before the individual parts are sewn together, the edges must be scarfed. This means that the leather is made thinner along the edges so as to ensure that there will be no bulges when the pieces are sewn together.

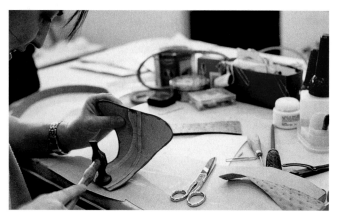

The curves of a bag are shaped by hand, with reinforcement on the inside providing the necessary support. This stage in the manufacturing process makes assembling of the sample model very expensive.

The pre-shaped side piece is joined to the main body of the bag, using a special pillar sewing machine. The bag must be guided very carefully to obtain an accurate seam.

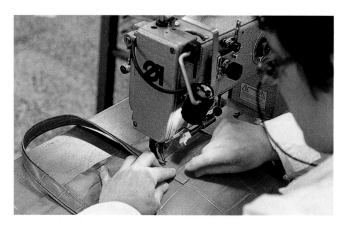

When the handles are attached to the main body of the bag, the seamstress must proceed with the greatest care. In this position even the smallest irregularities in the seam along the sides would catch the eye.

The inside is as meticulously finished as the outer part of the purse. A kind of bag is accurately made from the lining material. This is then carefully inserted inside the outer shell of the purse.

After the zipper has been sewn in, the top part of the bag is given the curves required on a wooden mold. Each model of bag has a different mold.

Before the side parts can be sewn together the seam allowances are beaten along the edges. This again is done on the wooden mold.

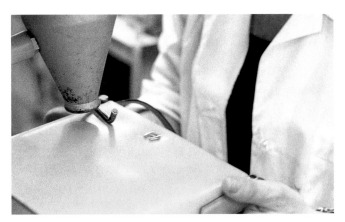

In the final finishing process the last traces of unevenness and any dirt are removed. Then the bags are given their beautiful shine—by hand, of course.

When you grab your purse in the morning you are unlikely to reflect on how many hours of craftsmanship have been necessary to make this classic ladies' accessory. But the quality will quietly demonstrate it.

The art of traveling

When a businesswoman travels today, she travels light. What does not fit in her purse, overnight bag or tote must be left behind. Even when she goes on vacation she tries not to exceed the airline's weight limit. In the past this would have been impossible because, even for a short trip, she would have taken enough clothes to fill a wardrobe trunk, as well as boxes full of shoes, toiletries, shoes, and hats. One might imagine that this kind of traveling has now died out but there must still be people who travel in this manner. Why otherwise would luxury travel stores still stock wardrobe trunks and cabin trunks of every type and size?

Admittedly, the items exhibited in the shop itself are only for display, so that clients may order what they want on the basis of these finished products, just as people used to do in the past. Musicians, actors, and show business stars who wish to take their valuable stage costumes from their home to the concert hall, opera house or television studio have luggage requirements that are out of the ordinary, and royalty and heads of state may use this oversize luggage because they need a vast array of outfits for all their foreign trips and banquets. For instance, the Queen of England always travels with a complete mourning wardrobe so that she can change immediately into black should the need arise. The third group of people who buy such large, luxurious luggage are rich people who always travel around the world accompanied by a vast wardrobe trunk and numerous suitcases. If you travel first class you do not worry about a few hundred pounds of excess weight.

It need not be as large as the Louis Vuitton wardrobe trunk that measures 55 x 22 x 25 inches. When you want to travel in style, a traditional case of normal size made of wood and leather is much more elegant than the practical, hard shell model. But many women who could afford handsewn leather cases prefer to do without such a luxury, since they are worried about what happens to it in the luggage hold and baggage conveyor. Even an aluminum suitcase will seem to have aged ten years after only a couple of flights, so how would a leather case react to such rough handling?

VIPs do not have to worry about such things because their belongings always receive preferential treatment when loaded. A scratch on Sharon Stone's suitcase? No airline would want to risk such damage to their image. Those who do not enjoy VIP status can still indulge themselves by buying hand-made cases for traveling by car, for which they are ideal. Apart from the remote risk of being damaged in a rear-end collision, these beautiful leather cases cannot come to any harm. The hard-shell suitcase is preferred when crossing the Atlantic, but here women can show their good taste with their hand luggage. Whether traveling business, club or economy class, a single piece of luggage such as a make-up case or small overnight bag may be taken into the cabin, and some business class flights allow two pieces. These and the purse should be as elegant as possible.

There is no doubt that elegant luggage is part of a successful image in the same way as stylish clothes and the right accessories. But there are still women who refuse to spend large sums of money on luggage. They consider a brand-new crocodile make-up case by Asprey & Garrard akin to showing off. If they do have expensive luggage, it will display a considerable amount of wear and tear, giving the impression that these beautiful handsewn cases have been in the family for generations. Only fashion victims would buy a complete matching set of toiletry bag, hold-all and shoe-bag with a logo design pattern. The less ostentatious prefer a hodgepodge of worn items of luggage because who would want to show off with their luggage? That is certainly the opinion of English ladies who often travel with very old cases and bags. But this understatement is not understood everywhere. "Couldn't the poor woman afford a decent new suitcase?" is the question many will ask themselves when they see such a woman on the train or plane.

People who do not mind being noticed will love the complete travel sets with their conspicuous logos because they are always perfectly finished and very long-lasting. However, they are often targeted by thieves, usually more for their intrinsic value than for the contents.

Types of luggage

The most famous hold-all in Vuitton's range of luggage is the Keepall, which was introduced in 1924. It was originally used to store dirty washing so as to keep it separate from clean clothes.

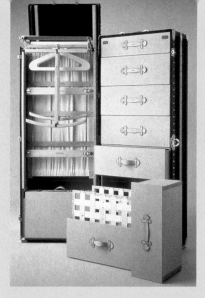

For elegant women crossing the Atlantic on an ocean liner, the wardrobe trunk was an indispensable piece of luggage. A real work of art, this trunk made of wood and leather can be used as a chest of drawers in the bedroom.

The British also know about luxury, as this portable wardrobe trunk by Asprey & Garrard shows. Naturally, this luxury shop based in London, also produces special designs to order.

As the name suggests, cabin trunks were taken into the passenger cabins of an ocean liner. Because space was at a premium, luggage had to fit perfectly in the space available, for instance under the bed or in the closet.

A special case for shoes? Why not? Then there is more room in the rest of luggage for clothes. However, it is evident that the model illustrated above would only do provided you are not too fond of shoes.

Suitcases are much smaller and more practical than a wardrobe trunk. The reduced size enables them to fit in the trunk of a car, and the smallest may be allowed as hand luggage on an airplane.

Aluminum cases are popular because they are very light and also quite tough. But they also mark very easily with scratches and dents, which can make them quite unsightly—something that the meticulous woman will not like at all.

Not particularly chic, but all the more practical for that: indestructible, hard-shelled luggage. It is almost indispensable for traveling by plane and may be fitted with wheels and a handle for easy transporting, as shown here.

Business women often like to keep their second outfit in a holdall that they can take on the plane with them. This saves waiting time in the baggage hall and eliminates the danger of misdirected luggage.

The "Rythmes du Monde" Hermès silk scarf designed by Laurence Bourthoumieux
for the 1999 autumn collection illustrates the signs of the zodiac. The highly detailed
rendering of the motifs and brilliant colors are typical of Hermès.

Silk scarves

If this book was to include just three classics of women's clothes and accessories, these would be the Kelly bag, the Chanel suit, and the Hermès scarf. All three are famous accessories for the sophisticated lady and they are still representative of a particular image. The Kelly bag is the epitome of the elegant handbag, the Chanel suit is the symbol of the perfect combination of skirt and jacket, and the Hermès scarf is the quintessential silk scarf. This all the more remarkable given that Hermès was originally a saddler and it only produced its first silk scarf in 1937, a century after it was founded. This brightly colored scarf soon became the indispensable accessory of international society women and almost a sign of identification.

The success of the Hermès scarf naturally prompted the firm's rivals in the luxury market into action. Fashion houses, couturiers, leather goods makers and tie manufacturers all began to design their own collections of silk scarves. Naturally the most famous names in the world of fashion did not simply copy Hermès but developed their individual styles. Often this consisted in using expressive and abstract motifs rather than the highly decorative Hermès style. For instance, in 1955 the couturier Jacques Fath designed a bright pink scarf with a bright yellow sun in the center, Chanel printed its logo in bold red, gray, and black on silk chiffon, and in 1965 Marc Bohan printed Dior's "Meilleurs Vœux," or Christmas wishes, to the world in stylishly calligraphic block letters on a silk square.

But however many silk scarves by Ferragamo, Dior, Loewe, Givenchy or Gucci a woman may have accumulated in her chest of drawers, whenever she means business she chooses a scarf by Hermès, the messenger of the gods. Why she does this cannot be rationally explained because many others in the luxury market produce scarves of equally wonderful quality. The preference of so many for Hermès is probably based on a phenomenon similar to the position of a Rolls-Royce. Mercedes might build better automobiles, but a Rolls is simply the ultimate luxury car. For a princess, blue blooded or not, it has to be Hermès.

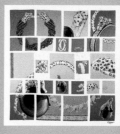

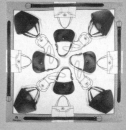

How a silk scarf is made

The starting point of any silk scarf is the designer's original idea, which is captured in sketches or developed from already existing motifs and discussed with colleagues. Often the designer is inspired by historical prints, illustrations or woven designs, or perhaps from antique furnishing fabrics, rugs or antique porcelain. The idea is still relatively vague at this point and it is therefore turned into a concrete drawing by a graphic designer. This drawing is then used as the basis for making a stencil for each color used in silk screen printing. As soon as the design has been approved the color effect of the composition is tested on paper. If the result is satisfactory, the type of silk will then be selected. It might be a twill silk with its characteristic ribbed texture, while in other cases it might be decided that a fabric with woven-in patterns or motifs such as logos or lettering that become visible in the light would be preferable.

When the pattern and the silk are ready, the process of printing can begin. First the fabric is laid out on a long table; a typical roll of fabric is about 35 inches wide and 120 feet long from which 40 scarves can be made. Then the silk screen for printing the first color is applied to the fabric. In the past this was invariably done by hand by two people who would hold the frame at each end and position it accurately on the silk. Color is then applied to the screen and distributed evenly with a squeegee, which forces it through the open areas of the screen. In this way the color pattern is applied in the correct position on the fabric. Then the frame is moved along the fabric and the procedure is repeated until the first color of the pattern has been applied to the whole length of the fabric. The procedure is repeated using a frame for each color until the motif is complete.

Although brochures and advertisements usually still show the scarves being screen-printed by hand as they were in the past, today this is usually done by a machine. In this case, it is not the screen that moves but the whole table on which the fabric is laid out. However romantic a hand-printed scarf may seem to us, most

manuufacturers favor the use of machines because the screen is automatically placed very accurately on the fabric and the amount of color is applied perfectly evenly.

There are two types of silk screen printing. In one all the colors are applied one after the other on natural fabric. In the other, known as discharge printing, the base fabric is dark in color and the pattern is achieved by "removing" or "taking out" the dark color in the relevant places and replacing it with lighter colors. Discharge printing is ideal for patterns with a dark background because the dark colors are more intense and deeper than if the black or blue was simply printed on.

In the case of "normal" silk screen printing the process is reversed, that is, the printing modifies the light-colored material by making it darker. The first stage consists of marking the outlines of the pattern on the fabric. This is followed by the application of the colors, which may include as many as 18 or more shades, depending on the design. After a color is printed on one scarf, the operation is repeated on the next scarf but one, leaving the space of one scarf unprinted at this stage, so that the fresh colors at the edges do not get smudged or run together. Thus the first stage consists in printing the outline of the first scarf followed by the third, the fifth, and so on up to the thirty-ninth scarf. When the colors are dry, the second, fourth, sixth and so on up to the fortieth scarf are printed.

When the whole length of fabric has been printed, it is important to wait until the colors are thoroughly dry. Then the silk is set and finished in order to give it shine as well as softness. The final stage of production is often carried out by out-workers. They cut the scarves and hem or "roll" the edges by hand. In the case of cheaper scarves, this is done by a machine, which is very obvious. Only hand-rolled hems have accurate corners and, in addition, the intervals between the individual stitches are always very slightly irregular, which adds a certain charm to the scarf.

Fashion designers and world-famous museums such as the Victoria & Albert Museum in London have their finest scarves printed by Beckford Silk in England.

Visitors are welcome. People interested in seeing how the screen-printing process is used on silk should make a visit to Beckford Silk, near Tewkesbury, Gloucester.

The pattern of many scarves is applied on a background of white silk twill that is supplied to the silk-printing factory by the weaving mill. Many companies buy their silk directly from China.

The cashmere shawl

Made in Germany: the label with the eagle

Since 1893 the German textile manufacturer Eagle Products has been producing the finest scarves, shawls, plaids, spreads and fabrics in wool, cotton and cashmere for exclusive specialist shops and fashion houses all over the world. The textiles produced by this quality-conscious, family-run company are used by numerous designer labels and own brands. In 1909 the company moved its premises to Hof an der Saale, a traditional center of textile manufacturing in northeast Bavaria. The words "Made in Germany" displayed on the label, together with the Eagle trademark are entirely justified, since the whole manufacturing process takes place in Germany, from weaving to dyeing and finishing, either in the factory itself or subcontracted to neighboring companies and outworkers in the immediate neighborhood. Eagle's range of products includes everything a lady might need.

A spring day in Paris, Milan or Madrid can often still be quite cool, which is why women often wrap themselves in large shawls when they hurry to the small corner bar for their morning café au lait or caffè latte or café con leche. Indeed, a light cashmere shawl looks very good with a skirt, shirt and pumps and will also protect you from the cold. They are very useful in winter when they can be worn over a coat and jacket to give further protection against wind and frost. They come in a wide range of patterns and motifs, such as warm earthy shades, swirling paisley patterns, Scottish tartan or plain pastels.

Cashmere shawls have been very popular with women all over Europe since the mid-18th century. At first these precious shawls were rare because the fibers had to come all the way from India by sea to England, so they were in short supply and expensive. Women loved them for their incredible softness and also for their exotic colors and patterns. These were inspired by a variety of plants that were represented in a stylized or realistic manner. Some of the best-known patterns were the "miribota" or eye motif that was supposed to protect against the evil eye, and the crown of the date palm, also known as the "palmette" motif, that was a symbol of life and fertility. Since the early 19th century the miribota motif has been known in Europe as "Paisley," after the Scottish town where "authentic ethnic" cashmere shawls were produced. However, the earliest imitations of the Oriental originals were not made in the British Isles but in France. There were also a few manufacturers in Vienna who concentrated on the production of this new fashionable accessory.

But women who wanted real cashmere shawls would not buy European-manufactured shawls because these were mostly made of wool. It was only in the second half of the 19th century that raw cashmere finally arrived in France so that cashmere shawls could at last be produced in Europe. This did not affect the price much because the raw material was very expensive and it made little difference whether the product was manufactured in Asia or in Europe. Slightly less expensive alternatives were shawls with patterns printed on materials made of wool, cotton, silk, and mixed fibers. Besides the traditional oriental patterns, other patterns, motifs, and colors were introduced that appealed to European taste. One of the largest producer of patterns was the Frenchman Antony Berrus who employed up to 200 designers in his workshop at the time. The great popularity of the cashmere shawl only began to decrease at the end of the 19th century when coats made their appearance on the scene and warm shawls became superfluous.

Even though this cozy accessory went out of fashion at the beginning of the 20th century, fine shawls and scarves remained popular. However, it was the last decade of the 20th century before the triumphant revival of this classic accessory took place. This time it took the form of the pashmina, the ultimate must-have of the late 1990s. These feather-light maxi-shawls made of cashmere or a mixture of cashmere and silk were available in a wide range of pastel or deep colors. They were mainly worn in summer when a sweater or cardigan would have been too warm but the conditions not warm enough for bare arms and shoulders. The first pashminas were seen in England in 1996. American women soon acquired a taste for these luxury accessories and the fashion spread from the United States to the European mainland where it reached its peak in 1999. But the great popularity of the pashmina also meant that it lost its "insider" appeal, and trendsetters consequently pushed it to the farthest corner of the drawer. But as soon as inexpensive imitations have disappeared from circulation, the original is bound to make a comeback.

A shawl is not easy to define but everyone knows what it means. Shawls vary in size, the type of fiber used, the weave, and the pattern. They are indispensable for the sensitive throat on cool days, and a wonderfully beautiful accessory.

The **plaid** is a tartan-patterned blanket, originally worn over the shoulder as part of Scottish Highland dress. In the past it was used by women to keep warm in drafty open automobiles or when snoozing on the train. Today plaids are mainly used as spreads on sofas or as rugs for a picnic.

Whether it is called a **cape** or poncho, this elegant combination of shawl and cape is another practical accessory. It is particularly popular with women in southern Europe where it can be worn almost all year round—on cool spring days over a shirt and skirt, suit or trouser suit, and in winter as an extra protection against the cold over a coat or jacket.

The fabric **stole**, from 15 to 30 inches wide and six feet long, is something in between a scarf and a cape. Depending on the color and material, it may be used as a warm substitute for a coat or an elegant accessory for an evening out.

The right hat

Ladies' hats are quite a controversial subject. It is a fact that few women can walk past the hat department in a large store without trying on a particularly daring model, but no one will buy it regardless of how well it suited them. After all, when would you wear a hat? With your business suit at the next meeting? Hardly, and even less when you opt for a smart casual look with a shirt, jeans, and fancy sneakers. That is why the elegant hat remains a dream that comes true for only a few seconds in front of a mirror.

In the 1950s the ladies' hat was an indispensable part of the elegant woman's outfit. Why it suddenly fell out of favor with young women in the 1960s is not easy to explain. It was partly because it was seen as a symbol of the austere, conservative, post-war era, and partly because it could not be worn with the new, voluminous hairstyles of the time. In addition, a wide-brimmed hat would have been very impractical in a car. But which of these three factors was the crucial one in the demise of the hat will probably remain a mystery—what is certain is that the once popular accessory plays a very small part in everyday fashion today.

A Laura Ashley model wearing a romantic dress and elegant hat that represents the English summer look.

"Dragon fly" is the name of this model created by the ladies' hat designer Sylvia Fletcher at Lock's in London.

Sylvia Fletcher's kingdom, her showroom for ladies' designer hats, is situated on the first floor of the oldest hatmaker's shop in London.

Called "Teardrop" by Sylvia Fletcher, this model has a name that might seem sad, but the name actually refers to its flowing shape.

But although ladies' hats were in theory declared clinically dead in the 1970s, they are still present in our fashion consciousness. This is partly due to upper middle-class women who remain staunchly loyal to this elegant accessory and the aristocracy who are equally fond of hats. Indeed, the two events most loved by high society—weddings and horse-racing—cannot be dissociated from the picture of women in hats. This is quite apparent in leafing through today's illustrated magazines and gossip columns, which regularly show women in hats at important social events. In addition, the wide range of hats still available in specialist shops and department stores confirms without any doubt the lively presence of the allegedly "dead" hat in society.

SYLVIA FLETCHER AT JAMES LOCK & CO.

The most popular hat parade is still that which takes place each year at England's Ascot races. But the most elegant and elaborate hats, by far, are to be found in the Royal Enclosure. The majority of the hats seen here are absurd, imaginative, completely over-the-top creations that are designed to attract the attention of photographers and television cameras. The woman with the most striking, unusual headdress will become famous for a few seconds in the television news report of Ladies' Day. But those who take pride in themselves would never exceed the boundaries of good taste in the matter of hats.

Because hats have found in Great Britain a kind of refuge for threatened fashion categories, London has become a major shopping center for both wearable and extravagant hats. Temples of consumerism such as Harvey Nichols, Fortnum & Mason, and Liberty offer women a wonderful range of hats. In addition, there are also the specialist hat shops such as Herbert Johnson at Swaine Adeney Brigg, and London's most famous hatters for both men and women, Lock & Co. This company was founded in 1676, and hat-maker Sylvia Fletcher creates her masterpieces on the top floor of the company's building. Naturally, those who cannot find what they are looking for can place a special order.

The model named "Pagoda" would be a perfect choice for a summer garden party, for instance, or a wedding.

The country hat

British women love country life and often feel more comfortable in rubber boots, sweater, and Barbour jacket than in a business suit. However, they still know how to be stylish when taking part in the sporting activities of the landed gentry. Admittedly, the simple term "hat" does not seem right to describe those remarkable objects that may be seen on the heads of women at steeplechases and other horseracing events. But that does not bother anyone, because these absurd, crumpled, tweedy headdresses were not designed to go to a royal garden party at Buckingham Palace. Above all, they are designed to protect against the icy cold winds of the high moors, style and elegance being very low priorities. You will see ladies wearing checked cloche hats with the wide brim pulled down, woven imitation fur hats, caps with feather ornaments, and Russian fur caps with sticking-out ear flaps. Some of these picturesque hats are family heirlooms; others may have been bought at the flea market or from an itinerant trader, or are even hand-knitted and hand-sewn. What they have in common is that they are all individual creations—and, above all, warm.

The umbrella

An umbrella is an indispensable accessory for any woman wherever she is—including rushing past Milan cathedral, as in this poster.

The umbrella has been reinterpreted many times as a female accessory in the course of the last 300 years. In the 18th century, the parasol was used to protect the pale complexion of women of the aristocracy against an undesirable suntan, while at the same time it was used as an expression of coquetry, similar to the fan. In the 19th century umbrellas were still mainly used as protection against the sun, although by then their value against the rain was also recognized. But using it to fight bad weather was "somewhat bourgeois," because upper class women did not need one. They traveled mainly in horse-drawn carriages and only went for walks when it was sunny. This restricted attitude toward fresh air survived until the early years of the 20th century, with the hackney carriage gradually being replaced by the automobile.

When sport and fitness became trendy in the 1920s, a pale complexion was suddenly completely out of fashion, and the parasol became almost obsolete. Admittedly, it did not disappear entirely from the picture but its continued use was mainly on the part of the older generation. The modern woman used her umbrella only in wet weather. Manufacturers soon adapted to the new situation and concentrated on creating interesting, imaginative umbrella designs. The resulting models had fanciful handles and fashionable printed fabrics but they never achieved the great variety of parasols. Meanwhile the umbrella had lost its stolid image. In the past it had merely been used by servants running errands for their masters because it kept them reasonably dry, but soon this practical accessory was also adopted by the elegant city-dweller, either as an umbrella the length of a walking stick or as a handy folding model, such as the Knirps developed in 1926 by the German manufacturer Hans Haupt.

The role of the umbrella changed again in the second half of the 20th century. While in the 1950s umbrellas were part of every woman's outfit in the same way as the hat, bag, and gloves, it suddenly became less popular among young

women in the 1960s. They preferred wearing a fashionable shiny plastic raincoat or using a folding umbrella. Manufacturers reacted by creating futuristic models made of transparent plastic that enclosed the carrier as if in a bell. In addition, they also developed a very practical model, somewhere between a walking-stick length and a telescopic umbrella in size, that could be carried hanging on the shoulder by a strap attached to the handle and the point of the umbrella. These innovations did not prevent the umbrella from becoming merely a practical object in the 1980s and 1990s that no longer needed to match the rest of the outfit.

Nowadays hardly any woman still owns an umbrella that matches her shoes and gloves. Instead she has various kinds of umbrellas for different uses: a golf umbrella for weekend outings, so large that the whole family can fit underneath it, a tartan walking-stick length umbrella with a wooden handle for walking in the park, an umbrella with a shoulder strap that might display a well-known logo pattern (in case of meeting people who might be impressed by this), a black folding umbrella for business or shopping trips, and maybe a classic ladies' umbrella of the 1950s inherited from her mother—no longer fashionable, perhaps, but still beautiful.

Anyone caught in the rain will be pleased to have an umbrella at all, no matter how old and scruffy it is. But it is much nicer to face the elements with a stylish umbrella.

Handmade umbrellas

The Milan-based umbrella manufacturer (and avowed umbrella enthusiast) Francesco Maglia runs the "Fabbrica Ombrelli," which has been in his family for five generations.

The term "handmade" is often encountered in the world of luxury accessories, but it is frankly unexpected in the case of umbrellas. Nonetheless, the best umbrellas are handmade like any other luxury product of the leading brands. They came from one of the handful of companies left that still make umbrellas by hand. With 100 companies, Italy, at the turn of the century, used to be a major center of umbrella manufacture, but the old-style ombrellaio or umbrella-maker has almost disappeared. There are only three companies left in Milan that practice this ancient craft of handmade umbrellas. One of these is the Fabbrica Ombrelli Maglia Francesco on the Corso Genova no. 7, which was founded in 1854. Connoisseurs regard it as the best umbrella manufacturer in the world.

There are three main reasons for Maglia's fame as an umbrella manufacturer. In the first place, they use only the best materials for the stick and handle, mostly fine woods that the owner and head of the company, Francesco Maglia, selects himself in Italy and Germany. Second, the fabrics are produced exclusively for the umbrella manufacturer so that the company is always able to offer unusual colors, patterns and textures. Third, the careful hand-crafting of the umbrellas' manufacture results in a sturdy and durable product that can also be repaired if necessary.

The exact time needed to make an umbrella is difficult to determine, since the orders are processed in batches instead of each umbrella being produced separately from beginning to end. But there is no doubt that many hours are spent because each umbrella goes through over 70 extremely elaborate production stages. First, the materials are picked and bundled together according to the orders. The core of the umbrella is a solid wooden rod or stick that in many models also forms the handle. In other models, the handle may be made of a different material that is then attached to the wooden stick. The parts needed to make an umbrella are a stick, sometimes a separate handle, the fabric, the struts, and other small parts such as rivets and the ferrule. When all the components of the umbrella are assembled, the fabric is cut out.

There are special patterns of different sizes for each model. These patterns are then arranged by hand on top of the fabric in such a way as to leave as few remnants as possible. Then the outline is traced with tailor's chalk and the fabric cut out following these lines. The cutter must also ensure that the patterns match exactly along where the seams will be. Besides requiring a good eye and a lot of experience, the process takes a long time. But this is not a problem because the 13 workers are allowed to take as much time as they need. While the fabrics are prepared, another worker prepares the stick, making holes to mount the handle if necessary, or otherwise bending the handle into the desired shape over steam. The wood is then polished. Another worker then mounts the struts on the wooden stick. This process is repeated by hand for each umbrella.

This is followed by one of the most time-consuming and labor-intensive stage in the production process. Depending on the model, the fabric is secured to the metal struts at up to 24 points, using the old-fashioned needle and thread method . In addition, the seamstress sews on small pieces of fabric as reinforcement at the joints so that the fabric does not tear. The final operation is to sew on the small strip of fabric with a small fastener at the end that secures the folded umbrella when it is tightly rolled. Here too the work must be carried out extremely carefully, because the slightest error would be picked up at the final quality control.

This is why the company's motto is that it is better to get everything right the first time and to allow a little more time for each stage in order to achieve this. The meaning of payment for piecework is unknown to them and the delivery time can take several months. But every customer eventually gets the umbrellas made to his or her own specifications, because Maglia has no standard models.

Some umbrellas waiting for their handles to be fitted. But most models are made in one piece, with the handle formed from the stick.

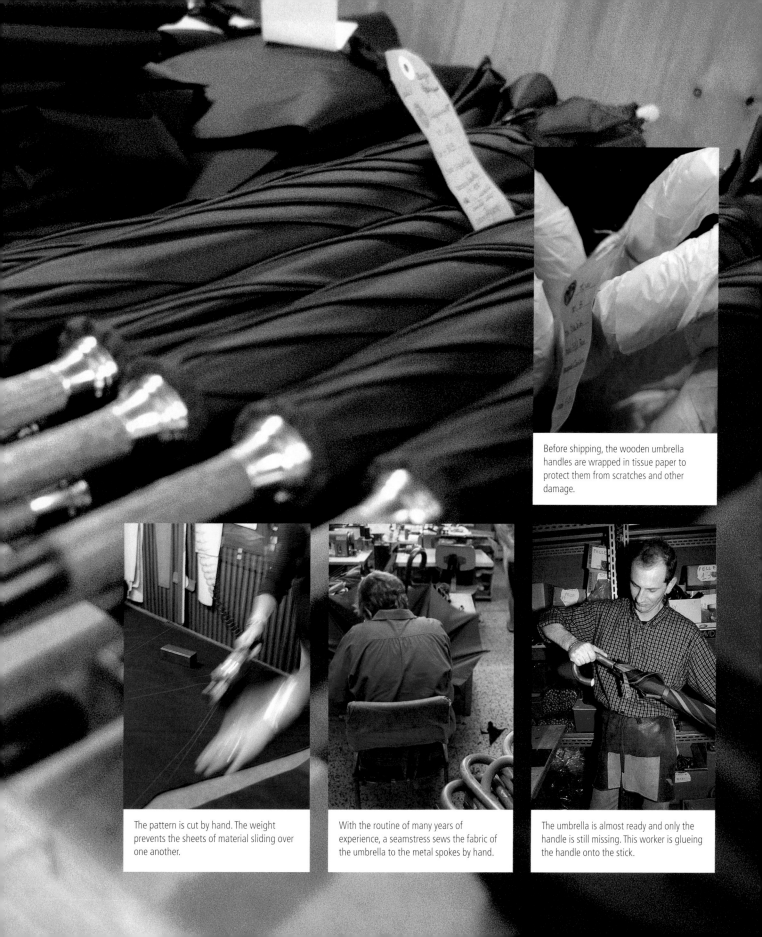

Before shipping, the wooden umbrella handles are wrapped in tissue paper to protect them from scratches and other damage.

The pattern is cut by hand. The weight prevents the sheets of material sliding over one another.

With the routine of many years of experience, a seamstress sews the fabric of the umbrella to the metal spokes by hand.

The umbrella is almost ready and only the handle is still missing. This worker is glueing the handle onto the stick.

Sunglasses

Sunglasses are a typical 20th-century accessory. Although colored glass was used as far back as antiquity to protect the eyes from bright sunlight, and tinted lenses were already quite widespread in the 19th century, no one ever thought of them as a fashion accessory because they were not considered particularly becoming. It was only in the 1920s when a suntan became the symbol of active, sophisticated trendsetters that sunglasses became part of the image. Sport, traveling, sea, and sand—it became the indispensable accessory of everything considered chic. But it was quite a while longer before "shades" developed a fashion identity of their own.

In the 1950s sunglasses were still mainly worn as a protection against bright sun, used when driving or on the ski slopes. To wear them as a decorative accessory in the hair, possibly even on a cloudy day, would only have occurred to the fashion avant-garde. But movie directors had already discovered the modern image of sunglasses—who does not remember Grace Kelly in *To Catch a Thief*, cool and unapproachable behind her dark glasses? The big screen was always ahead of its time, because the separation between the product and its purpose did not take place before the 1960s, when young people wore Ray-Ban aviator glasses just as Peter

The brown marbled framework of these gold-embellished Cartier sunglasses is particularly good for blondes women, since it is less harsh than black.

Fonda had done in the cult movie *Easy Rider*. In the 1970s movies and music finally elevated sunglasses to the rank of a "must-have" for the young, becoming a classy accessory. Obviously sophisticated women could not identify with the icons of pop culture, but they had their own icons whom they could imitate. The most important at the time was Jacqueline Kennedy. She turned sunglasses into her own trademark, at first unintentionally and under tragic circumstances, as the grieving president's widow hiding from the world behind dark glasses. Later, she wore them deliberately, when, as the wife of shipping magnate Aristotle Onassis, she adopted very large dark glasses in an effort to remain incognito. This was of course in vain, since the paparazzi immediately recognized the jet-setting American when she set out on her massive shopping expeditions in Rome, Paris and New York.

In the 1980s and 1990s sunglasses became a completely indispensable, matter-of-fact part of any fashionable outfit and, often worn regardless of the season or the weather. To see better behind the wheel? As protection against the glare of snow? Because of sensitive eyes? Because of a late night? These used to be the reasons why people wore sunglasses in the past. Today, sunglasses are worn because of the image they convey, whether the sun is shining or not. All that is needed is an elegant pair by Gucci, Cartier, Armani, or Ray-Ban & Co.

A trendy accessory in 2002: shades with pastel-colored lenses.

Fashionable pink sunglasses by Freudenhaus Eyewear.

Light-colored frames with a classic tear-drop shape.

Rimless sunglasses with colored lenses.

To see better or to look better?

Glasses or no glasses? This is a question that could never have been asked a few decades ago. Anyone with bad eyesight had to make do with large, inelegant spectacles whether they wanted to or not. These seldom did much for a woman's appearance because glasses in the 1950s and 1960s were frankly unbecoming. No wonder many women chose not to wear glasses at all and went through life in a misty blur—with the consequences demonstrated by Marilyn Monroe in *Gentlemen Prefer Blondes*. Today one can only shake one's head in amazement because the enormous range of glasses now available meets all requirements from a design and esthetic point of view. In fact, women who wear glasses are often envied by those who do not because glasses are now so stylish and sophisticated. In addition, people who wear glasses are, quite irrationally, often thought to be more intelligent. Since intelligence is no longer seen as a drawback in a woman, no one wants to risk being thought less clever simply because they have good eyesight. Perhaps that is why so few women who wear glasses choose to wear contact lenses, although in many circumstances they would be much more convenient than glasses. Could there be any better proof that women have made their peace with the spectacles that were once so unloved?

Gloves

The glove shop was much more important for women in the 1920s because gloves were then an integral part of a woman's outfit.

Do you wear an evening gown to go to the supermarket? Certainly not. Nor would you wear jeans and a T-shirt to go to your parents' golden wedding anniversary. In both these instances the outfit would not be appropriate for the occasion. Nevertheless, the motto "the occasion determines the outfit" is interpreted rather loosely. This was not always the case. In the 1950s, elegant women still had to cope with a complex dress code, so that what to wear with what and when was dictated according to strict etiquette. Moreover, the criterion of what was "appropriate" applied to every detail of a woman's appearance, starting from the finger tips, in other words, the gloves. Consequently, a well-dressed woman would have a pair of gloves to match every outfit and every circumstance. For shopping in the morning she would wear pale gray goatskin gloves, and for going out to lunch, beige kid gloves. In the afternoon mid-brown peccary gloves were called for, and in the evening three-quarter length black silk gloves were worn. As well as the material and color of gloves, their fit was very important. This is why the most discriminating women usually had their gloves made to measure, such a time-consuming process that even the most extravagant haute couture addicts of today would have been impressed. For instance, Marlene Dietrich's daughter Maria Riva tells how her mother had casts made of her hands in 1933 that were used as a model by the glove maker. After numerous fittings and many long hours, the glove maker created a masterpiece that fitted the plaster model like a second skin. When the star eventually slipped on these works of art, the impeccable fit was immediately obvious: there was not a single wrinkle, nor a smidgen of excess leather. There was only one disadvantage—the star could not move her fingers. This is something you no longer need to fear when you buy gloves from a store, unless of course you buy a size that is too small. Such gloves are cut more generously and functionality comes before elegance. Their first task is to keep your hands warm.

In the early part of the history of fashion, gloves were simply worn for protection. It was only in the 14th century that people slowly discovered the luxury potential of this accessory that had hitherto been considered mainly functional. But it took another 100 years before the glove became fully established as an elegant accessory and indication of a person's social rank, as is often seen in paintings. Because men and women in the 15th century already tended to keep their receipts, people's passion for gloves is well documented in spite of a relative lack of illustrations. For instance, it is known that in the Renaissance period the upper classes paid a fortune for elegant gloves.

The refinements were accompanied by strict rules of behavior. One of these was whether a woman should hold out her hand with or without gloves when shaking hands with a man. At first it was considered fundamentally improper for both sexes to shake hands without first removing their gloves. But soon the rule changed to what it is now: the woman keeps her gloves on to shake hands, but the man must remove his. However, this rule was devised at a time when ladies wore fine, elegant gloves and ski mittens had not yet been invented. So it is now advised that everyday winter gloves should be removed but elegant accessory models and long evening gloves should be kept on.

On cold winter days, gloves are worn to keep the hands warm. But the Munich-based label Aigner will also ensure that your gloves combine warmth with elegance.

A glove is sewn together

Every year when the days grow shorter and cooler and the leather gloves are taken out of the drawer for the first time, we are hardly aware of the craftsmanship that has gone into making these items. A pair of gloves consists of up to 24 separate pieces that may have required 2,000 stitches to assemble, at least in a hand-sewn design.

Glove-making is a difficult craft with a long tradition that today is practiced by only a few companies. One of the oldest is the German company Roeckl. It was established in Munich in 1839 by the glovemaker Jakob Roeckl. The small workshop with a sales outlet soon developed into a prosperous business with its own tannery and dye works. In order to expand, Jakob

Roeckl's son Christian built a large factory just outside the town in 1871 and opened shops in Berlin, Wiesbaden, Frankfurt, Cologne, and Bremen.

After the early death of Christian Roeckl, his 24-year-old son Heinrich took over the company, which prospered and expanded enormously under his management.

After World War II, Dr Heinrich Franz Roeckl, the great-grandson of the founder, rebuilt the factory, which then experienced a fresh boom. Today this family company is run by his children and grandchildren, and although much has changed since the early days, gloves are still made almost exactly as they were in the mid-19th century.

After the glovemaker has selected the leather from stock, he pulls it over the edge of the table, both lengthwise and crosswise.

Using a ruler, the glove maker measures the width of the hand. This determines the size of the glove.

There are patterns in various sizes for each model. The outline of the pattern is drawn on the leather.

First the thumb part is cut out of the leather. This is done by hand with scissors.

The side parts of the individual fingers are cut out by hand.

After the individual parts have been marked—there are 18 to 24 depending on the model of glove—the front and side parts are punched out.

Inside the glove an elastic band is sewn in by machine.

The ready-made thumb part is sewn into the punched-out opening. Great skill is required to stitch the thumb accurately into the round opening.

It takes over 2,000 stitches to sew a glove by hand. To make the work with the trihedron needle easier, the needle is being pushed through a triangular device.

The finished outer glove is pulled over the lining, which is then secured at the fingertips.

The glove is ironed on a hot mold, to smooth out uneven spots.

The final stage is polishing the glove. After a final quality check, the gloves are packed and dispatched to the stores.

Gold and silver:
precious jewelry for every day

The three kinds of gold in Cartier's Trinity ring symbolize friendship (white gold), fidelity (yellow gold) and love (red gold), which why it is popular as an engagement ring.

Chunky jewelry for a special evening out is very exciting, and no false modesty is needed because with an evening dress you can afford to wear sparkling jewelry. One shows what one has, it does not matter whether it is real jewelry or tasteful costume jewelry. But rings, chains, bracelets, earrings, and watches are also some of the most beautiful personal accessories for wearing during the day. However, jewelry should be simpler and more restrained when worn with a business outfit or casual wear. A diamond necklace to go to a meeting or to go and play tennis? That would not be right. But what are the classic pieces of jewelry suitable for everyday wear? All the strict rules that in the past clearly dictated who wore what jewelry on which occasion (young girls, married women, widows, women in mourning, classed according to social rank, and so on) were swept away in the 1920s by women's enthusiasm for costume jewelry. Also the rule that gold and silver should never be worn together is no longer slavishly obeyed. Everyone decides for themselves what they prefer. But a few rules have survived that most women still follow to a certain extent.

First, there is the time of the day: the earlier it is, the plainer and more discreet the jewelry should be, while in the afternoon a little more jewelry can be worn. Second, the pieces of jewelry must go together. This does not imply that a chain, earrings, and bracelet must be bought as a set, but simply that there should be stylistic harmony between the pieces. Third, the saying "less is more" often holds true, although there are some women who wear chunky jewelry at all times, having developed this into a "trademark" style of their own. But to do this one must have very good taste or at least be very individualistic.

Precious stones play a rather secondary role in plain everyday jewelry, but the metal is all the more important for that reason. Almost every woman wears at least one gold or silver ring, and if she is married, probably also a wedding ring. Additionally she may wear some stud earrings for pierced ears or plain clip earrings as well as a chain and bracelet.

Since time immemorial gold has been the quintessential precious metal for jewelry. This much sought-after metal with its warm glow is panned from alluvial sand in rivers or dug up in gold mines; both methods are very time-consuming and extremely labor-intensive. In the 16th and 17th century the Spanish conquistadors brought large amounts of gold from Central and South America back to Europe. In the 18th century large gold deposits were found in Brazil and Russia and in the 19th century gold was discovered in California, Australia, and Alaska, while today the gold mines of South Africa are a major source of the world's gold.

For jewelers, gold is an ideal raw material because it is wonderfully beautiful, it has high chemical stability, it does not tarnish or oxidize, meaning that it does not rust, and being highly malleable and ductile it is also easy—almost too easy—to work with. Pure gold is very soft and jewelry made from it bends easily so that it can quickly get out of shape. For this reason goldsmiths use alloys of gold, adding other metals such as silver, copper, palladium, and nickel to the molten gold. This makes the gold harder so that it keeps its shape better. However, the addition of other metals often changes the color. If gold is alloyed with 20% palladium or nickel, the gold turns gray-white, resulting in what is known as white gold. If the original gold color is to be preserved, equal amounts of silver and copper are added. If only copper is added the result is red gold.

The proportion of pure gold in a piece of jewelry is revealed by its fineness, which is expressed in thousandths. Pure gold has a fineness of 1,000 (meaning that 1,000 parts out of 1,000 are gold), but because of its softness pure gold is never used to make jewelry. Valuable pieces are made of 750 gold (of which 750 parts are gold and 250 parts are other metals). 585 gold is not quite as valuable, 333 gold has little in common with real gold. For this reason such jewelry is often gold-plated later. An alternative measure of gold content is the system of karats (not be confused with the carat unit of weight used for precious stones), indicating parts of gold by

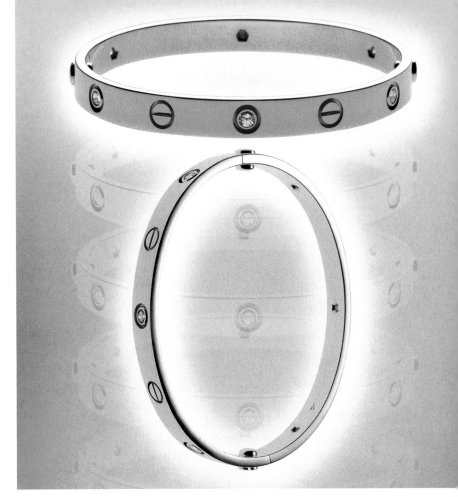

weight out of 24. Pure gold is therefore 24 karat, 18 karat corresponds to a fineness of 750 (three-quarters of it being gold), and 14 karat corresponds to 585 gold. The gold content of a piece of jewelry is indicated by a hallmark on the inside or back.

Silver, the eternal number two in the world of jewelry, is also mixed with other metals (mainly copper) in order to give it more strength. For more precious pieces, the alloy starts at 900 (of 1000 parts at least 900 are silver). Usually 935 or 925 silver, known as sterling silver, is used for valuable pieces. Here too you should always check the hallmark. Silver has the disadvantage that it oxidizes quickly so that it discolors and turns black. The reason for this is the presence of sulfur in the air, which reacts easily with silver and even more readily with the copper present in the silver alloy. There are silver alloys that do not oxidize but they are based on a high percentage of palladium, a metal that is part of the platinum group and therefore very expensive. Other ways of protecting against oxidation are blanching, whereby the copper particles situated on the surface of the piece of jewelry are removed, and rhodium plating, which covers the surface with a thin layer of bright, non-tarnishing rhodium.

Similar to silver in color but much more precious and expensive is platinum. Compared to gold and silver, this metal is a newcomer in jewelers' windows because it was first used to make jewelry only in the second half of the 19th century, usually in combination with diamonds. Platinum alloys are very pure, usually 950 parts out of 1,000 being platinum. For the alloy, related metals such as rhodium and palladium have been used, as have gold, silver and copper. The very high price of platinum jewelry is not only due to the intrinsic cost of the metal but also because of the difficulty of working it. It has a very high melting point, 3,214.9° F (1,768.3° C), and to achieve the necessary temperature the goldsmith needs special equipment and a special workshop, an expense that not every goldsmith can afford. Real platinum jewelry pieces have the letters "pt" engraved on them.

The "Love" bracelet by Cartier is a piece of real jewelry that can be worn every day because this thin bangle looks as good with a business suit as with jeans and a T-shirt.

Louis-Joseph Cartier, grandson of the company's founder, Louis-François, was the creative force in the company from the turn of the century until 1942.

Glossary of precious and semi-precious stones

Agate
Quartz, chalcedony, hardness 6.5 to 7. Brightly patterned or striped, transparent to opaque, brown, orange, gray, beige, black, bluish, greenish. Where found: various.

Amber
Fossilized tree resin, hardness 2 to 2.5. Comes in every shade of yellow, clear to opaque, often with inclusions. Where found: Russia, Poland, Denmark, and many other countries.

Amethyst
Quartz, hardness 7. Dark to pale violet, transparent to clear. Where found: various but especially in Brazil. One of the most popular semiprecious stones.

Aquamarine
A beryl, hardness 7.5 to 8. Blue or blue-green, transparent to clear. Where found: Asia, Africa, America.

Aventurine
Quartz, hardness 7. Comes in greenish shades, often red-veined, transparent to opaque. Where found: various but especially in Brazil and South Africa.

Beryl
Large group of gemstones that includes aquamarine and emerald, hardness 7.5 to 8. Comes in almost any color, clear to transparent. Where found: various.

Chalcedony
Quartz stone, hardness 6 to 7. Whitish, blue or gray, clear to transparent. Where found: various.

Citrin
Quartz stone, hardness 7. Yellow, often with a green tinge, mostly transparent. Where found: various.

Coral
Hardness 3 to 4. Red to pink, whitish, always opaque. Where found: grows worldwide in warm seas.

Cornelian
Quartz stone, chalcedony, hardness 6 to 7. Red, orange, red-brown, transparent. Where found: South America, Africa, Asia.

Diamond
The most precious of all gems, hardness 10. Mostly colorless, all other colors are very rare, clear to transparent. Where found: South Africa and other African countries, Brazil, China, Russia, Canada, Australia.

Emerald
Beryl, hardness 7.5 to 8. Various shades of green, transparent to opaque. Where found: various.

Garnet
Hardness 6.5 to 7.5. Mostly dark red, occasionally with violet tones, opaque to clear. Where found: various. A semiprecious stone rich in tradition.

Hematite
Hardness 5 to 6.5. Black, anthracite, mid-gray and black-brown, always opaque. Characteristic metal sheen. Where found: various.

Jade
Hardness 6.5 to 7. Dark to pale green, rarely in other colors, mostly opaque. Where found: China and elsewhere.

Jasper
Quartz stone, chalcedony, hardness 6 to 7. Comes in almost any color, mostly brightly patterned. Where found: various.

Lapis lazuli
Hardness 5 to 6. Dark blue, often with light-colored embedded particles, opaque. Where found: especially Afghanistan.

Larimar
Hardness 4 to 6. Blue to light blue, opaque to transparent. Where found: Dominican Republic.

Malachite
Hardness 4. Striped in various greenish tones, opaque. Where found: Congo, Zambia, Russia.

Moonstone
Feldspar, hardness 6 to 6.5. Whitish to bluish, mostly transparent with opal-like luster. Where found: Asia, Australia.

Obsidian
Hardness 5 to 6. Comes in several dark colors but also brightly colored or with light-colored embedded particles, opaque or transparent. Where found: volcanic regions.

Onyx
Quartz stone, chalcedony, hardness 6.5 to 7. Black, striped black and white, opaque. Where found: Brazil, Asia, Arabian peninsula.

Opal
Hardness 5.5 to 6.5. Often shimmering with many colors, clear to opaque. Where found: Australia, North and South America.

Pyrite
Hardness 6 to 6.5. Yellow to golden colors, opaque. Where found: various.

Rock crystal
Quartz, hardness 7. Colorless to whitish, clear to transparent, occasional inclusions. Where found: various.

Rhodochrosite
Hardness 4. Comes in shades of pink, striped or veined, opaque to transparent. Where found: various.

Rhodonite
Hardness 5.5 to 6.5. Shades of pink, often with dark veins, transparent to opaque. Where found: various.

Rose crystal
Quartz stone, hardness 7. Light pink to pink-violet, clear to transparent. Where found: Madagascar, Brazil, and many other countries.

Rubellite
Tourmaline, hardness 7 to 7.5. Pink to deep red, transparent to opaque. Where found: Madagascar, U.S.A., Brazil, Tanzania, Pakistan.

Ruby
Corundum, hardness 9. Comes in various shades of red, transparent to opaque. Where found: Asia, U.S.A., Australia, Europe.

Sapphire
Corundum, hardness 9. Usually blue, but also exists in all the other colors (except for red when it is called ruby), transparent to opaque. Where found: various.

Sodalite
Hardness 5 to 6. Comes in shades of blue and green with light-colored veins, transparent to opaque. Where found: various.

Tiger's eye
Quartz stone, hardness 6 to 7. Yellow, yellow-brown, red-brown, streaky, opaque. Where found: especially in South Africa, but also in other countries.

Topaz
Hardness 8. Yellow, yellowish-brown, pink or colorless. Where found: especially in Brazil, but also in many other countries.

Turquoise
Hardness 5 to 6. Light blue to green-blue or blue-green, opaque. Where found: U.S.A., South America, China.

Tourmaline
Hardness 7 to 7.5. Almost all colors, clear to opaque. Where found: Madagascar, U.S.A., Tanzania, Brazil, Pakistan.

Tourmaline quartz
Quartz stone, hardness 7. Colorless rock crystal with dark tourmaline needles, clear to transparent. Where found: Brazil, Madagascar, China, Australia.

Zircon
Hardness 6.5 to 7.5. Brown, red-brown, yellowish, also in other colors, transparent to opaque. Where found: Sri Lanka, Russia, Canada, U.S.A., Brazil.

Zirconium
Synthetic imitation of zircon, hardness 8.5. It is also used as an imitation diamond.

The power of stones

Mankind has always been fascinated by sparkling, dazzling stones that come in every color of the rainbow. People attributed special powers to these stones and used them in magic, in religious ceremonies, and for medicinal purposes. Even today many women still wear (of course without any esoteric motive) a particular stone on a ring or as a pendant because it somehow makes her feel better. Of course no one knows for certain whether the stones actually work, but they certainly do no harm.

In the past, only stones that were unusually large, beautiful, shiny, intensely colored, and rare were recognized as precious stones. They were therefore usually impressive finds that normally ended up in the royal treasure chamber or in the possession of the Church. But because these remarkable stones were few and far between, and as the demand for them rose, the terms "precious stones" or "gemstones" were extended to a number of different minerals and stones. Later, a

distinction was also made between precious and semiprecious stones. How precious a stone is depends to some extent on its degree of hardness. At the top of the list is the diamond, the most sought-after, and at the same time, hardest of all stones, defined as 10 (the maximum) in Mohs' hardness scale. It is followed at 9 in the hardness scale by the corundum family that includes sapphires and rubies, topaz at 8, and beryl, including aquamarine and emerald, at 7.5 to 8. With a hardness of 7, quartz, including amethyst, rose quartz, and rock crystal, are deemed rather less precious. Stones with a hardness below 4 are hardly ever used in jewelry, apart from amber (hardness 2 to 2.5), which is not a stone in the real sense of the word, but a fossilized tree resin, and coral (hardness 3 to 4), which is the lime secretion of living polyps in the sea. The value of a stone also depends on other criteria, such as its purity, brilliance, and size. For instance, a particularly beautiful emerald may be more expensive than a small, slightly imperfect diamond.

Precious and semiprecious stones are extraordinarily old natural products consisting of different combinations of minerals and trace elements. They have developed in the course of millions of years after the formation of the earth's crust as a result of chemical processes in the earth's interior or on the surface. Almost all countries in the world have larger or smaller deposits of precious or semiprecious stones that are mined, often under very primitive and dangerous conditions for the workers, and used for trading. Today, not all sparkling precious stones have been mined. Chemical laboratories play an important part in this field by creating synthetic gems to meet the demand of the jewelry industry. By using various methods such as the crystallization of solutions and flame fusion it is now possible to "create" synthetic precious stones by "assembling" the right chemical components. The layman will find it very hard to detect these replicas. The best criterion is the price—a sapphire ring that you can buy with loose change is highly suspicious.

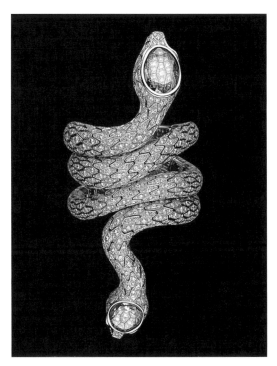

Platinum snake bracelet by Cartier. The two heads are embellished with diamonds weighing 6.38 and 6.68 carats, while the scales of the "reptile" are formed by 2,900 small diamonds.

18-carat white gold ring by Piaget, set with 200 diamonds 2.4 carats each and a heart-shaped sapphire of 5.33 carats.

Elegant, delicate platinum earrings embellished with 46 diamonds weighing 2.7 carats each and 14 emeralds 4.82 carats each. From the Piaget collection.

Diamonds

The hardest, most precious, most sought-after of all precious stones, a legendary symbol of power and the jewel of the powerful, supposedly the bringer of bad luck, as in the case of the "Hope" and "Regent" diamonds, a stone that cuts all other stones but is cut by no other: there are few people who remain unmoved at the sight of a large diamond, whether in reality or in a photograph, so great is the fascination of this object of desire. The legend started in India, in about 400 B.C., when the then rulers began systematically looking for precious stones for the first time. These treasures of the Orient only reached Europe much later. It was in fact only in the 17th century that the keen traveler and merchant Jean-Baptiste Tavernier sold a few of the pieces he had imported to Louis XIV, the French king. Diamonds remained a male prerogative until the 18th century when only kings, princes and other grandees wore them in their crowns, scepters, rings, decorations and the pommels of their parade swords. At that time the breathtaking beauty and proverbial fire of this most precious stone had not yet been discovered. The reason was that every diamond needs to be very accurately cut with facets in order to reveal its full brilliance, and that was neither understood nor possible at the time. It was only at the end of the 18th century that diamond cutting techniques were improved and the characteristic faceted diamond cut was developed. This highlighted the decorative aspect of the diamond, so that from being a man's stone it became a ladies' gem, well on the way to becoming a "girl's best friend."

All diamonds consist of crystallized carbon, an allotropic element that exists in two states. Usually it is encountered in the form of graphite, the soft, gray, opaque material that makes an excellent pencil lead. But when carbon is subjected to extreme pressure and a very high temperature deep down within the earth, the atoms form an extremely hard, transparent crystal. Eruptions in volcanic regions pushed these precious stones up to the surface, enabling the search to begin. In the past India was one of the major exporters of diamonds, but today the major exporting countries are Brazil, South Africa, China, Russia, and Sierra Leone. Diamonds are now also mined in other African countries, in Canada, and in Australia.

The largest diamond ever found is the famous Cullinan diamond. When it was discovered, in 1905 near Pretoria, South Africa, it weighed 3,106 carats, that is, slightly under 1 lb. 6 oz., or 620 grams. It was presented to King Edward VII, on whose instructions it was cut into nine large and almost 100 smaller stones by diamond cutters in Amsterdam. Cullinan I was, with its 530 carats, still the largest cut diamond in the world, and in 1910 it was incorporated into the royal scepter, the smaller Cullinan II was incorporated into the Queen's crown.

Cutting a diamond is an extremely difficult procedure that demands great precision and a lot of experience. In order to bring out the full beauty of a stone, the jeweler must sacrifice some of the carats. To ensure that this loss is as little as possible, valuable specimens are studied and analyzed for several months before cutting.

The value of a diamond is based on an assessment of the four Cs, that is carat, cut, clarity and color. Carat (abbreviated to ct) indicates the weight of the stone. A carat corresponds to 200 milligrams (about $\frac{1}{140}^{th}$ of an ounce). Cut refers to the cutting of the diamond. The cut should be of excellent quality with facets at specific angles so that it per-

fectly reflects the light and creates a "fire" inside. A diamond with at least 56 facets, a table and a point may be called a brilliant. That does not mean that other cuts are less precious, for there are many ways to cut a stone and to get the best out of it. Whether round, oval, tear-shaped or cone-shaped, the most important requirement is that the cut should be appropriate to the stone and the piece of jewelry it is intended for.

Clarity refers to the purity of the stone. The number, size, and location of any inclusions, transparency, and possible structural irregularities are assessed. In addition, a distinction is made between defects that are visible to the naked eye and those that can be seen with a ten-power magnifying loupe. The highest grading that can be reached is "FL" for "flawless" and this means that no imperfections can be detected internally or externally with a ten-power magnifier, so the stone is absolutely transparent. Then comes "IF" ("internally flawless"), meaning that there are no inclusions that are visible with the same magnifier. The grades below include "VVS" ("very very slightly imperfect") and "VS" ("very slightly imperfect") with inclusions only visible with some difficulty under a ten-power magnifier; these do not affect the stone's brilliance. "SI" ("slightly imperfect") and "I" ("imperfect") have inclusions that can be seen with the naked eye that may affect the stone's brilliance.

Diamonds are graded for color, with the ideal being colorlessness. This is an important, sought-after characteristic because it allows the white light to penetrate the stone unhindered, emerging as a rainbow. Most stones are situated between "D" ("colorless") and "Z" ("light yellow"). The color is determined by comparing the stone with an internationally fixed number of master stones. As well as the white-yellow range, diamonds also come in a range of other colors such as pinks and browns. The so-called "fancy diamonds" that may be blue, red, green, and almost black often fetch considerable prices from collectors. The color of a stone can be changed artificially through heating and radiation, but such diamonds are not particularly appreciated and this is reflected in their comparatively low price.

A diamond should be a wonder of nature, not of technology.

Tiffany & Co. charm their clients with its exclusive "Lucida" diamond cut which was launched in 1999.

Paris, Place Vendôme

The Paris headquarters of the legendary jeweler Cartier have been at the 13, Rue de la Paix since 1899. The company also has premises in the Place Vendôme, at numbers 7 and 23.

The royal wearers of crowns needed expert jewelers to look after them and their other precious regalia, as well as to create new pieces from time to time. For centuries, the great royal, imperial, and princely houses had an almost symbiotic relationship with the most famous goldsmiths and silversmiths of their time, and vice versa. For instance, Cartier is known to have been the official royal jeweler by appointment to 15 different sovereigns between 1904 and 1939. These included not only European royal houses but also legendary rulers of the Orient such as Rama V of Siam, who never ordered one bracelet at a time but boxes full of them, or the Maharajah of Kapurthala, a passionate watch collector who had his 250 watches wound every day by a specially appointed servant.

Toward the end of the 19th century, it was not only the old nobility who could afford to shop in these luxury boutiques, but also the new financial aristocracy who had made their fortune in the New World in banking, the railroads, and mining. It was a time when not

only blue-blooded ladies from Vienna and St. Petersburg, but also wealthy women from San Francisco, New York, Buenos Aires, and La Paz would plan stays of up to three months in Paris in their engagements calendars, during which they would order a complete haute-couture wardrobe for the new season, with the appropriate jewelry, of course. Many of them would stay at the celebrated Ritz Hotel that had opened in 1898, attracting the new cosmopolitan clientele like a magnet. As a result, the best jewelers opened sumptuous boutiques in the immediate vicinity of this luxurious hotel. Thus the Place Vendôme became a center of European jewelry. Today, some of the most famous jewelers such as Van Cleef & Arpels, Mauboussin, Buccellati, Piaget and many other well-known names are still established in the Place Vendôme. Boucheron's Chinese salon is now a protected historic monument, while the building that has housed Piaget since 1853 was where Chopin composed his last mazurka shortly before his death in 1849.

Who's who of the great jewelers

Boucheron

Founded in 1858, Boucheron was the first jeweler to realize the full potential of the Place Vendôme because of the wealthy clientele staying at the nearby Ritz Hotel. The store was opened in 1893, and at first the new premises had a magnificent marble floor. But after a client inadvertently pushed a large emerald off the counter to the floor, thus damaging it, wall-to-wall carpeting was installed.

Buccellati

Contardo Buccellati was already working as a goldsmith in the Via degli Orafi in Milan in the mid-18th century, but the house was officially founded in 1919 by Mario Buccellati. A jeweler and silversmith, he counted the Italian, Belgian, Spanish, and Egyptian royal houses among his clients, as well as the Vatican. In the 1970s, under Gianmaria Buccellati, the company opened boutiques all over the world, including their premises in the Place Vendôme. Today the company employs 250 people.

Bulgari

Founded in Rome in 1884, this celebrated house specializes in striking creations and opulent Italian elegance. Maria Callas always paid a ritual visit to the Bulgari boutique in the Via Condotti, without which a stay in Rome would not have been complete. The Bulgari family still has a majority shareholding in the company and it is the third-largest jeweler in the world, after Cartier and Tiffany, with 1,250 workers and 100 boutiques throughout the world.

Carrera y Carrera

This company was founded in 1885 by a member of the Carrera family, the young José Esteban, a small jeweler in Madrid. Since then the house has become one of the most famous Spanish jewelers, specializing in decorative art nouveau adaptations, reminiscent of filigree miniatures. The more sober-modern Ginkgo range is also very popular and includes among its many admirers Claudia Schiffer and Kathleen Turner, who have been seen wearing jewelry by Carrera y Carrera.

Cartier

Founded in 1847 by Louis-François Cartier, the house boasts many of the world's rich and famous among its clients. The panther, one of Cartier's best-known "symbols," was inspired by Jeanne Toussaint, a friend of Coco Chanel, who was nicknamed la panthère. In 1933 Jeanne Toussaint took over the management of the haute joaillerie department and made the wild cat a cult symbol. Cartier began to address a wider public in 1973 with the launch of Les Must de Cartier.

Chaumet

This is a house with a long tradition whose roots date back to 1780. In 1804 Chaumet (then Marie-Étienne Nitot) produced several pieces of jewelry for Napoleon's coronation. These included the famous "Regent" diamond of 140 carats, which he set in the emperor's sword. The actress Catherine Deneuve and the Moroccan royal family are among Chaumet's regular clients today.

Garrard

The roots of this long-established British jeweler date back to the early 18th century. Jeweler to the English royal family since 1843 by appointment to Queen Victoria, Garrard is responsible for the maintenance of the Crown Jewels, which are kept in the Tower of London. It was in Garrard's workshops that the legendary Koh-i-Noor diamond was re-cut to be incorporated in the crown that Queen Elizabeth II wore for her coronation in 1953.

Mauboussin

Founded in 1827, this is still a family-run business that is managed by Patrick Mauboussin, the sixth generation. This former jeweler to the French court was one of the first jewelers to combine diamonds with colorful precious stones and it also created beautiful jewelry during the art nouveau period. Some of Marlene Dietrich's most spectacular jewelry was made by Mauboussin.

Repossi

The Repossi family was originally Italian jewelers from Turin, but in 1977 Alberto Repossi opened his first shop in Monaco, having been appointed court jeweler to the princely family. Repossi is famous for its necklaces, close-fitting chokers, and engagement rings.

Tiffany

Tiffany & Co. has been a hallmark of New York and a representative of American culture since it was founded in 1837. The Fifth Avenue store was immortalized by the movie classic *Breakfast at Tiffany's* starring Audrey Hepburn and based on the novel by Truman Capote. The symbol of the company is the characteristic bright sky blue "Tiffany Blue."

Van Cleef & Arpels

The history of Van Cleef & Arpels began in 1896 with a wedding that brought together two families of goldsmiths and merchants dealing in precious stones. In 1906 Julien, Louis, and Charles Arpels together with their brother-in-law, Alfred Van Cleef, opened their boutique in the Place Vendôme. It was Van Cleef & Arpels who made the crown for Farah Dibah, Empress of Iran.

Chaumet's elegant salon in the Place Vendôme has been listed as a historic monument since 1927.

Empress Marie-Louise with jewelry by Marie-Étienne Nitot, Chaumet's founder.

Paloma Picasso has been an ambassador for Tiffany & Co for over 20 years.

Pearls

There is hardly any accessory that is so closely associated with the concept of ladylike elegance as the pearl necklace. For generations of women it has been an indispensable accessory of style that reflected well-groomed charm, good taste and a respectable background—or at least simulated it. The popularity of the pearl necklace and its amazing success story in the 20th century is linked to a discovery that enabled an extremely rare phenomenon in nature to a become a planned process that could be reproduced thousands of time: the culture of pearls. While people depended on the discovery of natural pearls, these shimmering, round little objects remained the most precious jewelry anyone could own and they were even more expensive than diamonds. At first, it was the laws governing dress codes that dictated that only members of the royal houses and aristocracy could wear pearls. Later, when dress regulations were abolished in the 19th century, pearls remained the prerogative of the rich aristocracy, their exorbitant price making their widespread popularization impossible.

Pearls are full of mystery. It is known that pearls are found inside a certain type of mollusk, the so-called pearl oyster, and that they are formed of mother-of-pearl, but what induces an oyster to produce a pearl is not known. The most frequent explanation is that it is caused by a grain of sand that has penetrated inside the mussel. In order to protect itself, the mussel encases this grain of sand in mother-of-pearl. This explanation does not seem to make much sense since most mussels are usually full of sand (but unfortunately not full of pearls). Natural pearls that have been broken or subjected to X-ray examination have never been shown to contain an inorganic center. According to the more recent theory on

A pearl necklace made from south-sea pearls by the New York jeweler Tiffany & Co. The platinum clasp is decorated with diamonds.

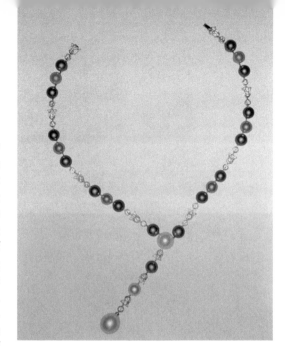

An interpretation of the traditional pearl necklace with a modern twist. Cartier has combined diamonds with pearls arranged by color gradation, thus creating a 21st-century piece of jewelry.

the formation of pearls, the process begins with marine creatures or parasites coming into contact with the mollusk, thus damaging the surface. This causes the transfer of mother-of-pearl forming cells from the surface of the shell to the inside where they continue doing what they were doing before, that is, producing mother-of-pearl. The culture of pearls is also based on this principle. A tiny core of mussel shell is taken and then coated with mother-of-pearl forming cells. Then, the piece of shell is carefully inserted inside a pearl oyster. Over the next few years the oyster then forms a pearl around this core. But this does not always go as smoothly as might be hoped because typhoons, water pollution, fluctuations in temperature, and diseases can all endanger the success of the whole operation. This is why pearl culture demands constant care and supervision, which is extremely costly. This explains why fine quality cultured pearls are also expensive.

The large-scale culture of pearls was developed in Japan in the late 19th century. This led to a boom in the popularity of pearls in the early years of the 20th century, which continues today. Pearls are very versatile and can be worn with all kinds of outfits. It is therefore not surprising that each era has interpreted pearls to suit its own fashion. In the Roaring Twenties, they were worn as hip-length necklaces, the more the better. In the 1940s and 1950s, they became shorter and consisted of only one to three rows, usually worn with a twin set, while in the 1980s Princess Diana made the choker with several rows of pearls popular throughout the world. Pearl necklaces are becoming for every lady, and whether they are natural or cultured is completely immaterial as far as style is concerned.

The nomenclature of pearls is strictly regulated. Only naturally-occurring pearls can be called "real pearls," "natural pearls," or "Oriental pearls." All others are called "cultured pearls." Real pearls are extremely rare and correspondingly expensive. There can be no objection against a good quality cultured pearl, since the only difference is that it was nudged a little to get it started. There are several types of cultured pearls that vary in size, shape, color, and therefore also in price. One of the best known is the Akoya, which is grown in salt water. The Biwa, on the other hand, is a freshwater pearl. China, like Japan, also has a long tradition of freshwater pearl culture. South Seas cultured pearls are among the most expensive. They come mainly from Australia but also from Burma, Indonesia, Tahiti, New Guinea, Thailand, and the Philippines.

Five criteria are taken into consideration in assessing the value of a pearl: luster, surface, shape, size, and color. Luster refers to the brilliance of the magical sparkle of the pearl. It must be shiny and clear, and the surface must be smooth and even, without scratches or flecks. The greater the regularity of its roundness, the more valuable it is. However, very irregularly formed pearls (baroque pearls) are also very sought-after. The size is indicated in millimeters. Very large pearls are rare and correspondingly expensive. The color of a pearl depends on the type of mussel and the growing conditions, so it does not really influence the value of the pearl. The natural color spectrum includes all shades of white, pink, champagne-color, bluish, and greenish. Black Tahiti pearls are unusual and therefore expensive.

This unusual duck-head brooch was created by Cartier in 1953 and belonged to the Duchess of Windsor. A strangely shaped blister pearl forms the head while the eye is formed by a sapphire, the bill by a coral with a brilliant-cut diamond as the nostril. The neck is decorated with emeralds and the feathers on the head and lower edge of the neck are made of gold.

Lady Mountbatten wearing four rows of pearls, seen here in a photograph dating from 1937 that was shown in Boston at an exhibition on tiaras.

Princess Diana in 1986 with her beloved choker. This consisted of several rows of pearls with a clasp embellished with an imposing sapphire.

Watches

Baume & Mercier has created the "Linea" model with interchangeable double bracelet so that it can be matched to the outfit.

Is a beautiful, expensive watch an important accessory in a lady's outfit? Absolutely, but not in the same way as it is for a man. Many women are not really keen on a watch with mechanical movement and even the legendary precision of a Swiss chronograph will impress them only moderately. Much more important than technical sophistication is aesthetic appearance. A woman sees her watch primarily as a piece of jewelry, so its importance as a horological masterpiece is only secondary. As a result,

women may be attracted by quartz watches, automatic models or even mechanically wound watches as the fancy takes them: for instance, for daytime wear, a mechanical bicolor Reverso, for evening wear a classic Cartier Tank, and when on vacation on the Costa Smeralda, an indestructible Rolex Oyster Perpetual in stainless steel. Or she may have been seduced by a trendy Swatch she saw in the duty free shop whose color perfectly matched a particular skirt, sweater or scarf.

The first wristwatch was produced in 1868 by Patek Philippe. Girard-Perregaux launched the first series-produced model in 1880, and in 1904 Cartier launched what was to become one of the most famous watches in the world, the Santos-Dumont. At that time all watches were mechanical with manual winding. With this system the energy needed by the watch to run is stored in the spring barrel. The tension in the mainspring supplies energy at a rate controlled by the balance wheel to the complex gear mechanism that drives the hands that indicate the time. When the tension in the mainspring has been completely released, the watch stops. To ensure a constant supply of energy, the mainspring is wound and tensioned again by turning the winding crown by hand. This operation is performed daily.

In 1923, the first automatic watch was launched on the market. These watches acquire their energy from the arm movements of the wearer. The watch contains an oscillating weight that swings as the watch is moved. The kinetic energy that it absorbs winds the mainspring through a special gear train. This means that there is no need to wind the watch every day—so long as it is worn throughout the day. Off the wrist they will inevitably run down after a day or so.

In the 1950s, the problem of the watch running down was finally solved by putting a battery inside the watch, providing a constant source of energy, regardless of movement. In the late 1960s and early 1970s the quartz watch became so successful that its triumphant progress seemed unstoppable. The principle of the quartz watch is that the electrical energy of the battery keeps a quartz crystal oscillating at a very precise frequency. This frequency is divided by electronic and mechanical means so that it moves the hands indicating the time with extreme accuracy. Some quartz watches have a digital display instead of a dial and hands, so they have no mechanical moving parts. All quartz watches will run for the lifetime of the battery, which is usually about two years.

There were two distinct watchmaking trends in the 1980s. In 1983 the Swatch was born, providing a large number of stylish designs at a cost so low that it became easy to own several watches for different occasions. At the same time the mechanical watch experienced a revival after the euphoria created by the great accuracy of the quartz watch had died down. Indeed, quartz watches have a number of disadvantages: the battery tends to run down at the wrong time when no replacement is available, and quartz watches cannot always be repaired, unlike their mechanical rivals.

The prestige of mechanical watches is probably higher now than it ever was, but this does not mean that quartz watches are necessarily lacking in style; quite the contrary in fact. Many watches in the top price range are beautiful jewel and luxury watches with quartz movements. But lovers of mechanical watches are not swayed by this. They believe that quartz watches are soulless and deficient in character, aspects for which their legendary accuracy cannot make up. In any case, the accuracy of a good automatic or hand-wound mechanical watch is sufficient for most purposes.

Wristwatches began to be worn by the lady in the 1920s when the rhythm and way of life suddenly began to speed up. The concept of "having no time" became synonymous with the modern age, and it was even considered chic with the "invention" of stress. From the start, ladies' models were inspired by men's watches and re-interpreted as slightly smaller, slightly more feminine versions. Even today many of these unisex designs have remained timeless. For instance, the large version with a broad strap of the much loved Reverso by Jaeger-LeCoultre is very popular with men, while the smaller version (which is just as beautiful) with a slender, discreet, or fashionably colored strap is much appreciated by all elegant women. There is also an evening version of this model, decorated with diamonds. Some makers offer separate ranges of ladies' watches, especially when their men's models are particularly masculine.

Precious watches, whether mechanical or quartz, should be sent back to an authorized dealer or an established specialist every four or five years so that they can be checked and any possible damage repaired. At the same time the watchmaker will clean all the parts, adjust the mechanism and check the accuracy. Water-resistant models should in addition be checked every year to ensure that the seal is still intact.

The dainty Louis Cartier Tank is a true classic ladies' watch. It is hard to believe that it was inspired by the armored vehicles of World War I.

For an all-purpose watch, the best choice is a timeless model with stainless steel bracelet because it can be worn on any occasion.

A few famous names in timekeeping

Patek Philippe
Patek Philippe is the undisputed number one among watch enthusiasts. The Geneva-based manufacture was founded in 1839 and is celebrated for producing outstanding, highly complicated watches of the highest quality, such as the Calatrava launched in 1932 and the Ellipse created in 1966.

Jaeger-LeCoultre
Founded in 1833, the name of this maker is virtually synonymous with the famous Reverso, designed in 1932. The case is mounted in such a way that it can turn 180 degrees. The company also produces other beautiful models such as the Master Control and the Master Geographique.

Rolex
Forget about its reputation of being a "show off" brand. Rolex produces fantastic watches and the water-resistant Oyster, produced in several versions, is a real classic ladies' watch. The entry-level models in stainless steel are not unusually expensive, but there is no limit at the top of the range.

Audemars-Piguet
Traditional maker of Swiss watches with numerous complications, that is, additional functions such as chronograph, calendar, second time zone, chiming mechanisms, moon phases, and so on that are very popular with men. There are also special ladies' models such as the Promesse, Charleston and Carnegie.

Breguet
Abraham Breguet (1747–1823) was one the most brilliant inventors in the field of watchmaking. Many of the watches produced by this legendary manufacturer (founded in 1775) can be recognized by the distinctive blued steel hands with an "eye" or ring, known as Breguet hands. The models in the Heritage range are especially beautiful.

Baume & Mercier
Founded in Geneva in 1830, Baume & Mercier produces elegant, classic watches for ladies and gentlemen, including some unisex models such as the sober, rectangular Hampton. The company belongs to the Richemont luxury group.

Cartier
The Paris jeweler Cartier started making watches in 1898. Since then it has produced several classics such as the Tank (1919), the Pasha (1932) and the Panthère (1983), which are available in countless versions. They also produce prohibitively expensive jewel watches.

Vacheron Constantin
Another venerable address in Geneva is Vacheron Constantin. Founded in 1775, it is the oldest watchmaker in continuous production in Switzerland. One of the most popular ladies' models is the Kalla 1972. Vacheron Constantin now belongs to the Richemont group.

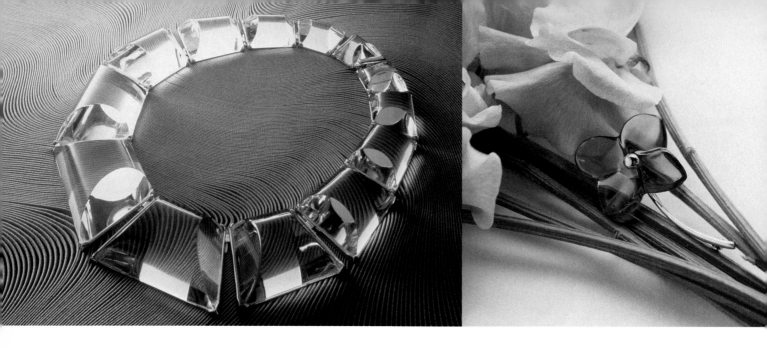

Costume jewelry

Is there a clear dividing line between real jewelry and costume jewelry? Real jewelry is defined as expensive works of art made from precious materials such as gold, silver, platinum, diamonds, rubies, sapphires, and emeralds, while costume jewelry are pieces inspired by these precious objects but using more modest materials. Nevertheless, costume jewelry is much more than a cheap substitute for the real thing that we all hope to own one day. Costume jewelry is a form of jewelry in its own right and in many cases an art form in its own right. Indeed many exclusive creations are often as expensive as "real" jewelry.

The desire for decorative accessories is as old as mankind and completely independent of culture and social status. The costume and fashion historian Ingrid Loschek once said, "there are people without clothes, but none without decorative accessories." In the 18th century, Paris manufacturers of costume jewelry, the bijoutiers faussetiers had already formed a guild of their own that numbered over 300 members. Those with expensive jewelry would go to these costume jewelry manufacturers to have their valuable jewelry copied to take with them when traveling. This was certainly not a bad idea at

a time when robberies were quite common with horse-drawn carriages. The glitzy theatrical jewelry used in opera, theatre, and variety shows also came from the workshops of these costume jewelers. Instead of gold and silver they used less expensive metal alloys with strass or paste gems such as rhinestones to provide glitz and sparkle.

The origin of the word "strass" is disputed. The French claim the invention of this convincing diamond imitation as their own, naming the jeweler G. F. Strass (1700–73) as the inventor. The Austrians, on the other hand, claim that the name comes from the Viennese goldsmith J. Strasser who had astounded the Empress Maria Theresia with his artificial gems. Whatever the truth may be regarding the identity of the inventor, strass is simply cut glass. The glass used is made from quartz sand, soda as flux, and lime or lead as a stabilizer. The art lies in the precise quantities of the individual substances, the recipes being well-kept secrets preserved by the glassworks. Equally important is the correct supervision of the melting and cooling processes. Finally, this glass is cut by experienced, skilled craftsmen. Until the end of the 19th century this was a lengthy process carried out by hand, which is why strass was expensive

and exclusive. The foundation stone of industrial production of glass jewelry was laid by the Bohemian glassmaker and crystal cutter Daniel Swarovski. In 1895, he settled in Wattens, near Innsbruck, where he founded his own company. The factory was equipped with special machines that he had developed on which the transparent stones could be cut quickly, accurately and inexpensively.

Around the turn of the century, costume jewelry became highly sought after and experienced a long-lived boom. First it was during the belle époque before World War I when women loved sparkling, chunky jewelry. It continued with the development of art nouveau and with it the revival of applied arts, when beautiful jewelry was created out of modest materials such as horn, copper, colorful precious stones, and enamel. Finally, in the mid-1920s, came striking earrings, bracelets, armlets, bangles, and decorative brooches, together with the characteristic and indispensable long pearl necklaces. Following the example of the art nouveau movement, the new arts and craft movement known as art deco continued to use contemporary fashion elements as well as unusual materials with great enthusiasm.

The then highly innovative synthetic materials such as celluloid and bakelite were considered very avant-garde. It was also at that time that fashion designers began to realize the importance of jewelry in the general appearance of a well-dressed woman. It was in 1910 that Paul Poiret designed long necklaces of French jet pearls to be worn with his flowing clothes. Madeleine Vionnet, Lucien Lelong, and Jean Patou also designed their own range of jewelry. But the real queen of costume jewelry was Coco Chanel, on the one hand because of the very original design of her jewelry, and on the other, and this was the real innovation, because of the way these colorful, striking pieces of jewelry were destined to be worn: not only for going out in the evening but also with casual daywear such as knitted suits, sweaters, cardigans and even beachwear. Chanel also challenged the rule that said that real and costume jewelry should not be mixed. She herself set the example: although she had a vast collection of precious jewelry and accessories— many of these were presents from her friend the Duke of Westminster, one of the richest men in the world—she also wore creations from her latest range of costume jewelry.

Above left:
The "Medicis" crystal glass ring by Baccarat is available in a range of elegant shades such as crystal, sapphire, honey, onyx or peony pink.

Above:
The attraction of costume jewelry lies more in its decorative and often unusual details, and less in its material value. Here is a set consisting of a medallion and matching rings, called "Eclipse".

Ladies' fountain pens

Aurora
Aurora is a traditional house that was founded in 1919 in Turin, Italy, as the Fabbrica Italiana di Penne a Serbatoio Aurora. It has been famous since the 1920s for its many remarkable models as well as innovative creations.

Montblanc
In 1906, a qualified engineer, August Eberstein, and a banker, Alfred Nehemias, joined forces in Hamburg to start a fountain pen factory that during the following decades developed into a world-famous producer of writing implements.

Namiki
This Japanese manufacturer of fountain pens was supplying its stylishly decorated fountain pens to the best stores in the 1920s. The elegant, hand-crafted lacquer Maki'e models are particularly famous.

Omas
The Italian brand Omas (Officina Meccanica Armando Simoni) dates back to 1919 when it was founded as a manufacturer of spare parts for fountain pens. They are now one of the few surviving fountain pen manufacturers that have been producing pens of the highest quality since the 1920s.

Parker
Parker is one of the earliest brands in the history of fountain pens, its founder George S. Parker having applied for his first fountain pen patent in the United States as early as 1889. This was followed by numerous innovations and pioneering design ideas with which Parker continuously set new standards.

Pelikan
Pelikan's history began in 1832 when it was founded as a factory manufacturing artists' paints. This developed into a very successful range of office supplies. It produced its first fountain pen only in the 1920s and the design of this decade still dominates the range of models presented by the house.

Waterman
Manufacturer of the original fountain pen, the company was founded in 1882 by the American Lewis E. Waterman. Since 1926, the company has also produced fountain pens in France under the label JiF-Waterman. This is now the only production site since the American works closed down in 1954.

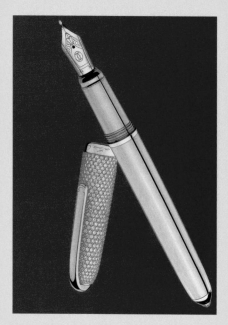

A luxury Cartier writing instrument. The fountain pen is made of solid white gold, adorned with 823 brilliants. Be careful not to leave it behind anywhere.

The writing lady

Watches, diaries, and fountain pens are accessories that many women clearly prefer to be traditional. Naturally, a quartz watch is more accurate than even a very expensive chronograph. Is that reason enough to replace your Patek Philippe with a Swatch? In the same way, a palmtop might perform many more functions than the traditional personal organizer, yet many businesswomen still prefer the conventional ring binder, bound in leather. Similarly, women also prefer to write and sign with a fountain pen or a silver automatic pencil even though fine felt-tip pens glide just as easily across the paper. So why is it that tradition is so often preferred to the most recent technology? Because modern classic pens, which are still the same as the writing implements of the late 19th and the first three decades of the 20th century, turn everyday writing into something special. It is true that a signature has as much legal power with a throwaway ballpoint as with a fountain pen, but only the latter will achieve beauty.

The dream of the plume sans fin, the fountain pen without end, in other words the pen whose flow of ink does not dry up, dates back to the 18th century. The constant dipping of the pen in the inkpot was a lot of trouble, but at that time there was no other way. Many devices were invented but none of them successfully ensured a lasting, continuous, even flow of ink. Then on February 12, 1884, the American Lewis E. Waterman patented his fountain pen feed that controlled the ink flow, thus establishing himself as the father of the modern fountain pen. His system was one of several that had been developed at the same time between 1880 and 1890 but his proved to be the best and thus was soon copied by many competitors. Waterman had solved the problem of ink flow, but the next stumbling-block was filling the pen. His countryman Roy Conklin found the answer in 1898 with his Crescent Filler, the first self-filling pen in the history of writing implements. The golden age of fountain pens embraced the first few decades of the

Mini-ballpoint pen from the "Must de Cartier" collection: pure yellow gold, decorated with diamonds. The entwined rings at the top are reminiscent of the "Trinity" friendship ring.

Infinitely more stylish than the inexpensive, leaking plastic ballpoints found free at gas stations, this luxury ballpoint pen with spiral motif is available in yellow or white gold according to choice.

Diamonds are a girl's best friend, so tell your beloved that you would rather like Cartier's leading model, decorated with 47 diamonds, for your next birthday!

20th century when some of the most beautiful and elegant writing implements were created. The decline of the traditional fountain pen started in the mid-1960s when the use of ballpoint pens began to spread rapidly. However, at the end of the 1970s the fountain pen experienced a great revival that developed into a real boom in the 1980s. Suddenly fountain pens were fashionable again and elegant Waterman, Parker, and Montblanc pens became a common sight in meetings, having replaced the common ballpoint. The lady much welcomed this revival because she had always preferred fountain pens.

Besides fountain pens, creative women also like pencils because they make it much easier to erase something during a hectic, brainstorming meeting. This is why every desk and meeting table should always have a good selection of well-sharpened pencils. But pencils are not very practical in a handbag. The point can damage or mark the lining, and it is easy to injure one-self when searching for it in the bag. Automatic pencils are therefore ideal for carrying around in a bag or briefcase. One possibility is to choose a model that matches the fountain pen, while those who appreciate authentic, traditional objects should look for classics by the house of Yard-O-Led, a company founded in England in 1934 that still specializes in hand-made writing implements using precious materials. The name is a corruption of "a yard of lead" because the reserve of twelve three-inch leads has a total length of one yard. When a lead is used up, the remaining stump is pushed out by turning and the next appears automatically. The Yard-O-Led is distinctive with its ingenious mechanism (it was invented in 1822!) and its elegant shell of solid silver. There are several patterns available, including plain, fine barleycorn, and Victorian, all of which are engraved by hand. Instead of silver you could always choose a gold version, either 18 karat solid gold or gold-plated.

The Montblanc "Bohème" fountain pen is understated in appearance despite its gold finish. Nevertheless, it looks solid and distinguished.

№ 8

Festive garments and haute couture

A lady in the limelight

Not every woman loves going to balls and receptions and many even fear such events. Nevertheless, even women who lead a rather secluded life know exactly what is expected on such occasions: a radiant appearance and a radiant smile. If it proves unavoidable, even the shyest will dress up to the nines and show themselves at their best to impress the other guests. They do not reveal that they would probably prefer to be digging in the garden, playing with their children or analyzing stock prices. They move around as if in total command of the situation in spite of being dressed in a way to which they are not accustomed. Along with those who only go out reluctantly, there are those who love these formal occasions. They will seize any opportunity to take out the little black dress, the elegant hat or the sumptuous evening gown. They do not find wearing extravagant outfits a boring task that they perform out of duty, but a pleasant occupation, and they enjoy the planning and buying of these clothes as much as they enjoy wearing them.

Men rarely play a decisive part in women's choice of clothes, except on formal occasions when their outfit is dictated by that of their partner. Traditional written invitations usually only indicate what the man should wear, on the assumption that the woman will decide for herself what outfit she should wear in this context. For instance, the invitation may stipulate "white tie" or "black tie." What does that mean? "White tie" means that the man will wear an evening tail coat with a white bow tie while the lady wears a long evening gown. What the man wears is precisely defined by the dress code. All he needs to worry about is buying or renting the right size and he will never go wrong. In contrast, the long evening gown is much more a matter of individual interpretation. But it is always a long, low-neck gown, worn with a jacket, cape or stole, evening gloves, and sumptuous jewelry. Within this specification, the choice of color, cut, fabric, and accessories are up to the woman. Things become even more vague in the case of the cocktail dress or dinner gown that the woman may wear when the invitation specifies "black tie." Every kind of evening dress is allowed here, from the little black dress to the timeless wine red velvet dress or the even latest confection from a designer boutique.

Dance floors are notoriously smooth and slippery and in view of the almost endless possibilities of the two categories of evening dress, it would be easy to flounder—yet the lady remains composed. Relying on her sense of style and good taste, she will select the outfit she deems the most appropriate one for the occasion. The lady will confidently look toward the upcoming party also because she has no logistical problems to contend with, especially not the crucial problem of where to buy her dress. In most cases she will already have a dress in her wardrobe that would be perfect for the occasion and if not, she knows where to borrow a sumptuous gown, fur stole or delightful evening bag. In fact, what are friends, sisters, mothers, and aunts with well-stocked wardrobes for? Whether the gown belongs to her or not is quite immaterial, she will wear it as if it was made for her—even if it is an Yves Saint Laurent model that her mother bought in Paris in 1977.

Whether you have called upon a couturier, hairdresser, make-up artist, and jeweler to help you achieve this wonderful appearance, or if you have done it all by yourself on a small budget, both ways can be very ladylike. What you yourself decide to do depends on many factors, the most important being the kind of occasion it is. The country where it takes place also plays an important part. The clothes worn for a high society wedding at the Plaza Hotel in New York will of course be different from a Redentore dinner at the Cipriani in Venice. Then, there is also the professional and social background of the guests. For instance, fashionable guests at a media event will be dressed differently from those attending the Queen Charlotte's Ball in London. Last but not least, age also plays an important part: women born in the first few decades of the 20th century will have a different view of what should be worn to those born in the 1980s. Nevertheless, ladies of all generations throughout the world do agree on one thing: one should always wear an outfit that is appropriate to the occasion. This shows respect for the occasion, for the other guests, and for oneself.

Audrey Hepburn wearing a long evening dress with a sophisticated low-cut back. This is a scene from the celebrated movie *Breakfast at Tiffany's* (1961).

Long evening dresses and ballgowns

Spanish designer Jorge Gómez believes that bright colors are perfectly acceptable for open-air summer parties.

Perfect for an opera ball or state banquet: a classic long gown by the German evening and bridal wear specialist Kleemeier of Hof.

There are many interesting phenomena in fashion. An example is the fact that the more festive the occasion the more traditional the dress code becomes. In other words: the more serious and important the social occasion, the more old-fashioned the outfit. Thus, the long evening dress is real "dinosaur" of fashion. Women could travel back 100 years with such a dress without feeling out of place in the past. In fact, the floor-length party dress with evening gloves, fur stole, evening bag, and tiara was the traditional dress for any event taking place after sunset. In spite of all the differences in details such as type of fabric and decorative elements, a modern woman in a modern evening dress would raise far fewer eyebrows in her time travel than she would wearing a modern casual look.

Why is this? Because the rules that to a certain extent still dictate the dress code for evening wear today are based on 18th and 19th century rules. These regulations mirrored the strict ceremonials of the princely and royal courts of the time. Particular clothes had to be worn in the presence of feudal lords and those who sought an audience had to dress up accordingly. Although these court rituals lost their meaning after the demise of the monarchy in most of Europe, they remained a guiding principle. How much evening wear is still influenced by this varies enormously from country to country. For instance, the United States are more influenced by Hollywood glamour than by royal examples of the past, while in Britain the dress code for evening wear is based on these courtly rituals. But even in the United Kingdom etiquette is sometimes ignored without serious consequences. At worst, the woman who is inappropriately dressed—that is, from a subjective point of view—is refused access. Admittedly, this happens much less often at a ball than at the strictly guarded entrances of discos and clubs. But because etiquette no longer provides a clear definition of correct evening wear and because old conventions have lost much of their meaning, women usually choose a dress from a purely esthetic point of view. Ladies who often wear evening dresses are usually careful to choose a dress that will also be practical for the purpose. For instance, she must be particularly careful if the dress is to be worn for dancing, especially in the select circles where dancing can become quite wild as the night progresses. This is why the cut and the style must be such that no unwanted bare flesh is exposed, and why experienced night queens usually try a few waltz steps to make certain that the straps are secure. If the woman only notices that her straps are constantly slipping on the evening itself, it will be too late to make any adjustments, and this could spoil the evening.

Of course, besides the right dress the right shoes are also needed. The best shoes to wear depend mainly on two factors: first on the fabric of the dress, and second on the type of event. If it is a sit-down event, elegance and beauty may take precedence over comfort because most of the time will be spent sitting down. On the other hand, if dancing is involved, pumps and strap sandals will be more comfortable. Tight shoes could damage the feet, making every step an agony, while excessively high heels may be dangerous when dancing. Nevertheless, the shoes are part of the outfit and, besides being suitable for dancing, they must also be appropriate for the occasion.

Right: In this creation by the Dutch label Lady Bird, the embroidery of the top and evening bag is emphasized by the simplicity of the skirt and stole.

Far right, above: The German designer Anja Gockel has chosen the reliable black and red combination but interpreted it in a very unconventional, wildly romantic manner.

Far right: The Spanish label Brunella includes trousers in its range of evening wear. The long, transparent stole worn here gives the outfit a particular elegance and festive touch.

Cocktail dresses and the little black dress

Wearing a long evening dress is very exciting but unfortunately there are very few opportunities to do so. Who goes regularly to balls and state receptions? Most events nowadays call for a short evening dress, perfect for elegant parties, the opera or a chic private view of a contemporary artist's exhibition. This is why many young women prefer to invest in a versatile little black dress or short cocktail dress rather than in a sumptuous long evening gown which they would only wear very rarely.

A well-made little black dress is a perfect example of timeless elegance, and thus it is no surprise that it has been around for a long time. Indeed, the knee-length black dress was created by Coco Chanel in 1926. The date of its creation

In the 1920s the "little black dress" was considered revolutionary, but today it has become a classic for festive occasions. This model is by Laura Ashley.

perfectly reflects the character of the little black dress, because only the 1920s could have produced such a modern article of clothing, being the decade that saw the greatest changes in women's fashion. It is therefore not surprising that evening wear should also have experienced revolutionary changes. Compared with the opulence of ball gowns, the little black dress is provocatively plain and unadorned. American Vogue described it as the "Ford" of clothes, because the automobiles from this maker stood for modernity and the democratization of luxury items in the 1920s.

As with many innovations, it took the little black dress quite a while before it became common property in the world of fashion. Its heyday arrived in the 1950s and 1960s when the image of the little black dress received a further boost: it was worn by Audrey Hepburn in Breakfast at Tiffany's and became a fashion icon for many women. However, by this time Chanel was no longer the only couture house producing this type of dress. Indeed, Audrey Hepburn had asked her favorite couturier Hubert de Givenchy to design her little black dress. But Givenchy was neither the first nor the last to adapt Coco Chanel's new look for his clients. Today the little black dress is still a firm favorite among designers and new interpretations of this timeless classic are seem on the runway every season.

While the little black dress reflects the modernism of the 1920s, the cocktail dress reflects the love of luxury of the 1950s. The idea was simple and effective: a dress with a very low neckline, with straps or even strapless like an evening dress, calf-length, worn with a little jacket, and which therefore could also be worn in the afternoon. Christian Dior was the acknowledged creator of the cocktail dress, first launching it in 1948. This look soon proved to be the ideal solution for the lady of the 1950s who wanted to be well dressed both in the afternoon and the evening. The transition between these two times of the day was marked by the removal of the jacket, so there was no longer any need to change for the evening.

Falke only intended to advertise stockings but the picture also shows a perfect example of the modern interpretation of the little black dress.

From Marlene Dietrich to Yves Saint Laurent: The tuxedo for women

Women's wardrobes are full of interpretations and adaptations of men's clothes. Even women's evening wear has been influenced by men's clothes, notably by the tuxedo, the traditional evening wear for men. It was first launched at the end of the 19th century as an alternative to the tail coat. How the idea came about to replace the tail coat by a lounge jacket with silk trimmings is not known with absolute certainty but the history of fashion has various theories as to its origin.

What is certain, on the other hand, is that this model also appealed to women. When avant-garde women began to wear men's clothes in the early 20th century, they also included the new tuxedo in their wardrobe. Marlene Dietrich was well-known for her passion for clothes inspired by men's fashion and this was one of her trademarks dating from that period.

When women wanted a tuxedo before World War II they had to have it made by a tailor, unless they were satisfied with a badly-fitting off-the-rack man's tuxedo. Being a fanatic for well-fitting, quality clothes, Marlene Dietrich would not have been prepared to make such compromises. Any woman who could afford it would have her "men's clothes" made by the best men's tailors possible. Although this may sound very eccentric today, it was not unusual at the time. Already in the 19th century women used to have their riding jackets, travel clothes, and forerunners of the suit made by men's tailors.

In the 1930s the Vienna-based custom tailor Knize was one of the most famous shopping addresses in Europe. Marlene Dietrich and her husband Rudolf Sieber used to be regular clients there until the annexation of Austria by Germany in 1938 forced its Jewish owners to flee. They traveled to Paris and then arrived in the United States, opening new premises in New York in 1941. In her biography of her famous mother, Dietrich's daughter, Maria Riva, describes how her parents ordered their clothes from this prestige custom tailor during a stay in Vienna in 1933. The first day was spent being measured and selecting the models, that is tails, tuxedos, chesterfield coats, morning suits, and shirts. The fabrics were chosen the next day, then many more hours were spent on fittings. But it was worth the effort because the diva was a loyal client who even after the war continued to have her tails and tuxedos made by Knize, albeit in their New York workshop.

Marlene Dietrich's tuxedo was a perfect imitation of a man's suit made for a woman. The tuxedo only became a truly feminine garment when Yves Saint Laurent created his legendary outfit. This brilliant fashion designer was ecstatically celebrated as the successor to Christian Dior in 1958, but two years later he was dismissed because he produced an excessively avant-garde collection and was replaced by Marc Bohan. Yves Saint Laurent set up his own couture house in 1961 and presented his first collection under his own name in 1962. In 1966 following the trend of the time—the 1960s were just as revolutionary as the 1920s in the field of fashion—he reinterpreted the tuxedo ("le smoking") and created the first true ladies' version of this classic that retained all the characteristic features of the tuxedo. Ennobled by the great fashion designer, the tuxedo now became part of many women's wardrobe. It was adopted by Catherine Deneuve, a loyal Yves Saint Laurent customer, and her example was followed with confidence. Today when a designer includes a ladies' tuxedo in the collection, it will inevitably be compared with the legendary Yves Saint Laurent creation of the 1960s. But that does not stop designers from including tuxedos in their collections. Its last revival was as a festive send-off to the 21st century and the next is certainly not far off.

Mulberry presents its light-colored ladies' tuxedo in a nautical setting. This is appropriate since a white dinner jacket was traditionally only worn at sea or outside.

Evening wear accessories

The Tutti-Frutti bag, created in 1930 by Cartier New York, would be the perfect accessory for an elegant evening out.

Show us your shoes! These gold sling-back pumps by Salvatore Ferragamo are far too beautiful to be concealed under a long dress.

This would be a wonderful birthday present: an 18-carat white gold necklace with 1,031 diamonds and 12 pink sapphires by Chaumet.

Chaumet tiara from 1908. It is a shame that such headdresses are so rarely worn nowadays because they turn every woman into a princess.

Evening gloves

Evening gloves are no longer compulsory accessories for evening wear but they are very elegant. What happens to jewelry such as bracelets when gloves are worn? Are they worn over the gloves or under them, where no one sees them? Etiquette experts say that jewelry should be worn under the gloves, but those who find this too plain should not worry since it is quite acceptable to wear a watch or bracelet on top. Evening gloves are not removed to shake hands or to eat. However, some glove designs have hand parts that can be removed separately before the meal.

Fur cape

Today, fur capes are mainly worn by older ladies, because the short cape made from valuable fur has not been considered a really modern accessory since the 1950s. Capes made from warm, woolly fabrics were worn by women to protect themselves from the elements until the 19th century. Indeed, coats would have been impossible to wear then because of the bulky clothes women wore at the time. Anyone who has ever tried to slip the puffed sleeves of an evening dress into the armhole of a coat will know why. On the other hand, the elegant fur version of the cape not only looks perfect with a sumptuous gown but will also protect from the cold.

Fabric stole

The design of the stole is very old and women were already wearing shawl-like capes in classical times. But it was only at the beginning of the 20th century that the stole became established as an accessory for evening wear. It was not a replacement for the coat or cape but to protect against draughts and the cool of the evening as well as to cover the low neckline on the way to and from the party. In fact, any large scarf can be used as an evening stole as long as it looks good with the gown. In the late 1990s pashminas became very popular and were often worn instead of a stole.

Fur stole

On hearing the words "fur stole" some women immediately conjure up a picture of soft mink, sable or ermine, while others think of the animal that prefers to wear its own fur. However this controversial item is a fashion accessory that need not be made of real fur. In fact, fake fur can look just as glamorous and be just as warm.

Evening bag

The evening bag is intended to be a decorative and practical accessory, with the decorative aspect undoubtedly being the most important. What does a lady need to take with her when she goes out? As well as make-up, she needs her cellphone, a clip with a few bills, some coins for tipping—and the invitation, of course.

Evening shoes

Silver, gold, velvet or silk—evening shoes made from precious materials sparkle with glitz. They may normally be concealed under the long gown, but they are very visible when the lady dances. This is why they must match the outfit perfectly, because shoes form an integral part of the ensemble.

Tiara

At the court of the French Emperor Napoleon Bonaparte it was the custom that on her wedding day the bride should receive a large dowry consisting of jewelry from her parents. This always included a diamond tiara. Today anyone who owns such a piece of jewelry usually keeps it securely in a safe deposit box, partly for insurance reasons, but also because of the lack of opportunities for wearing such a piece of jewelry. A gala night with a long evening gown is probably one of the rare occasions to wear this sumptuous piece of jewelry. In the past wearing a tiara was reserved to married women, because it symbolized the loss of innocence and the crowning of love. Today this convention is more flexible.

Diamond necklace

Women will take their most precious jewelry out of the safe deposit box to wear with a long evening dress, costume jewelry and imitation jewelry being out of place here. But what do you if you do not have a diamond necklace? The rich and famous usually have no problem, they just borrow a creation from a jeweler, who is happy to lend it in the expectation that the VIP will be photographed wearing it at the movie premiere or charity ball. But even less famous women may be able to rent jewelry under particular conditions.

Like the Countess of Bessborough in this historic photograph, elegant women would accompany a long evening gown with precious jewelry, a tiara, and, if they had them, decorations and medals.

Haute couture:
exclusivity made to measure

To understand the phenomenon of French haute couture it is best to start with the term itself. Haute couture means "high-class tailoring." The adjective raises the creations of the more famous houses above those of the "ordinary" ladies' dressmakers. In France, the designation "haute couture" is a term protected by law, and its use is supervised by the Fédération Française de la Couture, du Prêt-à-porter et des Créateurs de Mode. Only those who are listed by this association can use this title of the dressmaking nobility. In order to be accepted by the select circle of haute couture, the applicant must meet very stringent requirements. Among other conditions, the house must employ at least 20 people in its design department and workshop, and it must present a collection of at least 25 items twice a year. The comparatively large staff of designers and dressmakers guarantees that the clothes are designed and made by them according to the rules of the craft and that they also offer made-to-measure clothes. The regular presentation of collections is an indication that the house is seriously man-

aged. The ability to produce made-to measure clothes is for good reason one of the most important distinguishing features of registered haute couture houses. Indeed, the making of individual creations was the original purpose of haute couture houses, the collections serving only to inspire the clients. According to official figures, there were still 20,000 couture supporters in 1943, while today there are only 200. This does not mean that there are no longer any prosperous clients, but that buying habits have changed. In the 1950s, many fashionable women who had the necessary amount of money had their clothes made in a haute couture house, but since the 1960s, many prefer to buy clothes off-the-rack in fashion boutiques. Only the super-rich can still indulge in the luxury of the completely individual services that haute couture still offers.

Haute couture is often confused with designer fashion. The reason for this confusion is that since the 1960s haute couture houses have also been designing prêt-à-porter or off-the-rack collections. This was partly a reaction to the steep decrease in individual orders and partly to the emerging boom of designer fashion. Yves Saint Laurent was one of the first to venture into the direction of prêt-à-porter or ready-to-wear. He met with much criticism from the older, well-established houses who nevertheless almost all followed his example in due course. In reality, haute couture off-the-rack fashion does not really differ from ordinary designer fashion, whether the name of the designer is known or not. In the end, like designer fashion, prêt-à-porter produces clothes in various sizes rather than ones that are handmade to measure. Nevertheless, the prestige of an haute couture house is always carried over to its ready-to-wear collections and the name is a guarantee of the quality of their clothes. Although ready-to-wear contradicts the very concept of haute couture, it will attract the attention of new, young clients to the haute couture houses and possibly even arouse their interest in actual haute couture at a later stage.

Vienna in about 1925: society women choosing precious fabrics at Wilhelm Jungmann & Neffe. The dressmaker would then make these into dresses.

Bill dated 6 July 1894 addressed to Her Majesty the Empress Elisabeth, better known as Sissi, for three lengths of black fabric.

In addition to the confusion that surrounds the words "couturier" and "designer," the term "collection" also leads to misunderstanding. As already mentioned, haute couture collections were originally intended to be simply a source of inspiration for clients, because very few women had a sufficiently clear idea of what they wanted when they came to their couturier. Most women would know only what kind of clothes they wanted, for instance an evening dress or a dress for a garden party. Haute couture collections anticipated these needs by including a selection of designs which would be ideal for those occasions. All the wealthy client had to do was to select what she liked, whereupon the model would be made-to-measure for her as an individual order. Only if she could not find anything that pleased her in the collection would the couturier produce an entirely new design. This happened most often with very important women who needed a special gown or dress for one-off occasions, for instance an investiture or an official state visit. The prêt-à-porter collection has a completely different purpose, to present the collection of designs for the coming season to the fashion store buyers and the press. In this case, anyone who does not like the items in the collection will have to wait for the next show since individual orders are not taken.

Evening dress with transparent effect from the 2002 Gucci summer collection. Gucci is one of the most famous providers of "alta moda," the Italian counterpart of haute couture.

Fashion houses with "Appellation Haute Couture"

The first "couturier" in the modern sense was English-born Charles Frederick Worth, who worked mainly in France. He considered himself not so much a tailor as an artist and he put his own very personal stamp on his clothes. He decided what the garment should look like, not the client for whom he was making it. This immediately gave the couturier's role a creative, artistic status. At the same time it raised the question of intellectual property. Worth proposed an association of the Paris tailors' trade, which led in 1868 to the creation of the Chambre Syndicale de la Couture Française. Its task was to protect the creations of its members, to prevent unauthorized copying of patterns, and also to coordinate the activities of the haute couture houses. Many houses have been members of this interest group in the course of their history and a succession of famous couturiers held the presidency after Worth stepped down, including Jeanne Paquin and Lucien Lelong. The organization now operates as part of the Fédération Française de la Couture, du Prêt-à-porter des Couturiers et des Créateurs de Mode. Today, only twelve houses are entitled to trade under the "Appellation Haute Couture".

BALMAIN
PARIS

The haute couture house of Balmain was founded in 1945 by Pierre Balmain. After having trained as an architect, he worked at famous fashion houses, such as Christian Dior. As early as 1953, when the European lady still insisted on individual, made-to-measure clothes, Balmain designed a prêt-à-porter collection for the promising American market. His sphere of activity extended far beyond the luxury market, designing for the theatre and cinema as well as uni-forms for flight attendants. After Balmain's death in 1982, his assistant of many years, Erik Mortensen, took over the creative management of the house. Ten years later he was succeeded by Oscar de la Renta.

CHANEL

The story of Chanel began in 1909 when Gabrielle Chanel, known as Coco, opened a milliner's shop in a friend's house. In 1910 she moved her business to no. 21, rue Cambon, and nine years later she moved to no. 31 as her enterprise expanded with great success. This independent, self-willed young woman quickly made a name for herself with her unconventional, modern, very wearable fashion, a triumphant ascent to fame that was only slowed down by the world economic crisis of the 1930s. In 1939 Coco Chanel closed down her haute couture salon and until the end of the war she concentrated entirely on her boutique and the marketing of her perfumes. In 1954 she returned to her old premises (right behind the Ritz in the Place Vendôme) from where she launched a new haute couture collection that was very successful, first in the United States and then in Europe. After the death of its founder, the creative management of the house has been in the hands of several designers, most recently Karl Lagerfeld, who since 1983 has turned the haute couture house into an international cult label.

Christian Dior
PARIS

Christian Dior belonged to a generation of gifted amateurs, because he had originally been destined for a career as diplomat. He made his debut in the world of fashion with hat designs and fashion drawings until he began to work as a designer in 1938. In 1945, Christian Dior got the chance of a lifetime when the textile manufacturer Marcel Boussac appointed the newcomer as fashion designer of a new couture house in the distinguished Avenue Montaigne. Dior's first collection was launched in 1947 and it was enthusiastically described by the American fashion press as the "New Look." It also proved to be the foundation stone of Dior's meteoric rise to be one of the most successful labels. It also contributed to the prestigious reputation of Christian Dior himself as one of the most influential designer of the postwar years. After Dior's early death in 1957, the house was briefly taken over by his extremely talented assistant, Yves Saint Laurent, who was then succeeded in 1961 by Marc Bohan. In 1989 the scepter of France's most famous couture house was taken over by the Italian Gianfranco Ferré to the great horror of many traditionalists.

CHRISTIAN LACROIX

Christian Lacroix opened his haute couture house in 1987 at no. 73, Rue du Faubourg Saint-Honoré, and this is among one of the most recent addresses of the prestigious fashion mile. After studying history of art, Christian Lacroix took his first steps as a designer not far from his present headquarters, working for Hermès at no. 24. He then worked as artistic director of the traditional haute couture house Patou from 1981 to 1987. Lacroix loves opulent colors, striking patterns and luxurious fabrics that clearly reflect his love for the south of France and Spain. Although his creations are characterized by a daring stylistic mix, using unconventional colors and pattern combinations that do not entirely correspond to the traditional image of haute couture, Christian Lacroix is considered one of the finest Paris couturiers. This is especially because his fanciful creations were able to enthuse the young and rouse their interest in France's high art of dressmaking. But also his venture into ready-to-wear fashion in 1988 proved extremely successful, as reflected by the positive reaction of experts and the public. A year later, he launched an accessory range, in 1994 he introduced sportswear, and in 1995, jeans. In addition, Christian Lacroix has also designed costumes for the ballet and opera.

emanuel ungaro
COUTURE

The son of a tailor, Ungaro learned his craft from his father, earning his spurs as a fashion designer in the ateliers of Balenciaga and Courrèges. After running a small studio, he set up his own haute couture house in no. 2 Avenue Montaigne in 1965 with the financial help of the actress Sonja Knapp. Unlike many of his colleagues, Ungaro does not produce his designs on paper with a pencil but creates them on life models. From 1968 on he also designed his own fabrics for his creations. Ungaro's trademark is the unusual combination of colors and patterns, but it took a few years for the public to appreciate this look. Having successfully marketed his name under several labels, Emanuel Ungaro sold his enterprise to the Ferragamo group in 1996, but he continues to run his own fashion house. From 1997 he has been assisted on the creative side of the business by the designer Robert Forrest.

Louis Féraud
PARIS

Louis Edouard Féraud's career as a fashion designer was quite unexpected, since he was originally trained as a baker. But his remarkable aesthetic feel and infallible fashion sense led Féraud to open his own boutique in Cannes in 1945. Encouraged by his success in the south of France, he moved to Paris in 1953 and opened a boutique at no. 88, Rue du Faubourg Saint-Honoré. This became the headquarters of the Louis Féraud label. In the mid-1950s, Féraud presented his first haute couture collection, which stood out with its daring choice of fabrics and strong colors. On the design front he was increasingly supported by other designers, together developing the typical Féraud style: plain, straight-cut clothes with folkloric accents. In 1965 Féraud also began to produce prêt-à-porter clothes as well as his haute couture collections, and these were very successful in the United States and Japan. In 1995 the creative running of the house was taken over by his daughter Kiki.

GIVENCHY

Hubert de Givenchy has always been the gentleman among couturiers, and as Audrey Hepburn's favorite designer he also became well-known outside the world of fashion. At the beginning of his career he designed for Jacques Fath, Robert Piquet, Lucien Lelong, and Elsa Schiaparelli. In 1951 he set up on his own very successfully and in 1956 he moved to large premises on the Avenue George V. There he developed his own "counter-vision" to the almost overpowering style of Dior, thereby attracting many younger women, although the minimalism of the first Givenchy collections probably also reflected his limited means. Because his designs were so sought-after by the haute couture clientele, Givenchy was able to exclude the press from his presentations. This exclusion lasted for ten years but it did nothing to reduce his popularity; on the contrary, his creations became even more sought-after. In 1968 Givenchy also branched out into prêt-à-porter and perfume, including the famous L'Interdit. The scent was to have been called "Audrey Hepburn" but she prohibited it—hence the name of the perfume which means "the forbidden." Givenchy designed all the collections of the house until 1996 when the creative management was taken over by John Galliano. A year later he was replaced by Alexander McQueen.

HANAE MORI

The Japanese designer Hanae Mori was one of the first Asian designers to set foot on the Paris fashion scene, and she is the undisputed fashion queen of Japan for many years. Her debut in the world of fashion was quite unusual because she first studied literature in Tokyo. In 1950 she began designing clothes for movies and five years later she opened a fashion boutique. Her love affair with haute couture began in 1960 after a meeting with Coco Chanel. She soon set about realizing her dream with amazing success and in 1965 she was able to present her first collection. Her creations were soon available in many famous fashion boutiques. In 1972 she became known outside haute couture circles when she designed the skiing outfits for the Japanese Olympic team. She never forgot her dream of having her own couture salon in Paris and in 1977 she opened her own fashion house at 17–19, Avenue Montaigne. The recognition she received in France also benefited her in Japan, where she built a fashion empire that she runs from her imposing headquarters. Her customers are all wealthy and famous and come from all over the world. They include American First Ladies as well as the Japanese Crown Princess.

Jean Paul Gaultier

The notoriously "scandalous" designer of the 1980s began his training in 1970 and worked for several famous couture houses including Cardin, Patou, Goma, and Tarlazzi before presenting his first collection in 1976. However, success was not immediate and Gaultier experienced financial problems. He was eventually able to solve these with the help of a Japanese textile manufacturer and opened his own boutique. At this point the dramatic presentation of his collections aroused increasing interest. His fashion shows turned into sensational events that almost transformed this eccentric couturier into a pop star. Gaultier's mixing of street-wear, uniform, folklore, and avant-garde designs crossed all the boundaries of traditional fashion categories. Man or woman, trousers or skirt, these questions were and still are entirely meaningless for this fashion designer, who was raised in a Paris suburb. Even the current ideals of beauty do not interest him. This is why he sometimes uses ordinary people with far from perfect figures on the runway instead of flawless models. One of his most famous customers is Madonna, who frequently wears his designs onstage and has thus made Gaultier famous in the international music scene. Although his creations are neither classic nor ladylike, his fashion house belongs to the exclusive circle of the "Appellation Haute Couture."

JEAN-LOUIS SCHERRER
PARIS

Jean-Louis Scherrer is one of the most successful outsiders in the world of fashion because he actually graduated from ballet school before becoming interested in fashion design. Quite appropriately in view of his previous career as a dancer, he first designed theater costumes before attending the Paris École de la Chambre Syndicale de la Couture for two years in 1956. He then gained practical experience by working as an assistant to Christian Dior, Yves Saint Laurent, and Louis Féraud. In 1963, Scherrer found financial backers who enabled him to open his own fashion boutique on the Rue du Faubourg Saint-Honoré. In 1972 he moved to 51–52, Avenue Montaigne. Scherrer's fashion has always been sumptuous and lavish, often displaying oriental or Asian influences. But his elegant creations have nevertheless remained unmistakably French, which is why Scherrer is recognized as a classic representative of French haute couture. In 1992 he handed over the management to the Danish designer Erik Mortensen before retiring completely from the fashion house that he had founded many years earlier.

TORRENTE

When the world of fashion gathers twice a year at the Paris runways, the haute couture house of Torrente, founded in 1969, is always the center of interest because it regularly opens the round of shows with its sumptuous, elegant collections. But Torrente is more than a much respected and popular label among fashion experts and clients, it is also the last family business in the select club of fashion houses with the "Appellation Haute Couture," and above all, the only one run by a woman. Today the world of French couture is dominated by men although in the early days it was run by women

designers such as Madame Grès, Jeanne Lanvin, Madeleine Vionnet, Augusta Bernard, Callot Sœurs, Louise Boulanger, Elsa Schiaparelli, and Coco Chanel. Today, Rose Torrente-Mett, who worked as an assistant to Ted Lapidus until she founded her own fashion house in 1964, continues in the footsteps of these fashion queens. She also led the way in the ready-to-wear field. After setting up independently, she first concentrated on cocktail dresses and evening wear before later also including daywear in her collections. Madame Torrente's style is geared to haute couture clients who are looking for style, quality and a slight understatement in their clothes—but not too understated, because her clients do not want to conceal the exquisite origins of their outfits.

Haute couture would have probably come to an end in the 1960s if Yves Saint Laurent had not bravely rejuvenated it, virtually single-handed. The public first became aware of the young designer's talent in 1953 when his design for a cocktail dress was awarded the first prize by the International Wool Secretariat. A year later, the 18-year-old Yves Saint Laurent began working as an assistant to Christian Dior and he went on to succeed him after his death. He presented his first collection in 1958 with the so-called "trapeze" line. It caused a sensation because it broke with the traditional Dior look, but nevertheless it sold extremely well internationally. However, in spite of a promising start the cooperation between him and the house of Dior ended in 1960 after Yves Saint Laurent presented an excessively avant-garde collection. From then on this exceptional artist only designed under his own name, and he did so very successfully from the very start. In the 1960s and 1970s he fascinated and shocked the public over and over again while at the same time acquiring a growing following in the world of haute couture. In the 1980s and 1990s, this formerly rebellious fashion designer came to be seen as a respected creative artist whose genius was acknowledged by books and exhibitions. He finally withdrew from the business in 2002.

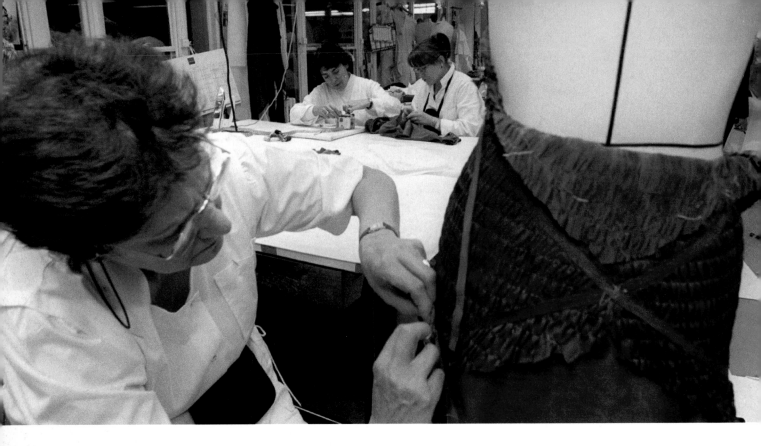

Haute Couture:
how the dress of dreams is created

Even the most accurate measurements cannot prevent the need for further adjustments on the mannequin.

A lady does not buy a haute couture dress, she celebrates its acquisition. The ritual starts with the invitation to her favorite couturier's fashion show. On the day of the show she will be ushered to her place near the runway, depending on, of course, her position on the client list. While the models present the designer's latest creations, she will note down her favorite designs in the collection, unless of course she wants to have the entire collection. The couture house then sets about adapting the clothes shown on the willowy models to fit the usually more normal figure of the client. If she is ordering for the first time, she will first be measured so that the workshop can adjust the pattern. The measurements of regular customers, on the other hand, are stored on the premises.

The next step is to cut the garment from an inexpensive neutral fabric, the so-called "toile" that is basted together for the first fitting. The real (and often very expensive) fabric only comes into play when the prototype fits perfectly. A new client must attend each fitting personally while a regular client only needs to attend the final fitting because the workshop has a dressmaker's dummy that replicates the shape of her body exactly. In this way the garment can be tried and adjusted until it fits perfectly without having to bother the client. In the case of a very important client, the couturier may go to her house, or indeed her palace, in person. This is a traditional service offered by the more prestigious haute couture houses in Paris and also abroad. For instance, Hardy Amies, the Queen of England's dressmaker, always used to go to Buckingham Palace for the fittings, not least for security reasons.

But most women prefer to go to the couture house and enjoy its exclusive atmosphere even when the time involved is quite considerable. It is said, for instance, that the Duchess of Windsor used to go twice a year to the fashion shows in order to acquire new outfits, in spite of her undoubtedly already sizeable wardrobe. The Duchess did not content herself with ordering creations from one designer only; she would order from up to six different couture houses. In the 1930s she was particularly fond of Mainbocher and Schiaparelli while after the war she showed a preference for Dior, Givenchy and Yves Saint Laurent. In order to survive the numerous, lengthy fitting sessions, she often brought a picnic basket with her containing sandwiches that she occasionally shared with the staff. Real enthusiasts of haute couture are happy to spend many hours obtaining an expert opinion, being measured, discussing the clothes and being fitted. The stressed-out businesswoman on the other hand will often prefer ready-to-wear fashion.

The epitome of exclusivity for the haute couture client is when the designer offers her exclusive designs that are not shown on the runway, being created with only her in mind. Princess Diana belonged to that very select circle of women who enjoyed this privilege. Usually she was first sent a few sketches from which she could choose, accompanied by designs for matching accessories. Because the couturier in question already had her measurements, the designs she selected could often be made immediately. Inevitably, this pleasant variation on the concept of home-shopping is not available to everyone…

Dietl in Munich is the most famous German couture house with a client list that reads like a *Who's Who* of German high society.

Fabrics used in haute couture

Batiste
Superfine fabric used to make light blouses and dresses, usually woven from cotton but also from linen. The best quality batiste comes from Switzerland.

Bouclé
Weave made from a variety of fibers with a knotty, ripply surface made from bouclé yarn. A typical fabric used for Chanel suits.

Brocade
Heavy patterned jacquard weave made from silk and metallic threads.

Cashmere
Soft, fine fabric made from the hair of cashmere goats. The best quality is extremely expensive.

Chenille
A particularly shaggy type of velvet with various decorative threads.

Chiffon
Extremely transparent silk weave.

Crêpe
Generic term for silk fabrics with a creased, puckered surface, such as crêpe georgette or crêpe de Chine.

Damask
Originally a silk fabric with a woven-in pattern, today it is a generic term for such patterned fabrics made from all kinds of fibers.

Gauze
Fine, net-like weave from various yarns, often used as a foundation for embroidery.

Gold and silver lamé
Shiny fabric with a silk or cotton warp and a weft consisting of silk or artificial silk with metallic thread.

Jacquard
General term for patterned fabric made from different colored yarns, named after the inventor of the special loom used to produce it, the Frenchman Joseph-Marie Jacquard.

Kasha
Mixed fiber fabric made from carded yarn and cashmere, used for suits and dresses.

Lace
Richly decorated fabric, woven in an open web, originally made by hand but now also machine-made. Depending on the technique used, it is called needle lace or bobbin lace.

Liberty silk
Fine, warp-faced woven silk fabric named after the Liberty department store in London where it was first sold.

Luste
Shiny, stiff, mixed fiber fabric with a cotton warp and mohair, alpaca or worsted weft.

Moiré
Fabric with a shimmering watermark pattern, created by warp and weft threads of different colors.

Muslin
Very fine, veil-like fabric, usually piece-dyed or printed, used for light dresses, blouses and veils.

Organdie
Transparent, batiste-like cotton fabric with a permanently stiff finish, frequently used for elegant day dresses and evening gowns.

Ottoman
Wool, silk or cotton fabric with broad transverse ribs.

Panné velvet
Shiny silk velvet.

Plissé
Fabrics with pleated, crinkled effect created during the weaving process.

Plush
Fabric similar to velvet but with a longer, less dense pile, often used for trimmings and accessories.

Pongee
Lightweight plain-weave silk fabric from China or India.

Rep
General term for various fabrics with a pronounced transverse rib effect, frequently made from fine fibers such as silk.

Sateen
Smooth, glossy fabric of warp-faced weave, made from linen or cotton in imitation of satin silk.

Satin
Strictly speaking, the term used to designate any fabric with a warp-faced weave, but it usually refers to a very shiny silk fabric.

Shantung
Plain weave fabric made from wild silk, with random irregularities.

Taffeta
Heavy, crisp, plain weave, matt fabric with a shimmering surface, made from silk or artificial fibers. It exists in numerous variations.

Tulle
Fine net fabric, woven in open web with hexagonal openings.

Velvet
Fabric with a short, shiny warp-pile on the surface of the fabric, made from various kinds of fabrics.

Voile
Plain weave, lightweight fabric made from cotton or silk.

Zephyr
Fine, shiny, plain weave cotton fabric used for blouses and dresses.

The haute couture suppliers

Anyone who wonders about the astronomically high prices of an haute couture garment should remember the enormous amount of time spent on the design and making of each individual item. Designs embellished with embroidery, sequins, and braiding take a lot of time to produce because they are sewn by hand and the decorations are sewn on by hand. For instance, embroideresses worked for 1,280 hours on the "Atys" dress designed by Lagerfeld for his 1997 summer collection, while Yves Saint Laurent's creation "Les Iris" required 600 hours. Of course, not every model is as time-consuming to produce, but each garment usually takes several dozen hours at least.

The high regard in which haute couture is held in France is not only due to its prestigious image but also because it is a major employer. The superexpensive creations on offer in the exclusive salons of the Rue du Faubourg Saint-Honoré may seem rather decadent but it should be remembered that many orders are placed with subcontractors who greatly benefit from this, thus securing jobs. In addition, it ensures the continuation of many crafts that have disappeared in other countries such as bobbin lace making, bead sewing, embroidery, and sequin artists. All these craftspeople make a living from the discriminating taste of wealthy ladies throughout the world. Indeed the entire fashion, accessories, and luxury goods industries benefit in addition to the direct suppliers to haute couture houses. Another point to be remembered is that fashion houses also produce ready-to-wear collections, perfumes, and licensed products of all kinds.

At first glance it would appear that suppliers are entirely dependent on the ideas and orders they receive from couture houses because, for instance, if the design does not include sequins it inevitably means that no one will be needed to sew them on. Nevertheless, haute couture actually has a mutually beneficial relationship with the related crafts and specialist industries. An excellent example of this rewarding interrelationship is the company Charles Lapierre, better known under the name Lesage. On the face of it, this company seems mere-

ly to supply couture houses with embroidery created by the fashion house itself, but in reality the supplier produces designs from its own collection that he had earlier proposed to the fashion house. So, in the same way that fashion designers are inspired by the creations of the weavers at the Première Vision French fabric fair, they are also inspired by the ideas put forward by embroidery experts. What Lesage is able create on fabric with patterns of beads, sequins, gold and silver thread, paste, feathers, and other decorative elements is something that even the most brilliant couturiers could not think up on their own.

It often takes hundreds of hours to sew pearls or other decorative elements by hand onto a haute couture dress.

The lady in white

At her wedding on February 2, 2002, Princess Maxima of the Netherlands wore an ivory silk dress by Valentino with a train more than 16 feet long.

The lady likes to see herself as someone who hates waste, nevertheless, a wedding is one of those few occasions when keeping costs down is not necessarily the right thing to do. To use an existing outfit and turn it into a bridal gown is rarely possible (few people have a white ball-gown in their closet), and the most you can hope to borrow from your mother, sister or aunt would be a veil or tiara that have been in the family for generations. Wearing your mother's wedding dress that she wore decades ago is out of the question. So the modern young woman is usually prepared to spend quite a lot of money for the "most beautiful day of her life." If she is getting married at a city hall she will probably splash out on a beautiful suit or an elegant trouser suit, and if she is having a church wedding she will need a beautiful bridal gown together with all the accessories. Sometimes another outfit is needed as well, the "going-away dress," an elegant outfit that is also suitable for traveling to the honeymoon destination.

White is today the traditional color for a wedding dress, and pastel colors such as cream, champagne or pale pink are also used. But that has not always been the case. Until well into the 19th century, brides wore brightly colored or patterned gowns. The advantage of such dresses was that they could worn again, as an afternoon dress or a ball gown, depending on the cut and style. Moreover, in strict Protestant countries the idea of a bridal gown as a "dress for only one day" was considered a luxury that was indecently extravagant. In fact, it was not unusual for women in those countries to get married in black.

The concept of the "bride in white" only became widespread in fashionable circles from 1880 onward. Initially, the church reacted to the introduction of civil marriage in the 19th century by stressing the Christian aspect of marriage, that the bride should remain chaste and innocent. The color white that until then had stood for perfection in the church's liturgy now also became a symbol of purity and virtue. In addition, the increasingly prosperous bourgeoisie wanted to display their wealth by endowing the bride with a lavish trousseau and gown that could only be worn for one day. The trend toward white bridal gowns was further accelerated by two royal weddings. In 1840, Queen Victoria wore a white satin bridal gown when she married Prince Albert, and in 1853 Eugenie wore a white velvet dress when she married the Emperor Napoleon III. Even today, people still look toward the high aristocracy for inspiration in matters of bridal fashion. Princess Diana's "fairy-tale" bridal gown became one of the most copied models of all time and started a trend toward romantic bridal wear.

This extravagant wedding dress by Oscar de la Renta recalls that until the 19th century women were married in dresses of any color, even black.

№ 9

Appendix

Fore ever and ever: Caring for the wardrobe

From morning to night everyone is bombarded with advertisements for detergents showing smiling women in beautifully cared-for cashmere sweaters. The labels of our favorite clothes carry many instructions such as "wash with similar colors," "no bleach," or "dry clean only," all strangely illustrated by hieroglyphs that may include a crossed-out wash basin, a pyramid or a circle with a P inside—washing instructions seem to be a science in themselves. But what does it all mean? What is the best way of caring for your clothes effectively without spending too much money?

There is one basic ground rule that must be observed at all times. The kind of care a particular type of fabric needs depends on how it is worn and how it is stored. Everyday underwear that is worn directly on the skin receives a lot of wear and tear because of frequent washing, but this also means that it can be stuffed in a drawer without being damaged. A handmade suit, on the other hand, only partially comes into contact with the body, at the collar and the cuffs, but nevertheless, dust, cigarette smoke, food odors, and pet hair often accumulate in and on the fabric. Dry cleaning with chemicals will clean the garment and remove these odors, but it also dries out the fabric, especially if done frequently. Even if the garment is treated with care and worn only very occasionally, the garment can still be damaged in the closet. Hanging for too long on a narrow hanger or hanger with pointed ends can damage the shoulders so that the jacket eventually becomes "flat." Then if the worst comes to the worst, the garment may be attacked by moths that make small holes in the garment. It is evident that looking after clothes begins in the closet.

Now we come to the actual cleaning of the garment. In theory, every garment can be washed by hand or in the washing-machine, because even the finest cashmere scarf will not suffer from being in contact with water. However there are three main reasons why most suits, dresses, coats, wool trousers, and skirts are always dry-cleaned. First, they may lose their shape if washed, and only an expert can restore their original shape by pressing. Second, the outer fabric and the lining and padding may shrink, each by a different amount. This would cause the garment to become out of shape, and worst of all, it would become unwearable. Third, watermarks and rings can occur during the drying process, for instance on the lining. So the golden rule is that cleaning instructions should always be followed to the letter, even when the reasons for dry-cleaning are not immediately obvious. Similarly, when cleaning instructions forbid dry-cleaning, it is just as important to follow them. Even if you do not like being told what to do, it is worth making an effort and showing some respect for the manufacturer's instructions. You will be repaid by clothes that preserve their original condition for as long as possible.

But washing machines, washbasins and the dry-cleaner around the corner are not the only way to maintain the well-being of your clothes. There are other ways of helping to keep them in good conditions. The simplest is to air your clothes thoroughly every time you have worn them, by for instance hanging your pantsuit on a suitably shaped hanger on the balcony or near an open window (but protected from rain, of course). The cool air will remove odors and also restore humidity and, as a result, the elasticity of the cloth. Another important way of maintaining clothes in good condition is to brush them thoroughly. Choose a good quality clothes brush with natural bristles whose degree of hardness is appropriate to the fineness of the fabric. There is no quicker or more effective way of getting rid of dust and dry dirt. Adhesive tape and similar means are not advisable since the adhesive may leave traces of glue on the fabric, so it is better to remove hairs and fluff by hand or with a brush. Last but not least, pressing is important. Instead of taking your suit to the dry-cleaners because of a few creases, you can press it yourself with an iron and thus restore its shape. It is important to place a cotton cloth between the iron and the garment so as to avoid creating shiny patches on the fabric.

Care and washing symbols: What do they mean?

 USA: •••
Machine wash HOT.
Europe: Machine wash at up to 95° C (200° F)

 Tumble dry with care, LOW heat

 Dry cleaning recommended

 USA: ••
Machine wash WARM.
Europe: Coloreds, machine-wash at up to 60° C (140° F)

 Do not tumble dry

Wash with similar colours — Danger of colors running or fading, only wash similar colors together

 USA: •
Machine wash COLD.
Europe: Delicates, machine wash at up to 40° C (100° F)

 Iron at high temperature

Wash separately — Danger of colors running or fading, best washed on its own

 USA: • Machine wash COLD, gentle cycle.
Europe: Machine wash at up to 30° C (85° F), delicate program,

 Iron at medium temperature

Wash inside out — Turn the garment inside-out before washing it

 Hand wash only in water at up to 30° C (85° F)

 Iron at cool temperature. Do not use steam! Use a pressing-cloth and proceed with care

Dry clean only — Do not wash

 Wash gently by hand or machine wash using gentle cycle

 Do not iron

If decorated don't iron on — Do not iron over the decorative elements (sequins, strass etc.)

 Do not wash, dry clean only

 All common dry-cleaning methods are permitted

If printed don't iron on — Do not iron on the printed parts

 Bleach may be used

 Special dry-cleaning symbol: perchlorethylene is recommended as the dry-cleaning agent

No bleach — Do not use bleach. Be careful with stain-removing agents

 Do not use bleach or stain-removers containing chlorine

 The symbol that dry-cleaners like least: the garment needs a very special, delicate dry-cleaning treatment

 Tumble dry MEDIUM heat

 No dry-cleaning is permitted and extreme care is recommended with stain-removing agents

Ladies' shoes made from fine leather should always be treated with cream polish while the slightly harder-wearing lace-ups and penny loafers should be cleaned with a good wax polish.

Looking after your shoes

There are people who like polishing shoes. Mostly they are men who take shoes seriously while women, even those who are passionate about shoes, do not seem to be very interested in shoe polish, shoe cream, brushes and cloths for shining shoes.

Nevertheless, your pumps, loafers, and sneakers do need a certain amount of care. First of all, clean shoes look so much better, second, the leather remains more supple, and third, regular cleaning will prolong the life of your footwear. Before you start cleaning your shoes, put on a pair of rubber gloves, so you won't have to spend much time getting your hands and nails clean again, and wear an apron.

Start by removing all particles of dirt and mud. Remove wet earth and mud with a cloth and a brush, or scrape off dried earth with the handle of a brush or a blunt knife.

Let us now look at shoe care products. For the fine leather that is used for fashionable ladies' shoes or elegant sneakers, use shoe cream of the same color as the shoes, usually available in a tube or a pot.

For heavier, more robust shoes, use wax shoe polish, which is usually supplied in a tin.

The cream should be applied sparingly with a soft cloth. Try out the color first on an inconspicuous part of the shoe—if the cream is too dark, it will create unsightly discoloration of the leather that would be extremely difficult to remove. As soon as you have applied the cream to both shoes, proceed immediately with the polishing. Use a soft horsehair brush, a duster or an old nylon pantyhose.

Wax shoe polish is applied with a cloth or brush but here too it is important to use it sparingly. Do not forget the underside of the sole, but only apply to the parts that do not touch the ground or they are likely to mark light-colored carpets. Unlike cream, shoe wax should be left to soak in for several hours, or overnight. The longer you wait, the easier it will be to obtain a good shine by polishing with a brush, followed by a soft cloth.

Never use shoe cream or wax on velour or Nubuk leather, instead scrub them on occasion with a special suede brush.

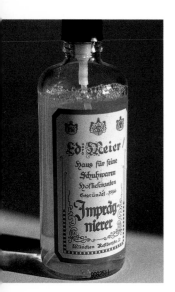

Suede shoes should be treated with a special suede product when necessary. Apart from this, only occasional brushing with a suede brush is required.

Clothes, accessories and jewelry: the most important care tips

Skirts, trousers, blazers, suits, and coats

Dust, light, and moths are the archenemy of all fine fabrics, especially those that are used all the time. But you can protect your clothes from these dangers very effectively by storing them in a closet (where they are protected from the sun and dust), leaving sufficient space between the clothes (so that air can circulate), and putting sufficient moth-killer (which should be renewed regularly) between the clothes. When clothes are stored away for several months at the end of the summer or winter they should first be washed or dry-cleaned. Should stains occur, it is worth remembering that the more delicate the fabric, the more careful one should be with stain-removers. If in doubt, entrust it to your regular dry-cleaner because attempts at home may make matters worse. Indeed many responsible dry-cleaners will refuse garments that have already been unsuccessfully treated at home with dubious products.

Silk scarves

Silk scarves should always be cleaned in accordance with the care instructions. If there is an indication that forbids hand-washing there must be a reason for it. The colors might run in water and watermarks often occur during the drying process, two good reasons why it is best for silk accessories to be dry-cleaned. But make sure the dry-cleaner is experienced in dealing with valuable textiles. Many wool scarves can be washed at home but do not wring them out too vigorously. More delicate items such as pashminas should be dry-cleaned rather than washed.

Gloves

Always smooth your gloves down after wearing them and arrange them spread out and flat. If the gloves are not to be worn for a while, then store them according to color. If they are wet, allow them to dry away from heat—not on a radiator or in the sun. Shiny patches on suede gloves can be roughened with a suede brush. Heavily soiled gloves may be washed with curd soap or special soap bought in a specialist shop. To wash the gloves, put them on and move your hands in the soapy water as if you were washing your hands. Then blow open the gloves while they are still wet and let them dry slowly. Finally pull them carefully into shape.

Jewelry and watches

Real jewelry does not need daily attention, but pieces should be cleaned and polished from time to time by a jeweler. At the same time, the security of the clasps and stone fixings can be checked. In general, the usual care should be taken to protect your valuables from damage, for instance, by not dropping them on a tiled floor. Mechanical watches should be wound occasionally when they are not worn regularly. Automatic watches can be kept going by a motorized winding box. Water-resistant watches with metal bracelets of steel, gold or platinum can simply be washed with soapy water. If you wear the water-proof watch in the shower or bath, the soapy water may harm the gasket.

Furs

Fur should never be allowed to get soaked in the rain to the point that the leather underneath is wet. Snow, on the other hand, does not damage fur. Just shake the flakes off the fur when you get home and hang the item on a shaped hanger. Never put it near a radiator or use an electric hair-dryer because excessive heat will dry out the fur. For the same reason, fur should be protected against high temperatures in summer. Fur is best stored in a cool, dark place. To protect against dust, put a light fabric cover over it. Do not use plastic because this can damage the fur. Alternatively, you can also take the item to a furrier who will store it in the right conditions. If you fur has a serious stain, it is advisable to take it an expert. Do not try and clean it yourself.

Practical tips for traveling and packing suitcases

The best way of ensuring that the luggage arrives at the same time as you do is to take it on board with you. But large suitcases on wheels are unlikely to be accepted and regulations restrict what is permitted as cabin baggage.

From a fashion point of view, a business trip is a state of emergency. The quantity of clothes that may be taken is limited, making it hard to cater for changing weather conditions and unexpected additions to the program, such as going to the opera after a successful meeting, hiking in the mountains, or going swimming. Sitting in an automobile, a plane or a train for a long time causes clothes to crease, and eating in any kind of moving transportation can lead to spilled food or drinks. Even worse, misdirected luggage may mean that the suitcase containing the outfit for the important meeting in Milan is on a plane to Thailand by mistake. In addition to these typical problems of a business trip, there is also the general stress caused by getting from the parking lot to the check-in counter and terminal in time, or the exhausting rush to the train track and the ungainly walk through a crowded train to a reserved seat, or the endless waiting in lines at taxi stands. Even the best preparation cannot protect you from these inconveniences, but it can help you cope with the troubles of a temporary nomadic life.

Before a seasoned traveler packs her bags and cases, she will consider every stage of her journey. It is important to decide how many outfits will be needed. This is not only determined by the length of the trip, but also by the appointments. If you are meeting the same people on three consecutive days, you will need three different outfits, but if you are meeting three different sets of people on those days, you can make do with one outfit, simply changing the shirt. In any case, it is important to travel with as little as possible.

This is especially true when traveling by plane because any bag that you cannot take on board the plane may go astray. If you can reduce your luggage to hand-luggage only, you will also avoid the tedious waiting and unpleasant pushing and shoving in the baggage hall. Similarly, if traveling by train you won't have to wait for the

return of your belongings in the station because you will have been able to keep your bag with you. Even so, you still have to carry your things, so light travel is recommended. It is also worth considering whether you will be able to change between arrival and your first meeting. If not, you must travel dressed ready for the meeting. This involves certain risks (such as the risk of spilling food or drink mentioned above) but on the other hand, you have to carry one less outfit in your bag.

Packing clothes is an art form that every woman has developed in the course of time with her own tricks and dodges. But basically it is a question of making sure that clothes stay as unwrinkled as possible—especially when there is no time to hang the clothes to hang out the creases before wearing them. The packing technique is of course also determined by the kind of suitcase used. Suit carriers are easiest to pack because suits, dresses, skirts and blouses can be packed directly from the wardrobe closet. Do not overfill the garment bag because the clothes could get creased. Cabin luggage requires a little more skill because clothes must be folded smaller. Blazers and jackets should be turned inside out (so that the lining is exposed), then one shoulder is pushed into the other and the jacket is folded lengthways. Then fold again at the waist so as to obtain a small rectangle. Finally stuff the shoulders with rolled-up underwear or pantyhose to prevent them from getting crushed. The collars of shirts and blouses should also be padded a little.

If you are flying and you need a suitcase because of the length of your trip or the number of meetings, you should also pack a complete business outfit separately in your carry-on, so that you have something to change into in case your suitcase goes astray. When packing the case you should arrange the clothes according to how delicate they are. Pants and skirts should go at the bottom because they will not be creased by the weight of the blouses and shirts. Shoes and your toiletry bag should also go at the bottom. Also take into account how gravity will affect the clothes and other objects when you lift the case. Shoes are best packed near the hinges, then they are at the bottom when you carry the case. The next layer should be the jackets. They can either be folded as a rectangle (as described above) or spread out flat. Then place the shirts, blouses, underwear or sweaters inside the jacket and fold the sleeves on top. They will prevent the jacket from being flattened.

If you don't have the time or the inclination to pack as described above, it does not mean that you are condemned to wear creased clothes at the conference table. There are several ways to remove the creases from your clothes. The simplest way consists in giving your creased suit a smoothing steam bath. Turn on the hot water taps and allow to run until the bathroom is filled with steam. Hang the creased garments in the steam-filled bathroom for twenty or thirty minutes. You can use this time to iron your shirt or blouse. (There may be an iron in the closet or one will be brought by the chambermaid on request. Alternatively, a travel iron is very useful and takes up very little space.) Once the garments have hung for long enough in the steam, let them cool down thoroughly (near the window or on the balcony) before putting them on. It takes no longer to steam your clothes to remove the creases than to pack with care, but you must include the necessary three-quarters of an hour in your schedule.

There still remains the question of what to take with you on a business trip. Because the concept of the correct business outfit varies from country to country and from one field to another, we can only give some general guidelines. When you do not know what you can expect at the other end, it is best to err on the safe side and be slightly more conservative than usual so that you do not run the risk of being under-dressed. Plain fabrics in traditional colors such as navy, charcoal or camel will make it easier to match accessories. If you choose a patterned fabric, go for subtle stripes or a classic glen check cloth. If you have some free time, be sure you also include a smart casual outfit on your packing list. If time allows, you can wear it for traveling instead of packing it and change into your business suit when you arrive at the hotel. This has advantages in all seasons, because in winter you will not freeze in a skirt and pumps while waiting for the train at the station, and in summer you will not crease your lightweight dress in the taxi. You will also be more comfortable in sneakers than in stilettos. Always try to arrive as relaxed as you possibly can—that is half the battle won toward a successful business trip.

Wardrobe trunk and hat-box? Few women use them nowadays. Today the art of packing lies in reducing luggage to the essential.

Index

Acknowledgements

With thanks to the following for their kind assistance:

Etienne Aigner AG, Munich
Alumo Textil AG, Appenzell
Arlington Socks GmbH & Co. KG, Schopfheim
Amadeus Fashion GmbH, Salzburg
Edizione Annapurna, Prato
Ascot Karl Moese GmbH, Krefeld
Asprey's & Garrard, London
Augsburger Knopffabrik Schneider & Söhne, Augsburg
Baccarat, Paris
J. Barbour & Sons Ltd., Simonside
Bass & Co., Melton Mowbray
Baume & Mercier, Geneva
Beckford Silks, Beckford, Gloucestershire
Beiersdorf AG, Hamburg
Belvest spa, Piazzola sul Brenta (PD)
Berk, Burlington Arcade, London
Bogner, Munich
Borbonese, Pianoro (BO)
Bower Roebuck & Company Ltd., Huddersfield
Harry Breidt GmbH, Munich
Calzificio M. Bresciani srl, Spirano (BG)
Clarks Shoes Vertriebs GmbH, Bingen
Brioni, Rome
The British Library, London
Burberry London, London
Cartier, Paris
Chanel, Paris
Chrysalis Clothes Ltd., Corby
AG Cilander Textilveredelung, Herisau
Ciro Paone spa, Arzano (NA)
Chaumet, Paris
Cordings of Piccadilly, London
Crockett & Jones, Northampton
Cutler & Gross, London
Daks, London
Da Vinci Co. Ltd., Tczew
Max Dietl, Munich
d-tails fashion research, Düsseldorf
Eagle Products Textil GmbH, Hof
Elbeo Vertriebs GmbH, Schongau
Emanuel Berg, Cologne
Escada AG, Munich
Falke Gruppe, Schmallenberg
Freudenhaus Eyewear, Munich
The Gates Rubber Company Ltd., Dumfries
George Michael of Madison Avenue, Cosma GmbH, Hamburg
Globe Worsted Company, Huddersfield
Gloverall plc, Wellingborough

Goldpfeil AG, Offenbach
Gucci Group Germany GmbH, Hamburg
Guerlain Parfumeur GmbH, Wiesbaden
Habsburg Kleidermanufaktur GmbH, Salzburg
Hermès, Paris
Hilton Vestimenta, Mattarello di Trento (TN)
Emma Hope, London
Igedo Company, Düsseldorf
J. P. Tod's, Milan
Wilhelm Jungmann & Neffe, Wien
Peter Kaiser GmbH, Pirmasens
Kleegräfe Strothmann, Gütersloh
Lacoste Yello Sport GmbH, Cologne
Laura Ashley Limited, London
Lamarthe, Paris
Les Copains, Bologna
Gabriela Ligenza, London
James Lock & Co. Ltd., London
Loewe, Madrid
Longwood Finishing Company, Huddersfield
Lanificio Ing. Loro Piana & C. s.p.a., Quarona (VC)
Louis Vuitton, Paris
Maglia Francesco, Milan
Malefiz Großhandels GmbH, Münster
Manufactum Hoof & Partner KG, Waltrop
Max Mara, Reggio Emilia
McGregor Fashion Group, Driebergen-Rijsenburg
Moncler, Grenoble
Montblanc, Hamburg
Mulberry, London
Musée Chaumet, Paris
Museo Salvatore Ferragamo, Florence
Mustang Bekleidungswerke GmbH & Co., Künzelsau
O'Neill Europe, Voorschoten
Piaget, Paris
Palmers Textil AG, Vienna
Peek und Cloppenburg KG, Düsseldorf
Peter Scott & Co. Ltd., Hawick
Pringle of Scotland Limited, Hawick
Revlon, Marbert AG, Düsseldorf
Rimowa Kofferfabrik, Cologne
Roeckl Handschuhe GmbH & CO., Munich
Salvatore Ferragamo, Florence
Samsonite GmbH, Cologne
Calzature Santoni s.r.l., Corridonia (MC)
Saga Furs of Scandinavia, Vedbæk
Scabal SA, Brussels
Schneiders Bekleidung GmbH, Salzburg

Stephane Kélian, Paris
Stephanie Rapp, Munich
Verlag Otto Sternefeld GmbH, Düsseldorf
Superga, Rivoli (TO)
Teresa Kopias, Lask
Tibbett plc, Wellingborough
Tiffany and Company, New York
The Timberland Company
R. E. Tricker Ltd., Northampton
Triumph International AG, Munich
Tumi, Middlesex NJ
W. P. Lavori in Corso S. r. l. , Bologna
Wolford AG, Bregenz
Woolrich, John Rich and Bros., Pennsylvania

Special thanks to Daniel Breidt, John Booth, Mark Fisher, Georg Gaugusch, Mark and Tom Grütters, Robin Guinness, Barbara Hagen, Herman Hasler, Markus A. Heller, Anne Hopkins, Corinna Kowalewsky, Sylvie Lenderoth, Francesco Maglia, Carolin Schlemmer, Dr. Claudia Schulz, Jaroslaw, and Petra Szychulda.

Picture credits

Page 13: Tibbett plc (photo: Terry Ryan); page 14: Revlon (photo: Herb Ritts)/page 16: Revlon (photo: Herb Ritts); page 18/19: Beiersdorf AG; page 20: Revlon; page 21 t.r.: E. O. Hoppé/Corbis/Picture Press; page 21 t.l.: Douglas Kirkland/Corbis/Picture Press ; page 21 b.: Revlon; page 22: Revlon; page 23: dpa (Deutsche Presse-Agentur GmbH); page 24 : dpa; page 25: Revlon; page 26: Mitchel Gerber/Corbis/Picture Press; page 28/29: Cartier 2001 (photo: Xavier Rebaud); page 29 t.: Cartier 2001 (photo: Xavier Rebaud); page 29 b.: Cartier; page 31: dpa; page 32/33: Guerlain; page 33 b.r.: Piras/Roetzel (photo: Bernhard Roetzel); page 34 l.: Bettmann/Corbis/Picture Press; page 34 r.: Falke; page 35: dpa; page 36/37: dpa; page 38/39: dpa ; page 39 b.r.: Bettmann/Corbis/Picture Press; page 40/41: Revlon; page 42: Falke; page 44: Picture Press Hulton-Deutsch Collection/Corbis/Picture Press; page 46: Falke; page 47: dpa; page 49 l.: Frommel photodesign (for Stephanie Rapp); page 49 r.: dpa; page 50: Triumph; page 51: Palmers (photo: Steen Sundland); page 53 background picture: Elbeo; page 53: Falke; page 54 t.l.: Palmers (photo: Steen Sundland); page 54: Triumph; page 56: Hulton-Deutsch Collection/Corbis/Picture Press; page 57 l.: Falke; page 57 t.r.: Palmers Archiv (Grafik: Gerhard Brause); page 57 m.r.: Falke; page 57 b.r.: Palmers Archiv (Grafik: Paul Aignee); page 58/59: Wolford; page 60: Emanuel Berg; page 61: Ullstein Bilderdienst (photo: Ullstein); page 62: Bettmann/Corbis/Picture Press; page 63: Falke; page 64: Belvest; page 66: Falke; page 67: Bettmann/Corbis/Picture Press; page 68/69: Belvest; page 70: Belvest ; page 71: Laura Ashley Limited; page 72 l.: Belvest; page 72 m.: Aigner Munich; page 72 r.: Escada; page 73 l.: Aigner Munich; page 73 m.: Laura Ashley Limited; page 73 r.: Belvest; page 74/75: Kleegräfe Strothmann; page 76: Max Dietl; page 78: Scabal; page 80: Belvest; page 82–85: Piras/Roetzel (photo: Bernhard Roetzel); page 88/89: Peek & Cloppenburg; page 90: Hulton-Deutsch Collection/Corbis/Picture Press; page 91 l.: Amadeus Fashion; page 91. r.: Belvest; page 92: Hulton-Deutsch Collection/Corbis/Picture Press; page 93: dpa; page 94: Belvest; page 95 l. and b.r.: Aigner Munich ; page 95 t.r.: Igedo (mo-

del: Trastornados, Gran Canaria); page 96 l.: Aigner Munich; page 96. r.: Belvest; page 97: Belvest; page 98: Emanuel Berg; page 99: Da Vinci; page 100/101: Cilander; page 102 l.: Falke ; page 102 r.: Belvest; page 103: Belvest; page 104 t.: Daks Piras/Roetzel (photo: Bernhard Roetzel); page 105: dpa; page 106: Salvatore Ferragamo; page 107: Belvest; page 108: Emanuel Berg; page 109 l.: Da Vinci; page 109 r.: Mustang Jeans; page 110: Piras/Roetzel (photo: Bernhard Roetzel); page 111 t.: Burberry London; page 111 b.: Piras/Roetzel (photo: Bernhard Roetzel); page 112 t.: Aigner Munich; page 112 b.: Lacoste; page 113: Louis Vuitton; page 114: McGregor Fashion Group; page 117: Bettmann/Corbis/Picture Press; page 118/119: Peter Scott; page 120: Laura Ashley Limited; page 121: Pringle Scotland; page 122/123: Loro Piana; page 125: Edizione Annapurna, Prato (photo: Dietmar Henneka); page 126 t.: James Lock & Co.; page 126 m.: Eagle Products; page 126 b.: Bresciani (photo: Bart Herremann); page 127: background picture: Burberry London; page 127 t.r.: Chrysalis Clothes; page 127 b.r.:Tricker's ; page 128/129: Chrysalis Clothes; page 130 t.: Aigner Munich; page 130 b.: McGregor Fashion Group; page 131: Hilton; page 132: Mustang Jeans ; page 133: Bogner Jeans; page 135: dpa; page 136: dpa; page 137: Lacoste; page 138: Hilton; page 139 l. and m.: Escada; page 139 r.: Joop; page 140: Chrysalis Clothes; page 141 t.l.: Aigner Munich; page 141 t.m.: Crockett & Jones ; page 141 t.r.: Cordings of Piccadilly (photo: Alex Roggero); page 141 b. l.: Cordings of Piccadilly (photo: Alex Roggero); page 141 b.m.: Aigner Munich; page 141 m. r.: Tricker's; page 141 b.r.: Piras/Roetzel (photo: Bernhard Roetzel); page 142/143: Bogner; page 143 m. and r.: Bogner (photo: Hubs Flöter); page 144: Piras/Roetzel (photo: Bernhard Roetzel); page 145: McGregor Fashion Group; page 146: Schneiders; page 147: Habsburg; page 148: Kiton (photo: Daniel Breidt); page 150: Barbour; page 152 l.: Brioni; page 152 m.: Les Copains; page 152 r.: Belvest; page 153 l.: Loro Piana; page 153 m. and r.:Schneiders; page 154: Kiton (photo: Daniel Breidt); page 155: Max Mara ; page 156: Barbour; page 157 l.: Mustang Jeans ; page 157 r.: Burberry London; page 159 t.l. and r.: Sa-

ga Furs of Scandinavia; page 159 b.: Loro Piana; page 160: Roeckl; page 161: Aigner Munich; page 162 l.: Barbour; page 162 m.: Woolrich; page 162 r.: Barbour; page 163 l.: Moncler; page 163 m.: Chrysalis Clothes; page 163 r.: Woolrich; page 164 t.: Belvest; page 164 b.: Falke; page 165: Revlon; page 166: Gloverall; page 167 l.: Gloverall ; page 167 r.: Mustang Jeans; page 168: Falke; page 170: Emma Hope; page 172 background picture: Piras/Roetzel (photo: Bernhard Roetzel); page 172 l.: Salvatore Ferragamo; page 172 r.: Aigner Munich; page 173 Salvatore Ferragamo; page 174 t.: Aigner Munich; page 174 b.l.: Stephane Kélian; page 174 b.r.: Aigner Munich; page 175: d-tails fashion research (photo: Clemens Kerkhof); page 177 from t. to b.: Tanguy Loyzance/Sygma/Picture Press, dpa (2 x), Museo Salvatore Ferragamo, Firenze (photo: Locchi); page 179: Verlag Otto Sternefeld (photo: Monika König); page 180/181: Verlag Otto Sternefeld (photo: Monika König); page 182: Falke; page 185 t.: Salvatore Ferragamo; page 185 b.r.: Gucci; page 185 b.l: Chanel; page 186: Bass & Co ; page 187 t.: The Timberland Company; page 187 m.: Superga; page 187 b.: The Timberland Company; page 188/189: Hunter; page 190/191: Crockett & Jones; page 191 r.: Piras/Roetzel (photo: Bernhard Roetzel); page 192 t.l., m.l.: Clarks; page 192 b.l.: Aigner Munich; page 192 r.: Gabriela Ligenza; page 193 t.l.: Berk ; page 193 t.r.: O'Neill Footwear; page 193. b.l.: Piras/Roetzel (photo: Bernhard Roetzel); page 193 b.r.: Manufactum; page 194/195: J. P. Tod's; page 196/197: Santoni; page 198: Chaumet (photo: Gustavo Ten Hoever); page 200: Cartier (photo: J. P. Charbonnier); page 202: Louis Vuitton; page 203: Cartier (photo: Nick Welsh); page 204 from t.l. to b.r.: Hermès, Hermès, Goldpfeil, Aigner Munich, Lamarthe; page 205 from t.l. to b.r.: Ferragamo, Cartier, Borbonese, Gucci, Chanel; page 207 from t.l. to b.r.: Aigner Munich (2 x), Stephane Kélian, Sony Ericsson, Louis Vuitton, Cartier, Piras/Roetzel (photo: Bernhard Roetzel), Cartier (2 x); page 208 t.: Montblanc; page 208 b.: Stephane Kélian; page 209 from t.l. to b.r.: Aigner Munich (2 x), Loro Piana, Montblanc, Aigner Munich, Louis Vuitton; page 210/211: Aigner Munich; page 212/213: Aigner Munich; page 215 from t.l. to b.r.: Louis Vuitton (2 x),

Asprey & Garrard, Louis Vuitton (3 x), Rimowa, Samsonite, Louis Vuitton; page 216: Hermès; page 217 from t.l. to b.r.: Louis Vuitton (2 x), Ascot, Cartier (2 x), Aigner Munich (3 x); page 219: Beckford Silks; page 220: Eagle Products; page 221: Eagle Products; page 222 t.l.: Laura Ashley Limited; page 222/223: James Lock & Co.; page 224: Maglia; page 224/225: Aigner Munich; page 226/227: Piras/Roetzel (photo: Bernhard Roetzel); page 228: Cartier; page 229: Freudenhaus Eyewear; page 229 b.: Cutler & Gross; page 230 t.: Roeckl; page 230 b.: Aigner Munich; page 231 t.r.: Roeckl; page 231 Bildergeschichte Verlag Otto Sternefeld; page 232: Cartier (photo: M. Feinberg); page 233:Cartier; page 235 b.l.: Cartier; page 235 r.: Piaget (2 x); page 236 l. Cartier (2 x); page 236 r.: Piaget (photo: Jean Daniel Meyer); page 237: Tiffany & Co. (photo: Monica Stevenson); page 238: Archives Cartier; page 239 t.: Musée Chaumet; page 239 m.: Chaumet (photo: C. Fleurent); page 239 b.: Tiffany & Co. ; page 240 l.: Tiffany & Co.; page 240 r.: Cartier; page 241 t.: Cartier (photo: Nick Welsh); page 241 b.l.: The British Library; page 241 b.r.: dpa; page 242: Baume & Mercier; page 243: Cartier; page 244 l.: Baccarat; page 244 r.: Baccarat (photo: A. Strouk); page 245: Baccarat; page 246: Cartier (photo: Panséri); page 247: Cartier (photo: Roberto Badin); page 247 b.: Montblanc; page 248: Kiton (photo: Daniel Breidt); page 250: AFE (photo: Pietro Servo); page 252/253: Igedo; page 254: Laura Ashley Limited; page 255: Falke; page 256: Mulberry; page 258 from t. to b.: Cartier (photo: Nick Welsh), Salvatore Ferragamo, Chaumet (2 x); page 259: Chaumet (from the exhibition "Crowning Glories: Two Centuries of Tiaras" at the Museum of Fine Arts in Boston); page 260: Archiv Wilhelm Jungmann & Neffe, Vienna; page 261 l.: Archiv Wilhelm Jungmann & Neffe, Vienna; page 261 r.: Gucci; page 266: dpa; page 267: Max Dietl; page 269: dpa; page 270: Stewart Mark/ Camera Press/Picture Press; page 271 dpa; page 272: Burlington; page 276: Piras/Roetzel (photo: Bernhard Roetzel); page 278: Tumi; page 279: Louis Vuitton

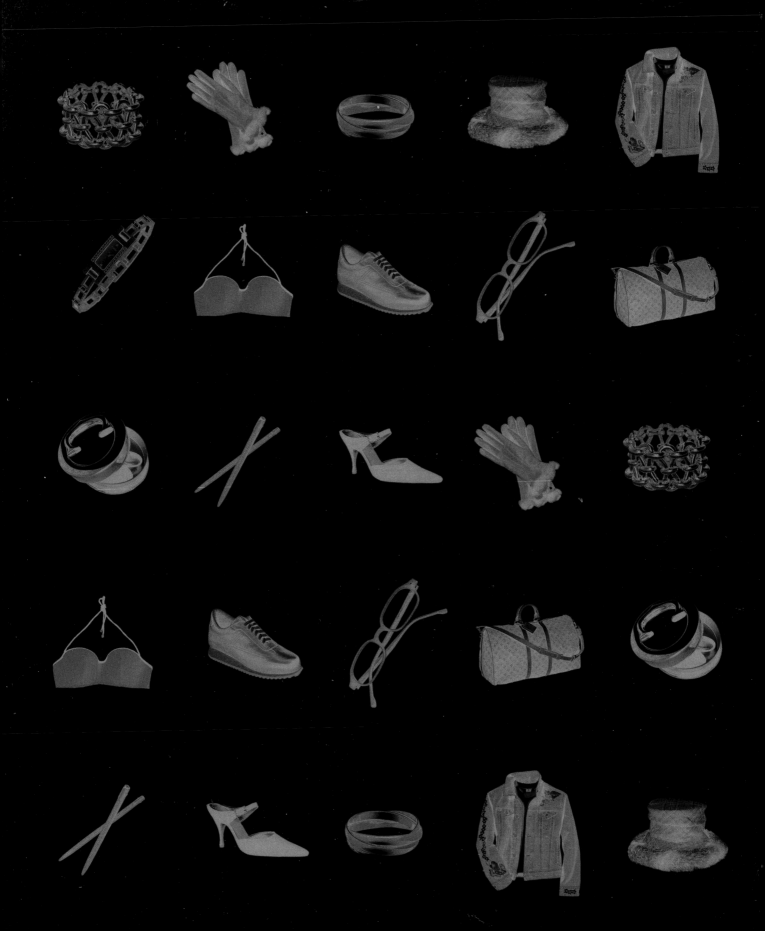